I USED TO BE NICE

I USED TO BE NICE

Sexual Affairs

SUE O'SULLIVAN

CASSELL

For a catalogue of related titles in our
Sexual Politics/Global Issues list
please write to us at the address below

Cassell
Wellington House
125 Strand
London
WC2R 0BB

215 Park Avenue South
New York
NY 10003

First published 1996

British Library Cataloguing-in-Publication Data
O'Sullivan, Sue
    I used to be nice: sexual affairs
    1. Lesbianism
    I. Title
    305.9'06643

    ISBN: 0 304 335711 (hardback)
             0 304 33572X (paperback)

Typeset by Ben Cracknell Studios

Printed and bound in Great Britain by Biddles Ltd of Guildford and King's Lynn

CONTENTS

Sue O'Sullivan's writing includes *Out the Other Side: Contemporary Lesbian Writing*, *Positively Women: Living with AIDS*, *Turning the Tables: Recipes and Reflections by Women*, *Women's Health: A Spare Rib Reader* and *Lesbians Talk (Safer) Sex*, which she co-authored with Pratibha Parmar.

Acknowledgements

Is it cool or uncool to write long acknowledgements? Who cares? I welcome the chance to make known the importance of colleagues, friends and loved ones.

Ruthie Petrie, dear old friend, consummate editor, first suggested this collection. I blanched but was persuaded and Ruthie gave me excellent critical and practical advice. Ruthie and I will hobble into the sunset together with our canes some day.

One of my most important ongoing friendships is with Susan Ardill, whether we are in England or Oz. We have collaborated in feminist projects and a number of writing ventures, some of which are published in this book. I love writing with Susan – it's an adventure and not remotely like 'writing by committee'.

Pratibha Parmar is another valuable friend with whom I have collaborated. I like the way we can get together after months apart and fall almost seamlessly into a close conversation. I have included sections from our short book, *Lesbians Talk (Safer) Sex*, in this collection.

Both Susan and Pratibha generously allowed me to include work which is equally theirs in this book and I am grateful to them.

Friends on three continents sustain me. Among my loved ones in Britain are Sue Katz, Sara Dunn, Nel Druce, Janet Hadley, Jean Smith, Ruth Wallsgrove, Alice Henry, Sona Osman, Amanda Sebestyen, Michelle McKenzie, Val Wilmer, Kate Thomson, Robin Gorna and Araba Mercer. (Karen Goldman lives in Israel but we always meet in London.) My first family, John, Tom and Dan, remain close to my heart.

In my long ago homeland I remain connected over miles and years to Nancy Jonas (my best friend for forty-eight years), Karen Slaney, Jill Posener, Barbara Ridley, Nancy Worcester, Sarah Schulman, Joan Nestle and Carole Vance. Visits with my parents and extended family in Maine remind me of how much I love them and the rocky coast.

In Australia I thank Michele and Pam O'Neil, Anne Mitchell, Roxy McGuire and all the GINAs, Jane Calvert, Peter Moraitis, Julie Peters and Jane Langley, the LOIS girls, Crusader and Rowland, Lesley Podesta, Louise Lovett, the shrink and the surgeon, Kelly Gardiner, Annie Pearse, Deb Tyler, Philomena Horsley, Sonya Tremellon, Wendy Young, Diane Hamer, Michael Hurley, Di Otto, Lloyd James and my precious friend, Bev Greet.

Wherever I am, Mitch Cleary is in my heart. She continues to surprise me, love me, demand the best from me. She is my love and my comfort.

I had the good fortune to spend two weeks finishing this book at the women's work space, Brisons Veor, on Cape Cornwall. It was a magic place to work.

I want to dedicate this book to two women, Vicki and Lela Breitbart. Vicki's and my friendship has endured and grown for thirty-five years. Her intelligence and humour have always delighted me; her feminist and radical work always impressed me. Her first born, Lela, was an extraordinary young women. Lela was independent yet connected to our older feminism, separate from her mother, yet wonderfully loving to her, occupied with her own life and friends, yet able to be attentive to her mother's concerns and friends. Lela was killed in a freak accident in the summer of 1995. I still can't believe she is dead. I think of her and I think of my dear friend Vicki; I mourn Lela and celebrate two vibrant women's lives.

Permission to reproduce essays from the following books is gratefully acknowledged:

Very Heaven by Sara Maitland, (Virago, London, 1988).

'68, '78, '88 by A. Sebestyen, (ed.) (Prism Press, Sturminster Newton, 1989).

Turning the Tables by S. O'Sullivan, (ed.) (Sheba Feminist Publishers, London, 1987).

A Certain Age by J. Goldsworthy, (ed.) (Virago, London, 1993).

The Good, the Bad and the Gorgeous by B. Budge, and D. Hamer, (Pandora, London, 1994).

Serious Pleasure by Sheba Collective (ed.) (Sheba Feminist Publishers, London, 1989).

Lesbians Talk (Safer) Sex by S. O'Sullivan, (Scarlet Press, London, 1992).

Introduction

I am a feminist and cannot imagine otherwise. Feminism informs my life; it has impelled me to engage with class and race; it demands criticism of itself; it has taken up home in my heart and head. The feminism I am describing may be attracted to rhetorical answers but sooner, rather than later, cannot abide them. Through feminism I have met women with wit and wisdom, lifetime friends, lovers and workmates. I have met spiteful, envious, destructive women through feminism. I have met dogged, determined activists; I have met dedicated party girls, mums, dykes, married women, socialists, separatists, Jewish feminists, Black lesbian feminists, old women, young women, fat and thin. I have known witty destructive women and wise mundane girls. I have engaged with theories, ideas, collectives, actions and embroiled myself in strategies and tactics, defended and attacked political correctness, made friends and enemies.

It isn't all serious. I love comics, magazines, TV, films, food, violent murder mysteries, the sea, sex, dressing up, hats, shoes, fashion, making and collecting jewellery, far-flung travel, day-dreaming, parties, lesbian erotica, second-hand shops, laughing till I think I'll wet myself, orgasms, the comfort of familiarity, music, dancing, the relief of silence.

Contradictions and ambivalences are old companions; I wouldn't be without them now. Years ago I wished them gone, envied total certainty. Friends joke about Sue and ambivalence – a joke I take with a grain of salt and a dollop of acceptance. They are an integral part of my feminism now, not unwelcome disruptions. Now as I ponder this collection, the final writing choices laid out in print, it is those two words, contradiction and ambivalence, which settle into view. If these 'conditions' affect the way I approach or experience life, can I lay claim to feminism, to left politics, to anything, with certainty? My answer is yes and I hope the writing in this book will convince the reader too.

Let me make it clear: I am not articulating a recent conversion to the uncertainties of postmodernism, throwing its net back in time and reframing my understandings of what I believed fifteen or twenty years ago in its light. The 'conditions' I refer to were alive and well long before I understood (what little) I now know about postmodernism. I never was on the forefront of academic fashion. I'll illustrate my uneven journey.

Sixteen and a Quaker pacifist in 1957: trying to explain to a handsome young sailor I met on the beach why the bomb (and war and killing) was wrong. No meeting of minds or emotions, maybe a tingle of sexual attraction. Fury and frustration. I want to attack him, hurt him, beat him (kill him?) because he cannot and will not understand my heartfelt pacifism. I worry about this later.

Young fucking: I'm dying for sex – dreaming of men and penetration. I get wet and dizzy as much with my fantasy as with any real life boy. Even at eighteen, having had variations on these day-dreams since I was twelve, I know nothing about wanking. I go out with boys and even older men. When I start having intercourse it is (what I don't know then) a classic disappointment. I remain wet, hopeful and disappointed.

School and college: I am in love with history and literature. Get all excited by discussions in and out of our small tutorials. I don't work very hard. I don't think I can write. I see myself as second rate, good enough to get by. My excitement is mine and is shared by some of my friends, it means nothing about what I might achieve academically and in the world. What will I do in the future? 'I suppose I could always teach school.'

College: a professor of history, a woman of a certain age who is fantastically attractive. Sophisticated and European, black sheath dresses, clunky silver jewellery, dark hair in a thick bun, red lipstick. My old friend Dodo and I sigh as she walks past us, smelling her perfume. Her views frustrate and confuse me. She is a sophisticated conservative who scoffs at my naive belief in the UN, my liberal woolliness. I can't stand what she believes but she knows a thousand times more than I; she is invincible and I know she's wrong but I am enthralled by her person and she addresses the subjects I find most fascinating. I fantasize about being able to refute her effectively.

Where is home? I am a North American who hasn't lived there for over thirty years. I talk like an American. I understand the USA, it's my right to make outrageous generalizations about Americans. Visiting the USA is wonderful, but live there? I wouldn't know how or where. I am a naturalized Brit. I belong here. It is the place I know best. I know zilch about British history, couldn't name its counties if you paid me, and am always identified as an American. I live in Australia. I miss London, its proper city density, miss my friends and children. I definitely can't make a transition to a third continent. No way, not even for love. Back in London I suddenly miss Melbourne, can't stop praising it, delighted with my life there. What's a girl to do?

Bad girl/good girl: I have a checkered relationship with smoking and drinking. Addicted to smoking, not to booze, but partaking of both in big doses. I'm also a trained health educationalist. I know inside-out all the data and all the right ways to cut down or give up. No excuses for me. I keep on, trying to give up the noxious weed, supporting non-smoking policies, aware of the power of the cigarette multinationals. And then I'm out back, puffing away, spending a fortune, loving it and plotting the next big quit. I worry about my weight. I shouldn't drink so much. It's easy to stop but it's fun to imbibe. I only get the moderation thing right sporadically. I misbehave and am indiscreet. It embarrasses my girlfriend and I feel remorse. I'd lose weight if I cut it out. I do and I don't lose weight. I don't judge people on how fat or thin they are. I judge myself. I can't stand the way it feels in the summer if my thighs rub together. I'm post menopausal. Love your pounds and cellulite. I can't. I adore food, eating out, cooking at home, reading recipes. I keep worrying around the dizzy puzzle of acceptance, resistance, pleasure and the fear of disease. This is my unstatic state. Love the state and not the conditions?

The essays in *I Used to be Nice* stretch back over twenty-five years. There are only a few from the first few years; many more come from the last ten. My confidence grew and my fears receded as I lived through more and more years of involvement in politics – in feminism, anti-racism, social-ism, activism, study. It grew as I negotiated my way through personal misery and happiness. As I tried to get to grips with loving my children and hating motherhood, loving their father but desiring relationships with women. I got knocked around a bit in most everything I plunged into and didn't forget it. Niceness used to cloak not only my insecurities and confusions but also my anger and frustration. Trying to behave with integrity is not the same as being nice. I still am nice – sometimes.

I have gathered my work here under five thematic umbrellas. These themes are often connected and certainly broad enough to incorporate changes and shifts in how I have approached a particular subject over the years. This is most clearly illustrated in my HIV/AIDS writing, where I have come back several times to the relationship of sexuality and the meaning of AIDS.

The writing in this book is a developing, ongoing attempt to understand and explore conditional truths, changing contradictions, articulated and unarticulated ambivalences. I am prepared to admit differences, question dogma and fight for my ideals. I still want to be part of collective change. I am prepared to be wrong (I don't particularly want to be), but I am conscious of the strength of my beliefs. I take faltering responsibility for myself. I do not stand alone. The work here is mine, and mine and others, particularly Susan Ardill and Partibha Parmar who co-wrote some of the pieces.

PART ONE

Telling It My Way

With the exception of a short item in a British lefty/anarcho newspaper about women disrupting what we saw as the male-dominated Festival of Revolution at London's Round House in the late 1960s, the only things I ever wrote were for 'women's liberation' publications. These were simply produced, cobbled together newsletters, and the monthly women's liberation journal whose editing and production was circulated among the proliferation of women's liberation 'small groups' through much of the 1970s in London. Far from seeing these contributions as anything to do with 'creative writing', I (and many others) wrote to share our experiences in the name of the personal being political. It was this impulse which made it possible to consider publication.

In that context, I wrote 'Rambling Notes' not long after the birth of my second child, Dan, in March 1970. In those first years of women's liberation many of the women involved were mothers and our concerns were reflected in our emphases on the privatized and often lonely nature of the family, on childcare, on issues of radical child-rearing and in our dismissal of biological determinism.

Although we asserted that capitalism alongside sexism created the lonely mother endlessly recleaning the house and servicing men and children, we also mercilessly attacked men for shirking childcare and housework. Implicit in this perspective was our own intimate knowledge that women were often isolated and miserable when stranded at home with babies and small children. However, it was unusual for a woman to stand up and state that being a mother might not be her cup of tea in any circumstances. As I remember it, I was driven to explain the depth of my unhappiness in this simple little piece which, however clumsily, rejected a simple notion of some future revolution.

It's striking to me reading this all these years later how much my own language has changed. Although I still call myself a socialist, still believe that it is important to understand and oppose capitalism, I also am not so easy with the rhetoric and labelling we so confidently applied back then. In part this nineties' discomfort may be due to a despicable streak of cowardice, knowing how unpopular the rhetoric has become. But I don't believe it was experienced as rhetoric in 1970. That language, used in relation to women in the domestic sphere, didn't feel tired or over-used – quite the opposite, it felt daring, invigorating and challenging.

For me, some things remain constant – but understandings and contexts change. How do you remain true to your beliefs and yet speak with a voice which plugs into the time, even in opposition to much of what is *of* the time? How do you snap out of your own ruts but not sway boringly to the loudest tune? All I know is that what has lasted for me when I read this over a quarter-of-a-century-old piece is the feeling of despair and confusion which I opened up to the readers of *Shrew*, hopeful that they would connect with me and be part of what rescued me. Naive perhaps but not despicable.

In the original article, painfully typed on an old typewriter and corrected with Tipp-Ex, I used the initials WL instead of women's liberation or feminism, WL because that was our shorthand; not feminism because none of the small groups used that word then. For clarity in 1995, I have spelled out what was initialled in 1970.

Ten years after writing 'Rambling Notes' and I'm still contemplating motherhood. I'm at *Spare Rib* magazine, a member of the all-consuming collective since 1979. I had recently finished a full-time health education diploma and didn't have a clue what came next. I wasn't looking but a friend asked if I were applying for the *SR* job which had recently been advertised. I didn't even know one was going, nor had I ever thought of working on the magazine, but that started me thinking. I'd been involved in women's liberation publications for most of the 1970s, including *Red Rag*, a socialist-feminist journal. I was already in love with women's publications but had never dreamed of getting paid even the pittance *Spare Rib* offered to work on a feminist magazine. One nerve-wracking interview and six weeks later I was at the door to *Spare Rib* at 9a.m. on a Monday morning, ready to go. No one turned up until after 10, no one had prepared a place for me to sit. It was, I soon realized, chaos as usual.

Spare Rib was an emotional roller-coaster. Every controversy or development in the women's liberation movement ended up in our endless collective meetings, sometimes brought in from outside by individuals or groups who all believed we should give the magazine over fully to their concerns, and sometimes originating from within the collective itself. We were embattled every way you looked.

But not only embattled. There were moments, weeks, months even when we sailed along, entranced with the magazine and engrossed with the possibilities *Spare Rib* afforded us. We had fads like eating lunch together at the Indian café on Old Street, or ending up in the little pub with the open fire after the inevitable late night's work. In the untidy office we all shared, the issues which drove us apart also pulled us together so we had gripping conversations in meetings or over fags in the hall about sex, race, class and the meaning of feminism, sprinkled with liberal amounts of gossip and whether or not we shaved our legs.

Whatever the mood, somehow it worked because each month the

bloody magazine came out. Within its pages we managed to include some interesting and innovative material, things which mainstream women's magazines didn't touch then. These might be weighty and deep or cranky and crackpot, but ponder them all we did. I still admire the way in which we tried to take an issue, such as the scary and wild assertion by a few women that boy children be banned from women's spaces or even that feminists refuse to rear boy children, and turn it into a serious exploration of some of the problems boy children present to feminists. My article on the problem of boy children was part of this process.

Today I would have less patience, would be less 'nice' about the women who believed that boy children were, by virtue of being born male, a threat to women's liberation. Some of those same women today have given birth to boys and changed their minds about the irredeemable nature their babies' genitals will lead to. But the not-so-funny final twist is there are no guarantees about kids. Whoever their mothers are, whatever they say and do, some boys grow up to be shits, others don't and some are shitty one day and great the next.

By 1980 I had been having sexual relationships with women for several years. I didn't call myself a lesbian, not because I didn't think I was one but because I was still living the longest part of the week with my husband and children and still didn't know what to do about it all. I loved them but knew it was with women that my sexual future lay. I don't reveal much of that in my article about boy children, perhaps because I was endlessly extricating myself from a painful, knotty, disastrous relationship with a much younger and totally fucked-up dyke. Although not confused about lust, I was in a quandary about identity. If I desired women but lived with my husband who I still loved and my kids who drove me nuts but I also loved, what was I? Bisexual felt all wrong. Without a woman lover, I imagined one or more in the future. With a very specific husband, I imagined no other men, nor had I since marrying him.

It wasn't until 1982, in the throes of a serious but troubled relationship with another woman that the contradiction was forced into a resolution of sorts. Being a dyke about town for half the week and spending the other half in the married home was impossible to sustain and left the people I loved confused and angry. I sublet a tiny, short-life flat in London's King's Cross and discovered the joys of living alone. Painful and hurtful times, but my children and husband handled the situation mostly with grace and goodwill.

I like to think I write against the grain of jargon or facile rhetoric. But in 1995 I wince at my use of the word patriarchy in 'Boy Children' – it feels glib, unexplained and unnecessary. As in 'Rambling Notes', I am aware of using language now out of fashion. Ten years after 'Rambling Notes', in 1980 I have a confident feminist vocabulary which fifteen years later, in 1995, also sounds out of tune. Yet I knew exactly what I meant when I used certain words and if political realities or fashions have shifted, many of the situations women face in the 1990s still need words which indicate the seriousness of change necessary.

In 1980 I could still refer to 'our movement' as a source of possibility and radical change even if the fragmentation we all became so familiar with was already in evidence. Today such optimism would appear caught in la-la land. However, new configurations of militancy keep popping up, often originating from lesbian political and social life. A frustrating flux but one not without hope.

In 1980 when *Feminist Review (FR)* asked me to write what turned into 'Passionate Politics' I was filled with fear and trepidation. I went to college in the United States and majored in modern dance. I thought of *Feminist Review* as an academic journal. Would my approach fit in? I didn't understand at the time that *FR* was trying to shift its academic emphasis to include more popular intellectual approaches. I agonized over the essay, pouring over my hoarded newsletters, diaries and pamphlets, trying to structure something adequate for the journal.

Later in 1984, the *FR* collective asked me to join and I was similarly afflicted with the urge to look over my shoulder to see if they were talking to someone else. I has recently left *SR* and wanted to be involved in other feminist publishing projects. I said yes to *FR* and imagined a new period of exciting intellectual development. I fantasized about the scary but mesmerizing discussions I would partake in, about how I would now get a handle on theoretical developments within socialist feminism, including psychoanalysis and postmodernism. Hmm. I've learned a lot but not quite in the way I imagined.

'Passionate Politics' has afforded me the chance to look back. I am glad I wrote it when I did because I couldn't do it now – the haziness is greater, events have overtaken my memories. It would be a different essay.

Amanda Sebestyen asked me to contribute a piece to her anthology, *'68, '78, '88*, covering women's involvement in feminism from the end of the 1960s until the end of the 1980s. I ended up working on it in tandem with my piece for Sara Maitland's collection, *Very Heaven*, which looked back at women's lives in the 1970s. The areas I was contemplating for each book overlapped yet I ended up with two chapters which differed in style, tone and emphasis. I didn't realize this at the time because I was running so fast to meet deadlines, but later it reminded me how one telling of a certain history is bound to leave things out, how a full understanding of that history, even from one individual, would be played with many notes.

The worst response I ever received was in a review by Maureen Freely of *Very Heaven*. I sat reading the Sunday papers one morning, enjoying the relaxation, browsing through the book review section. Wait a minute – there was a review of the book. Amazing. I don't think I'd ever been in a book which was reviewed in a big-time Sunday. Obviously I immediately dived in, filled with curiosity – I was mentioned and incredibly dismissively. Maureen Freely put me down for describing my sexual past explicitly. Who on earth would be interested, she sneered. My feelings were exactly the same as in the distant past when my mother brusquely rejected my childish self-consciousness in public. Reading the review, my face flamed and down the slippery slope of humiliation I slid. I got over it and was intrigued when, some years later, Maureen Freely published a much-touted erotic novel. Had the times changed?

Turning the Tables – Writing and Recipes by Women was the most enjoyable publishing project I've ever been involved in. It was fast and fun and exhausting. In 1986 at the International Feminist Book Fair in Oslo, a few of us from Sheba Feminist Publishers where I was working at the time, sat around in the flat we were staying in, deep into talk about food. We described favourite dishes, hated flavours, how we had learned to cook (or not), what place food and mealtimes held in our families. We joked about the stereotypes of British food and recalled culinary disasters. And we dissected the differences between cultures around food and meals. Someone said it was time for a feminist cookbook and there was a simultaneous rush of agreement. A feminist cookbook which included a melange of dishes, a mix of experience and a collection of different women's writings and recipes.

I edited the book, half in Sheba time and half in my own. It would be a Sheba fund raiser – 5 per cent of any royalties to Sheba and the remaining $2^{1}/_{2}$ to me. On this basis I felt confident about asking women to donate their contribution to the book. Many women we asked agreed at once. We decided we needed at least a few famous women to help sell the book, and the rest could be more like ourselves. We even wrote to Madonna. A few amazingly generous women responded, including Angela Carter, Julie Christie and Miriam Margolyes. A number of Black women writers and activists from Britain and the USA came through, and other friends of Sheba sent recipes. The whole book took a year to complete from beginning to end. We commissioned an introduction from a feminist cook book scholar, and we joked that one of the unique qualities of *Turning the Tables* is the untested nature of the recipes – no quality control kitchen for us.

From cooking and eating to the menopause, mine. *A Certain Age* was Joanna Goldworthy's anthology of writings about the menopause. I wrote my piece in the third person as an experiment, to see if I could do something different. That distancing made me feel more as if I were writing a story and I enjoyed the process. I had read Germaine Greer's book, *The Change*, and found it exasperating and only intermittently inspiring. It seemed that everything and everyone had to fit into her grand design. Lesbians were hardly mentioned although one of her theses was that menopausal women are finally free to shake off the leg irons of men's sexual demands. What about those of us already without men's sexual demands at menopause? Were we to abandon our pleasing sex lives with women? I thought that women, of any sort, were probably as wildly diverse in their physical and emotional responses to menopause as in any other life event.

The pieces in this section either come out of highly personal experiences or are my individual recollections of a particular historical period: motherhood and menopause, reflections on a few years at the beginning of the women's liberation movement in Britain, and on to a longer vista of politics and personal life – with a *soupçon* of cooking book flavour thrown in.

Rambling Notes

– FROM *SHREW*, 1970

Women's Liberation here (in Britain) is good in so much as it can raise consciousness. That's exciting and necessary but ultimately it can be only depressing if that's all it can do, even in our present society.

Why did I come into Women's Liberation? It took about six months of hearing about it from friends in the USA and at first not paying it much attention until about Christmas time 1968 it hit me what it was all about. It took that long for my particular point in life (intellectual, emotional *and* actual) for the concept of WL to germinate in my resistant mind but once it managed to break through that was it … I was committed in all ways. At times I could falter over WL intellectually but emotionally I knew it was right.

From the beginning most of us involved in the women's groups felt a need for action and numerous discussions followed… What kind of action? directed at who? with what end in mind?, etc. The actions we actually did do were usually demonstrations of some kind or else talking to people in different situations – schools, colleges, theatres. The hope behind everything we did was that the women we reached would begin to question their roles in all sorts of ways and also begin to question the very system we live under.

From the start of my involvement in WL I questioned from time to time how much it had changed my own life. I knew it had changed the way I looked at almost everything, but had the way I lived my life undergone any change? As my baby grew older I learned to manage better and could be involved in things which took me away more. My questioning of whether I changed my own life through my new analysis of woman's role in the home, in the whole of society, and my sharpened knowledge of what socialism was really all about, although real, were not felt to be immediately needed in my own life. I *knew* that one should try to put into practice what one believed but still I mostly talked.

The excitement was mostly going out of WL for me but the commitment remained and still does. After a summer (1969) in NY and much talk and experience of WL there I felt that in London we had very good possibilities because we were not split up into factions, and were interested in many issues at once.

Then I had my second child. The birth, unlike with the first child, was extremely fast. I still did not find it (the birth) 'beautiful' or 'meaningful' and was very pleased when it was over. It was again something of a shocking experience for me. I haven't really worked out what I feel about giving birth … it's a very primitive thing which takes over your body, and we are not primitive now. The whole thing about maternal love does not necessarily go along with the physical process of birth. You can successfully push the baby out and be presented with a healthy squalling baby and feel nothing except relief that it's over and some interest in the small creature in your arms. But that's ok. It's when the depression sets in that things become unbearable. And in my experience when you ask a doctor about it they just sympathetically nod and say it's 'normal' and will pass. Big help. For me the depression started after I got home from the hospital. I had been depressed after my first baby but it was not so intense and mainly concerned my feelings for the baby … I didn't really love him at all for the first six weeks. This time the depression pervades my feelings about everything … the new baby, Tom, and John and mostly my life – what am I doing, how can I go on, how can I cope, what should I do? I know that my actual position is much better than most women's. I know what 'post-natal' depression is all about. I know that the irrational depression will pass. I know that the baby will probably stop continuously screaming when awake at three months. None of this helps. I feel isolated, helpless and depressed.

Where I am is nowhere. I'm not living a radical life and there are no socialist solutions in Britain for my problems. What also has been brought home is that WL as it exists now offers few solutions. My old group, Tufnell Park, has split up. My place in the new Tufnell Park group has not yet developed, but I feel confused and so feel that so far I've not been positive in the new group because of my ambivalent feelings towards it.

I can't even effect middle-class solutions to my problems, although those are possible (e.g. mother's helper, nursery school, helpful husband).

Somehow we've got to do something about our lives … make possible some sort of change in the fucked-up way we, as well as everyone else, are forced to live under capitalism. I know that basically things can't be changed now, but some alternatives should be able to be created.

When I was in school, from primary through college, I had very close and good friendships with other girls. One woman who lives in the US has been a close friend since we were seven – twenty-two years of friendship. Other friendships go back fifteen years. Those friendships always meant a great deal to me although I never consciously realized this until I left college and got married. Then my friends weren't around. We went where our different men were or stayed in the big city. From that time till this I've only made a few women friends and I don't see much of them. Why is this? I don't seem to be able to develop close friendships anymore although I'd like to have them. I suspect this is true even within our women's group. I feel close to the women in the old Tufnell Park group but hardly ever see them except at meetings. A division between political life and private life. We discuss many things about ourselves in our groups but I still don't know anything about the lives of most of the women in the group ... things I would know if we were friends. But how does this friendship grow? In the past through being in school together ... doing things together ... being involved in work together. I guess I'm too isolated from people now to have friends. And there's something in me that helps to maintain that isolation.

Thinking About Boy Children

– FROM *SPARE RIB* 96, JULY 1980

An argument has been going on in parts of the women's liberation movement for the last six months or so concerning boy children, their mothers and other feminists. Some women are meeting specifically to discuss being mothers of male and female children. *Spare Rib* has received letters received deploring any possible policy in the women's movement which could keep out male babies and children (and by default their mothers) from women's events and places. It's made me ponder (not for the first time) about my boys, my feelings about motherhood. Whether or not it's only a handful of women who want to exclude male children from women's movement events, it's a debate which involves and raises thorny questions for many of us.

In 1970 I wrote, from the depths of post-natal depression, in *Shrew* '... what am I doing, how can I go on ... I feel isolated, helpless and depressed.'

During those years motherhood was a subject we discussed endlessly – ourselves as mothers, our own mothers and our children. Part of my recognition of women's oppression and my commitment to women's liberation was the growing understanding that our society made impossible demands on us as privatized, individualized mothers; made impossible demands on children as dependent 'future citizens' of a sick society. This ambivalence many of us felt about our children was slowly worked out in our consciousness–raising groups. We weren't failures or selfish because we couldn't live out an advertiser's dream life with them, or find satisfaction in an earth mother alternative. We wanted something more, something different for ourselves and for them. We'd have to change a hell of a lot to get there.

Thinking about it all, I remember the question of excluding boy children cropping up as a bitter rumour in the mid '70s, when it was pushed out of sight rather too quickly. Sighs of relief as embarrassing voices receded. It was outrageous for any woman to say that little boys should be excluded from a women's centre – obviously an overwrought reaction to children who hadn't asked to be born boy or girl.

I think now that this discussion ended too soon because obviously it's been simmering under the surface all along – not finished business at all. Perhaps this time we'll be able to take it through and resolve more completely the politics and emotions of it all.

For myself, it's a painful and complicated task. Right in the middle – having two boy children, being a feminist and socialist – looking for answers but knowing there aren't any simple ones.

I find myself dissatisfied with some slogans of feminism and the left. Any man could be my enemy, but what strategies, what tactics follow politically from saying 'men are the enemy'? But I won't absolve men from their sexism because it's all the fault of 'the system' and conditioning. Nor do I believe the destruction of capitalism will take care of women's oppression although I believe it is one of the preconditions for women's liberation. And although I want to work with and for women, I don't believe all men are a lost cause.

I have talked with women who believe that men are the enemy and that boy children are only 'little men' in the process of becoming full blown enemies – oppressing us in smaller ways as befits their size and age, but oppressing us nevertheless. Some of these women believe that biology is destiny and others, like me, believe that men are not born but 'made' by society. But unlike me they think the force of male power and privilege is so great that no boy child will escape this 'making'. If this is the case, they say, women must bond together in order to defeat men. For them, a rejection of boy children would be part of the price of that necessary war.

Other women, like me, who hope and try to combat sexism and

privilege in the boy children in their lives, hold up the possibility of change, of bringing up boys who reject their expected role as men and do not oppress women. Some radical feminists, too, hold this position and, believing that the struggle between men and women is primary, envisage militant and powerful interventions into male-dominated society and within personal relations with men.

I'm torn in different ways. Unlike some feminists, I believe that boy children are a problem, will remain so. We are asking the improbable of us and them when we hope to create them as our future perfect men, if only we try hard enough and get enough support from other women. But unlike the women who want to exclude boy children, I believe that daughters are a problem too; they may reject us and our feminism. I believe that the possibility of rejection by boys and girls (for different reasons and taking different forms) may be exacerbated if we try either to force them into a prepacked view of the world or attempt to isolate them from what *we* know is sexist and wrong. A boy with feminist influence in his life may stand a better chance than most, but the lure of the patriarchy is not something we can exclude or do battle with for the soul of an individual child.

I respect women who are investing energy into bringing up non-sexist children but I fear that unless we develop a concept of how anyone becomes and sustains themselves as a rebel within our society, we set ourselves and our children up for disappointment. Unlike some feminists who think that by rejecting things *for* children we help them, I believe that children have to come to grips with it all, have finally to understand it, in order to work out a criticism and rejection which is *theirs*.

None of us are outside patriarchy or capitalism. Any ideal image we offer to individual boys or girls is bound up with the possibility of failure. My goal in relation to my children is not to make them into non-sexist men, but to make a society which will make it impossible for them or any other boys to become sexist. That process may take more than my lifetime but the force of an ongoing collective struggle can influence and reverberate in individual lives, including my sons'.

The debate as it stands now over the future of male children often falls into the trap of 'either/or' thinking. Either you are/become a perfect non-sexist or you wallow in piggery. You are good or bad. But growing up and forging identities is very much about struggle and conflict. I see a society and people in it full of contradictions which are not necessarily static. I expect influences from school, friends, other adults, books, toys, films, music. All those things and people, taken in total, are showing my children that to be male, white and middle class offers them the most advantageous position.

At the same time they are suspicious and resentful of adults' power, of the grown-up world which is being held out to them as 'the way things are'. Their sense of 'unfairness' is acute. After all, their position and privilege as males are incomplete and tenuous. They're children and to them adults have the power, and that includes women. And there are people who offer alternative ways of seeing things, other ways of acting. Through these their acceptance of the official message is challenged and subverted. I demand some forms of behaviour and at the same time try to convince them that they can and will continue to change. I don't think it's the end of the road for them when they make a sexist remark and I don't think this is woolly liberalism.

I have to be honest about myself. Sometimes I too hanker after today's privileges but I understand that and know the fight is double-edged – against what's out there *and* in me. So if my boys are fascinated by soldiers and toughness, or harbour doubts about girls' abilities and roles, although these things make me furious and sad, I know that they're only one part of how they're thinking and acting. They also pick out and criticize the sexism in telly ads and programmes, the stupidity in thinking only women can cook or clean and the ridiculousness of super 'macho' men.

The daughters of feminists sometimes develop a fascination with clothes and make-up, the more 'feminine' the better, and become obsessed with boyfriends and families. It's only part of what they're grappling with and I don't think they're lost causes at all. As women, we can only confront them with our movement and argue about ways of seeing, thinking and behaving which will give them the tools to make the choice to make common cause with us.

But all this is fraught with difficulties and inconsistencies. I must admit that there is the possibility that my attitude about boys developed partly because I couldn't manage to try very hard for successful individual solutions. I didn't and don't want the burden or responsibility of proving I can bring up two non-sexist, anti-capitalist boys. The attempt could too easily become an intensification of a traditional mother's role. I rebel as much against the time and energy it would take as a mother to try and go against the tide as I do against the traditional roles of a mother. My boys' father happens to play the sustained 'caring' and taking-care-of role in their lives. This may be partly luck but it is also a reflection of the impact of feminism. If it hadn't happened, would I have left, or broken down, or stayed on?

As it is, I often end up by attempting to deny the family, my family, a very important place in my life. It suffocates me and closes in around me. However 'free' I seem, however much I am not oppressed personally by the men in my life, the force of male-dominated society becomes embodied in my family, 'my' men. The fact that they don't oppress me is countered by the fact that they could. At certain points, even the fact that they all sit and watch football infuriates me. The irony of being inside one of the institutions I want to work with other women to change turns to anger. It's because of the nature and role of the family within our society and because I am a women that I feel anguish over being IN it most acutely. At the same time I realize my relative privileges – economically and in terms of education I'm in a better position than many women.

Sometimes I go mad. Since they were little I've experienced horrifying feelings towards them. Their maleness has often alienated me. I also love them. I would relate differently to girl children, but I know they would suffocate me too. I must work with other women to change the society and the families in it that close us in. The women I want to be with will be mothers of girls or boys; they'll be women who have chosen not to have any children. They'll live with women. They'll live with men or alone. I believe that children don't have to weigh us down or close us in, nor we them. I want a society where all relationships have been transformed.

═══════════════════════

Passionate Beginnings: Ideological Politics 1969–72
– FROM *FEMINIST REVIEW*, NO. 11, SUMMER 1982

These days, in different circles of feminists and in feminist publications and conferences, there are various assertions about the ideas and actions from the beginning years of the women's liberation movement. Many of these assertions have taken on the air of received 'truths'. 'Socialist feminists never paid any attention to sexuality.' 'Radical feminists don't take class into account.' 'Lesbian feminists forced heterosexual feminists to accept the necessity of an autonomous movement.' And so on. None of these statements (I've actually heard them all at one time or another) take into account the vast differences which existed (and still exist) between women identifying as socialist feminists, radical feminists and lesbian feminists, nor any of the other political groupings of feminists. Instead they have seized upon statements of one group or individual and produced an all-time label. Non-aligned socialist feminists have been continuously branded with the economism of some of their aligned sisters' political positions – from the absurdity of the early Maoist groups to the more complex opportunism of some Trotskyist women's single-issue campaigning.

Radical feminists, because they proclaimed the primacy of sex-class oppression of women, were assumed to have no position on class divisions and no matter how often they rebelled against this label (*Feminist Practice*, 1979), it stuck. And the false assumption that heterosexual feminists were not active in the early days in creating and defending an autonomous women's liberation movement helps to obscure the more substantial questions of heterosexual privilege and anti-lesbianism which were (and are) dividing women.

Another problem is that some feminist intellectuals appear to have cornered areas which have long been concerns of the women's liberation movement and have, by dint of the obscure way in which these issues are now presented, temporarily scared many women off the areas they pronounce so seriously on. I recognize that theories cannot always in themselves be 'easy' to understand, but surely it is necessary to re-assert the earlier emphasis feminists put on the link between theory and practice and to remember how deeply rooted early discussions and actions were in questions of ideology. What is the point of developing sophisticated feminist theories of ideology if these appear as incomprehensible and irrelevant to many and also end up fuelling a general anti-intellectualism which feminists are not immune from.

I want to recall that the concerns of the early women's liberation movement were grounded in issues of ideology: in questions about the construction of femininity, motherhood and sexuality, in grappling with internalized inferiority, and a ghettoized 'private life'. Many of the actions taken by women in those years were around those areas. 'Consciousness raising' was, after all, about consciousness and change: about collective exploration of personal experiences and emotions, in turn leading to the necessity of struggle for personal and social change. Whether or not consciousness raising took place in a small group or in a larger meeting, at a national conference or in action, it represented part of a unique politics and one which we forget – to our disadvantage – today.

Although the tendency to label was there from the beginning it was more or less irrelevant for the first few years. Our early discoveries and ventures into action were intuitively and spontaneously imbued with and fired by ideas and issues which came from our own specific experiences as women as well as from a large and eclectic melting pot of 1960s radical politics. Of course there were different ideas, different analyses, but they were not yet exclusive. Women belonging to sects or parties were often viewed with suspicion by the non-aligned, exactly because they were assumed to have worked-out 'lines'.

By recalling where some of our ideas came from, I'd like to pull out the way in which other people's revolutions and struggles moved us, whether it be the Chinese revolution or Frantz Fanon's observations on colonialism in Algeria. And I want to think about some of our early concerns and actions – from leafleting the Ideal Home Exhibition to the Miss World demonstration. Why? Partly because many feminists now weren't around then; partly to identify times and places I think were influential; partly to start at the beginning and see what relevance, if any, those beginnings have to our politics today. In light of an economic crisis, a crisis in politics, and the various voices from within our movement which are telling us what we must do, think, experience, I think it will help to reflect on our emergence as a movement which significantly broke with previous ways of defining politics, allowed women to speak for themselves from their own experience, and, in doing so, reached thousands of women.

The early collective uncovering of women's oppression – the *necessity* and commitment to changing and challenging the world – bound feminists together in sisterhood. Throughout history movements for social change have given their members a world view which made sense of life and created solidarity in struggle. The women's liberation movement did this. The difference was our focus on the divisions between men and women in all areas of life, and our insistence on the political nature of the family, 'private' and personal life, and sexuality.

My personal evocation of the early years runs the risk of appearing nostalgic. That I do not want to be. Feminism changed my life in a way nothing else ever has. But if some of the strengths of the early years have been lost, there is much to be critical of in a retrospective look as well.

In this article I am being selective in my attempts to explain and describe aspects of the early women's liberation movement. I am *not* trying for a comprehensive overview. I've chosen to focus on the years between 1969 and 1972 and to relate them to today because I feel, more than I can prove, that that was a relatively cohesive time.

Nothing changed suddenly in 1972. Much of what happened came out of the necessity feminists felt by then to try to move beyond spontaneity to a more sophisticated level of analysis and long-range strategy. I know there are traceable, although complex, interactions and tensions which led to the muting of early insistence on the interdependence of theory and practice. After all, we didn't have a lot of theory and we certainly wanted to reach more women with our practice. But that must be the work of another article.

Looking back to 1969, 1970, 1971, 1972; remembering those early years. Many of us, in London at any rate, didn't even call ourselves feminists. We had responded to women's liberation on the basis of our own contradictory experiences of the world and with men in that particular historical period. Our knowledge of the long history of women's oppression and struggles against it, our own recognition of ourselves as feminists, came later. At that point it was the desire for liberation for all oppressed women which overwhelmed us. We righteously proclaimed our disdain of the possibility of being equal with unfree men. We wanted much more than that.

This is what is so exciting about the ideas generated by this movement ...
it leads you on to question everything ... all our social institutions, the
whole way our society is structured. (Camden Women's Liberation Open
Meeting. Hampstead Town Hall, 7 July 1971)

We don't want to demand an equally bad education as men – we want
equal resources, not equal repression. We want to fight for real education,
to make our own jobs and opportunities. (*Women's Newspaper*
No. 1, 6 March 1971)

I do not intend to justify my struggles for liberation. I am oppressed and
that is sufficient. I do not intend to ask permission from Pekin before
proceeding, I do not intend to neurotically consult Marxengelslenin
before baring my teeth or my teats. I do not intend to give ladylike (read
suckass) reassurance to male radical chauvinists during the course of this
struggle; even if it means losing their friendship (i.e. patronage!). ('The
Female Separatist', *Shrew*, July 1969)

Looking back ... those early years are vivid and alive. I imagine the
spinning feeling that we had stepped into something which had to change
history, but brought with it frightening doubts that we'd personally be
able to change as much as our ideals demanded. But today how and what
do I recall so vividly from yesterday? All these years later, how do I filter
and translate, magnify and minimize what I lived through? The tension
between my objectivity and subjectivity makes *me* tense; this article is no
listing of truths, although I have gone through my rat-pack bags of early
newsletters and magazines to try to check and match my memories with
the memorabilia. I am wary of pronouncements on the way things were.
Still ...

At the beginning of the women's liberation movement, we faced
problems about our identity as an oppressed group – especially when we
tried to go beyond the deeply felt gut knowledge that it was true. If
women were oppressed because of their sex, why was there, in
comparison with other oppressed groups, so little history of collective
rebellion? Feminist history came later and most of us weren't academics.
The history of struggles around class and race formed, however
erratically or with whatever mystification, part of those groups' identities
– general strikes, revolutions, slave revolts, anti-imperialist struggles.

The way in which many women came to articulate their oppression as
women, to perceive their subordination in the world of men, was *partly*
through empathy with others' struggles. By the late 1960s the politics
coming out of such struggles included observations, analysis and practice
which women in turn seized hold of to help them define themselves ...
Mao, Black power, Fanon, Vietnam, Reich, libertarianism, sexual
liberation. All this was double-edged, for although complacencies of the

old left and the establishments were being shaken up around issues such as leadership, democracy and sex, women and 'private life' were left out. Not only were they left out, women were oppressed. So we were using the male-dominated politics of revolution to help us define our own politics of revolution but these same events, texts, ideas, with their overall negation of women, propelled us towards the formation of the women's liberation movement itself.

Some of these diverse influences came via the United States. There, by the late 1960s, many women were familiar with the politics of liberation from the Black movement, the new left and the anti-Vietnam movement. These three areas expressed, within male domination, questions of consciousness – 'Black is beautiful', opposition to hierarchy and dogma, and challenges to imperialism from 'within the belly of the monster' itself. These three movements (never totally separate) in turn had their influence on politics in Britain. The experiences of American women active in these movements played a significant part in the formation of women's liberation groups and influenced us in Britain. But this was always in play with our own history – the long struggle for equal pay within the labour movement, and a Marxist intellectual tradition which had already produced feminist writings by the mid-1960s. None of this is to imply that white British feminists had transcended racism or a middle-class bias.

At around the same time, the brief and dramatic risings in France of 1968 brought forward some specifically European left-wing but 'alternative' politics which drew our eyes towards China of the Cultural Revolution. Also we were aware, within the European/Third World tension again, of the work of Frantz Fanon, who raised issues of consciousness, oppression and liberation within the framework of the Algerian revolution. Even considering his stunning lack of recognition about the oppression of women, these issues reverberated in the small groups of women I knew. We were devouring any literature we could find if it helped us to understand and name our own oppression and the contradictions our new consciousness brought to light in our own lives.

Finally, the libertarians and the 'situationists' of the 1960s and the 1930s 'sexual politics' of Reich, all found a place in our armoury of books and ideas. Looking back, it's all too easy to see the faults, the gaps and the false pictures we sometimes took from what we read in our rush to find explanations, descriptions, which made us say 'Ah yes! That's it. That's true for women too.'

Our growing collective recognition that all men of all classes and races oppressed at least some women, plus our appropriation of the descriptions and analyses of oppression from male writers and participants who totally ignored or put down women may appear now as a contortionist's act. It led, in some cases, to an appreciation (sometimes ironic) of the contradictions inherent in liberation struggles, without necessarily writing them off, and to an empathy (sometimes simplistic), usually open-eyed, with the struggles waged around imperialism and class. But all along we insisted, 'no revolution without women's liberation'. Feminists held up the essential nature of *women's* liberation ... no more taking the back row. And as we sharpened our understanding of the depths of women's oppression, some women despaired and rejected any of the male-dominated politics which were initially compelling.

At that point we found in Mao and Fanon ideas about consciousness and change which related to our practice of consciousness raising. Women took note when Frantz Fanon described how even in situations of overt repression in Algeria the people could internalize their oppression and believe they deserved it.

> For unconsciously I distrust what is black in me, that is, the whole of my being. (Fanon, 1967)

> ... that the total result looked for by colonial domination was indeed to convince the natives that colonialism came to lighten their darkness. (Fanon, 1965)

Couldn't we say that women had been colonized by men and through that and their isolation within the family came to identify with their oppressors?

> One has to deal, for example with the uneasiness that comes with a shift in loyalties from one's husband or lover, maybe, to the group. The safety and reflected power that makes it comfortable to identify with one's oppressor has to be given up and strength found to identify with one's oppressed group and other oppressed groups. The group itself should provide this strength. (*Shrew*, 1971)

It was the difficulty of explaining why women participated at all in their own oppression at whatever level which led to descriptions of marriage as a 'gilded cage', to discussions of 'the man in our head', to debunking for ourselves as well as others the accepted 'truths' of human nature. We explored and rejected traditional and deeply ingrained beliefs, particularly as they applied to motherhood and sexuality ... the myths of the vaginal orgasm and female passivity and 'natural' fulfilment through maternity and childcare. Fanon in Algeria and Black power groups in the USA expressed the necessity of oppressed people turning over their consciousness in order to struggle effectively. Women understood that they too had to struggle against guilt, conditioning and internalized self-hatred in order to begin new definitions of being women ... new definitions of liberation.

In the late sixties and early seventies, when looking at China, it was clear that the gap between the feudal patriarchal life of Chinese women in pre-revolutionary China and the relatively privileged lives of British women was vast. However the overt, totally accepted subservience and inferiority of most women in traditional Chinese society, which was reflected and recognized in poetry and literature, struck chords with western women who had no such totally clear cultural history of their own oppression to refer to. When we read books like *Fanshen* in our small women's group, it was *not* identification we experienced as the story of one Chinese village's passage from bondage to revolutionary beginnings unrolled. It was more a sense of connection and a thrill of admiration that the unambiguous oppression of women in China was being shaken. We felt a connection across thousands of miles and years of different histories:

> Women said 'Our husbands regard us as some sort of dogs who keep the house ... After we get our share we will be masters of our own fate.'

And:

> By 'speaking pains to recall pains', the women found that they had as many if not more grievances than the men and that once given a chance to speak in public they were as good at it as their fathers and husbands ... (Hinton, 1966)

We took inspiration from the fact that even the most intense material deprivation interwoven with the most deeply ingrained beliefs about women could, by dint of enormous effort, passion and upheaval united in revolution, be shifted. Cracks existed and could be widened – change was possible.

Some of us went on to find out more about the Chinese revolution and to be inspired by it, but even women who did not take a special interest in China were curious (and a little dubious) about it and about the subsequent Cultural Revolution in the 1960s. The cultural revolution, as we understood it, spoke volumes to feminist insistence that the seizure of economic power was not enough; that women had been badly served after the revolution in the Soviet Union and that prolonged and intense struggle would be necessary to change what went on (and on) in people's heads after any revolution.

One chapter of the 1949 classic, *China Shakes the World* (Belden, 1970) made the rounds of feminists as a little pamphlet called *Gold Flower's Story*. On her wedding night when she was fifteen, her husband

> ... almost tore her head off with a blow of his fist. Blood ran down Gold Flower's face. She lay back exhausted and in a quick fit of passion he raped her.

At eighteen, when the revolutionary Eighth Route Army entered her village and cadres came to organize, things began to change for Gold Flower. She heard women talking of struggling against their enslavement as women.

> 'That's right. Ah, that's right!' Gold Flower said to herself over and over again, as she listened to this woman who seemed to be speaking directly to her heart.

At a meeting of the village women Chang (Gold Flower's husband) was asked if he was ready to bow to women. His answer was not sincere.

> As if by a signal, all the women pushed forward at once. Gold Flower quickly went in back of her husband. The crowd fell on him, howling, knocked him to the ground, then jumped on him with their feet. Several women fell with him, their hands thrashing wildly. Those in the rear leaped in, tore at his clothing, then seized his bare flesh in their hands and began twisting and squeezing till his blood flowed from many scratches. Those who could not get close, dove under the rest and seized Chang's legs, sinking their teeth in his flesh.
>
> Chang let out an anguished howl. 'Don't beat me! Don't beat me!' he bleated in terror. 'I'll reform. Don't hurt me any more!'

But it was clear that Chang had not really changed.

> The chairwoman went up to the roof of her house and called through a megaphone. 'Comrade women! Come at once! Something of import-ance!' Out from nearly every clay hut in the village tumbled a woman. Rushing toward the Women's Association Building, they heard the chair-woman explain: 'Gold Flower's husband is bad again! Get ropes and catch him!'
>
> With Gold Flower in the lead, forty howling women ran through the village. But her husband had already fled.

Gold Flower's Story was both audacious and moving and also more extreme than most of us would have ever dared to imagine. I remember feeling a mixture of real malicious pleasure at the descriptions of man-beating but also feeling a bit guilty and voyeuristic. As she 'stood up', Gold Flower confronted her oppressors and most directly that meant her husband. However, her actions were only possible in the context of monumental social upheaval. In my 'small group' many of the women were aware of the contradictory nature for women of life 'in and against' advanced capitalism and male domination. A monumental social upheaval was not around the corner in England, and many women in purely material terms were not desperate. It was in exploring those contradictions as women that we began to develop our own political confidence.

Gold Flower was part of a movement against overt terror and repression. While stunned by her courage (the courage of the Chinese masses) we realized we had to break through an ideological stranglehold within a very different economic situation. Confronting the man in the house who was 'sympathetic' was not easy. In a March 1971 issue of the London Women's Liberation magazine, *Shrew*, an article described a 'confrontation'.

> Her husband was sympathetic on the theoretical level to the general tenets of Women's Lib but these views were not, from the woman's point of view, being translated into reality in their home and particularly in the care of the small children.
>
> … it was clear that both she and her husband were not alone in their failure to work out together the tensions and practical aspects which arose from childcare and housework and also out of her struggle to begin to define herself and her needs. These problems were made more acute and pressing for all the women in the group because of their involvement in Women's Lib.

After discussing the problem and considering a number of possibilities, the women decided to ask all the men they were in relationships with to attend an 'emergency' meeting. The meeting was held and was an anticlimax … 'puzzled' sympathetic men and nervous evading talk. I am not guessing about any of this because it was my 'small group' which called the meeting and wrote the article afterwards.[1] We were feeling our way in fits and starts towards being a 'person in my own right'.

> I challenged him on the hypocrisy of his political attitudes. Wasn't I oppressed too? He hadn't even come to terms with this fact, let alone the fact that he was my oppressor. I looked after the home and kids so that he could be free to do what he liked. (*Shrew*, March 1971)

Being aware personally of one's desire and need for liberation was seen as a collective process. In the *Women's Liberation Workshop Manifesto* which was pulled together at a meeting of fifty to sixty women before the first women's liberation conference at Ruskin College in February 1970, the emphasis was on the necessity for social change:

> Each small group is autonomous, holding different positions and engaging in different types of activity. As a federation of a number of different groups, the Women's Liberation Workshop is essentially heterogeneous, incorporating within it a wide range of opinions and plans for action. We come together as groups and individuals to further our part in the struggle for social changes and the transformation of society.

Women were in the process of defining their own political perspectives and entering into actions which helped them define aims. Between early 1969 and 1972 in London small groups spread, growing in number from two to over eighty. We continued to express the contradictions and anger of our daily lives in our rotating monthly magazine, *Shrew*. We got into the straight press through our actions and 'outrageous' views.

> We decided to have a sticker campaign which would be concentrated in the Underground and would among other things, publicize the Equal Pay rally to take place in May. Our first batch of stickers were made by the Poster Workshop but were so huge that it was impossible to strike quickly and run. The next batch was much smaller and had already sticky backs. Each set was aimed at exploitative and/or blatantly anti-woman or women-as-object advertisements. One was designed to be placed specifically on the Temp ads in the trains. For one week we saturated the escalators, station and train ads. And we did get publicity but not one paper mentioned the sticker which had all the details for the Equal Pay rally and most articles made a joke out of the attacks. Also some people were misreading the stickers. My baby-sitter, a Catholic school girl, thought they were the work of puritanical, crazed nuns racing through the subways in outrage at the display of nudity in the posters. (From a paper of my own, written in December 1970)

We continued to explore how we and others saw ourselves. What sort of actions should we undertake? What was our attitude to the media?

The nature of the politics we were developing was bound to stir up contradictory emotions and situations. It was generally agreed that society had to change in order for women to be free. But we were very confrontational about men. We weren't going to wait for a revolution before we tried to change our lives. We said it could begin now ... that the more we could transform ourselves, our relationships, our consciousness, the more we would move towards a possibility for fundamental change. The back and forth tension between our consciousness and our actions arising out of that consciousness elevated our perception of the necessity for women and ultimately men of breaking through the stranglehold of male-dominated bourgeois ideology. We were impatient with suggestions that we work within existing power structures, although not averse to exploiting contradictions in order to get money, for instance, to set up an alternative childcare project. We were saying that women's struggles *now* were essentially revolutionizing – without struggle now we'd be sold-out and co-opted and anyway we felt we had no real choice; we could not wait.

We were becoming clearer, though, about what a long, uneven process gaining a new consciousness was: overthrowing the old system would not simply be a matter of taking up the new. The contradictions in the process, the revelations of reactionary and progressive ideas and impulses in each individual as well as in all social relations, made us in turns pessimistic and optimistic. From *Bird* (the precursor of the *London Women's Liberation Newsletter*) in 1969:

> They talked at length of women being second-class people, questioned our every belief about the family and children by questioning the organization of society in general, tackling the whole thing with honesty and thoroughness. Afterwards we were split. For some of us Hilary and Juliet had shown up our middle-class meanderings for what they really were – rubbish leading to a dead-end. For others they were branded as dangerous militants ... But all in some way felt they didn't really feel second class in every cell of their bodies, and refused themselves any real feeling of fervour, possibly because in some way it might mean betraying their men.

Later:

> Gradually, though minor actions, through more group discussions, through more reading and learning we are all becoming militant. The skin over our eyes is peeling back, and people are trying to emerge out of passive female shells.

We'd read about Chinese women 'speaking bitterness' and thought that as part of raising political consciousness, this served a similar function for western women even in our very different circumstances. The insistence on focusing on our own experiences and on our 'private' lives was one of the most important forms of women's politics to come out of the movement. It created solidarity and sisterhood between women.

> By the present separation between private life and social life, women are persistently thrown back into individual conflicts requiring solution in the private sector. Women are still being educated for private life, for the family, which, for its part, is dependent on the conditions of production against which we are struggling. Education for a specific role, the inculcated feeling of inferiority, the contradiction between their own expectations and the demands of society, all generate a constant feeling of guilt prompted by an inability to do justice to the many demands, for having to choose between alternatives which in each case involve the renunciation of vital needs.

Women can

> only emancipate themselves if their own conflicts, which are suppressed into private life, are articulated. (Helke Sanders, Student for a

Democratic Society Conference, Frankfurt, September 1968. Translated and distributed here 1969)

Ironically this new form of politics was most despised by the various British Maoist sects who had picked up very quickly on the woman question, only to lambast the new movement (which they tried to control) as totally reformist. In the *News of the World* on 15 November 1970 members of the Women's Liberation Front (a mixed Maoist sect) were quoted as saying

> To me [The Workshop] seems just a group of people so hung up on sex that they just use their sessions as group therapy. They spend all their time sitting around contemplating their bodies. We don't want to be associated with their ideas. They're just man-haters, and that we certainly are not. Their magazine *Shrew* some months is full of dirty jokes and four-letter words – totally irrelevant to any issue of inequality. Their meetings are barred to men, while we welcome men at ours. I mean, if you want to change things then you've got to educate men to accept things too, haven't you? At the conference we had in Sheffield, they would not allow any men to be present and when they didn't agree with one of the speakers they barracked her with yells of 'Man – you're a Man!' They were so ridiculous and childish it wasn't true.

In a letter to the Women's Liberation Front (WLF) from the London Workshop came the following response:

> It seems to us, from reading other material put out by the WLF, that you do not really understand either the politics of the workshop or the importance which we attach to aspects of women's oppression like sexuality and the family.

At the national women's liberation conference at Skegness in 1971, which was organized primarily by the Women's Liberation Front and the Union of Women for Liberation (another Maoist group), the differences between 'feminists' and the Maoists erupted into plenary violence. From my own notes made at the time:

> Too much! My god. We lost the vote to exclude men from the first session in *order* to get the creche and literature stalls 'manned'. So now pleas for women to come to 'man' these things. The Front and Union *much* in evidence *but* since vote went to them guess IS [International Socialists, now SWP], Socialist Women [IMG], other city's groups must be weak on this point or are afraid of 'feminism' – Maysal, from the Union, does her best to put across the view that feminists are stupid.

But later at the conference women, many of them lesbians, attempted to get rid of the men who continued to operate from the stage ... mayhem.

Maysal grabbing mike from women – women grabbing it back. Brar (a man) rushing in to really be a shit – kicking and shouting. The whole session shouting 'out', 'out' and voting almost unanimously to have him leave and him REFUSING – Union women really fighting to keep him in. So sick – hysteria and screaming was incredible. He finally was ejected by a combination of women, the management and one Maoist man.

All this at a trade union conference where IS was also having a national conference and a strip show was being put on in the evening.

In December 1971 the Union made its position clear on at least one area of feminist concern:

In this class society which maintains the basic inequality of the bourgeoisie and the working class many groups of people are *victims* (sic) of injustice, moral hypocrisy, social ostracism, etc. These groups which form the lumpen-proletariat may be thieves, prostitutes, the 'mentally ill', tramps, beggars, homosexuals, etc. But each of these groups is not maintained directly to serve the ruling class; they are merely the by-products of bourgeois rule. (Concerning the Gay Liberation Front and the Women's Liberation Movement, 7 December 1971)

At that point, most left groups had no time for the direction the women's liberation movement was heading. Going to the Ideal Home Exhibition in 1969 with leaflets and trying to interview women we could persuade to stop and talk to us was not quite what they had in mind as 'real' political activity. Our leaflet said:

Properly manipulated ('if you're not afraid of that word') housewives can be given the sense of identity, purpose, creativity, the self-realization, even the sexual joy they lack – by the buying of things. (From an interview with Ernest Dichter, head of multi-million pound motivation research firm. Issued by Women's Liberation Workshop, 31 Dartmouth Park Hill, London NW5)

Our questions asked, 'Do you think Ideal Homes is aimed specifically at women? Why?' 'Do women control much money?' 'Do you think you could trade places with your husband, boyfriend, if you had equal training? Would you want to? Why? Why not?' 'Do you feel men and women should be equal? Why? Why not?' We weren't really clear about what we were doing at the Ideal Homes, but obviously felt it was a public manifestation of women's oppression. However, there were doubts: 'How liberated are we from advertising and other influences? We may have rejected the cruder forms of acquisition but are we really free of it?' (my own notes for discussion in the Tufnell Park small group).

The very fact that we believed out of our own experience that women could be reached politically in their roles as housewives, consumers and mothers, and also emphasized the way in which those roles captured women and slowly and steadily sucked their identity away, went against any frozen notions of the proletariat and/or point-of-production politics.

When women demonstrated outside the Miss World contest in November 1969, they wore sashes printed with the following slogans:

MIS-FIT REFUSES TO CONFORM

MIS-CONCEPTION DEMANDS FREE ABORTION FOR ALL WOMEN

MIS-FORTUNE DEMANDS EQUAL PAY FOR ALL WOMEN

MIS-JUDGED DEMANDS AN END TO BEAUTY CONTESTS

MIS-DIRECTED DEMANDS EQUAL OPPORTUNITY

MIS-LAID DEMANDS FREE CONTRACEPTION

MIS-GOVERNED DEMANDS LIBERATION

MIS-USED DEMANDS 24 HOUR CHILDCARE CENTRES

MIS-PLACED DEMANDS A CHANCE TO GET OUT OF THE HOUSE

MIS-TREATED DEMANDS SHARED HOUSEWORK

MIS-NOMER DEMANDS A NAME OF HER OWN

MIS-QUOTED DEMANDS AN UNBIASED PRESS

Although the demonstrators were not aiming their protest at the contestants ('whoever becomes Miss World is more than just a trade mark. She is a woman. She is a person. She has a mind.' From a leaflet, *What Price Miss World?* put out by the Women's Liberation Workshop), they did not take enough care to ensure that this was completely clear in their publicity. The impact on the media was unexpected and women were not prepared for it: 'To everybody's astonishment the TV and Press turned up in numbers, with much snapping, popping and aggressive interview technique' (*Shrew*, Nov/Dec 1969).

The next year events were better planned and publicity expected, although the explosion of a bomb under a BBC Outside Broadcast van parked outside the Albert Hall early on the day of the contest was a shock. 'MISS WORLD SABOTAGE BID' was the full top-page headline in the *Evening Standard* of 21 November 1970, and the day after the contest *The Times* said, 'Police, who had been ringing the Albert Hall from before the contest began, joined security guards and stewards to remove the demonstrators, most of them girls. Mr Hope returned on stage to say: "This was good conditioning for Vietnam".' *The Times'* leader that day said:

And a powerful antidote to women's liberation lies in the plain fact of biological function, with all the deep differences in the behaviour and life-experiences which this entails. Perhaps the real criticism of the Miss World competition should also be applied to the Women's Liberation movement: that they both exalt an essentially functionless feminism.

Five women were arrested during the evening's events and four went on to stand trial. Three of them defended themselves, all received fines, and in the long process the trial received an enormous amount of publicity. The women produced their own pamphlet, *Why Miss World*, a fascinating document which integrated the history of businessman Morley's Miss World competition, the demonstrators' feelings and preparations before the event, the evening itself and finally the trial and the participants' final assessments of the venture:

THE COMPETITION WILL SOON BE OVER ... WE HAVE BEEN IN THE MISS WORLD CONTEST ALL OUR LIVES ... JUDGING OURSELVES AS THE JUDGES JUDGES US – LIVING TO PLEASE MEN – DIVIDING OTHER WOMEN UP INTO SAFE FRIENDS AND ATTRACTIVE RIVALS – GRADED, DEGRADED, HUMILIATED ... WE'VE SEEN THROUGH IT.

MECCA ARE SUPERPIMPS SELLING WOMEN'S BODIES TO FRUSTRATED VOYEURS UNTIL AGEING BUSINESSMEN JUMP YOUNG GIRLS IN DARK ALLEYS – BUT THEY'RE ONLY SMALL-TIME PIMPS IN OUR EVERYDAY PROSTITUTION: WOMEN'S BODIES USED BY BUSINESSMEN TO SELL THEIR GARBAGE – LEGS SELLING STOCKINGS, CORSETS SELLING WAISTS, CUNTS SELLING DEODOR-ANTS, MARY QUANT SELLING SEX ... OUR SEXUALITY HAS BEEN TAKEN AWAY FROM US, TURNED INTO MONEY FOR SOMEONE ELSE, THEN RETURNED DEADENED BY ANXIETY. WOMEN WATCHING ... WHY ARE YOU HERE?

THE MAN'S MAKING MONEY OUT OF US.

WE'RE NOT BEAUTIFUL OR UGLY WE'RE ANGRY.

The women writing said:

We were dominated while preparing for the demonstration by terror at what we were about to do. To take violent action, interrupting a carefully ordered spectacle, drawing attention to ourselves, inviting the hostility of thousands of people was something that we had all previously thought to be personally impossible for us, inhibited both by our conditioning as women, and our acceptance of bourgeois norms of correct behaviour.

They too made it clear that they were not opposed to the women in the competition: 'The pre-contest planning meeting had unanimously rejected the use of any slogan or action that could possibly be constructed as an attack on the contestants, or that might lead us to any violent confrontation.' But even though there was much more thought and political sophistication involved in the Miss World demonstration, those involved could see weaknesses and problems afterwards.

This lack of positive strategy towards the media revealed the confusion and ambiguity that surrounded the Miss World Action. There was an irresolvable contradiction in its conception. On the one hand because the contest was an ideological target, the intention of the demonstration was propaganda by deed, i.e. we were not deliberately recruiting, but we were attempting to make our politics and ideas accessible to other women. On the other hand we were firmly against any co-operation with the bourgeois media. There is something self-defeating in the politics of a movement which is prepared to burst onto the screen of seven million viewers one minute, but withdraw the next into a jealously guarded privacy.

And the 'big-splash' politics of the demonstration was finally criticized as the basis for sustained politics:

> We've worked more in the communities we live in – fighting for nurseries, playhouses for our kids, working with unsupported mothers in the Claimants Union, meeting in small groups. Some of us have tried to live in collectives, some have worked with the Gay Liberation Front. Most of it has been slow, painstaking organizing compared with the Miss World demonstration – but it's in the home around kids, sexuality, that our oppression bites deepest, holds hardest. The 'left' have always said the economy – our exploitation has to be changed *first* before our lives, our oppression. We say both have to be changed at once – the struggle against internalized oppression, against how we live our lives, is where we begin, is where we've been put. But we can't end there – it's through that initial struggle that we understand that we can't live as we want to until the power structures of society have been broken. (*Why Miss World*)

By the next year, the inevitable demonstration at Miss World was assured publicity and on 10 November 1971 *The Times* carried a little news item: 'Police with a search warrant issued under the Explosives Act search the "Women's Lib" headquarters in Little Newport Street, Soho, yesterday. The search was made a few hours after threats of disruption at today's Miss World contest by militant women.' The bourgeois press went to town; the radical and semi-radical press covered the event. In fact it was the last big Miss World demonstration. This was not because, as one radical feminist wrote in 1972, '…we must realize that women (we) act in our own self-interest within the meagre choices offered us. No blame attaches to self-interest, or why did we want a movement of our own? Miss World actually offers the competitors a chance of limited self-expression – *very* limited admittedly …' (*Why Not Miss World*, 1972) but more because it was becoming a predictable ritual which actually appeared to add a bit of spice to an occasion the media had a taste for anyway.

In the first years, though, angry women, women in small local groups, women tentatively and unevenly trying to come to grips with the intertwined social relations of class and sex, quickly understood how political their voices and actions were, if only because of the force of reaction from left to right. It was understood that 'We have no line. As of yet we have no heavy theory. We are a beginning and a tremendously exciting one' (Sue O'Sullivan to meeting of 'housewives', 1971). The women's liberation movement needed to go somewhere, develop out of its early years ... I'm not saying we should have remained where we were – at an only partially conceptualized state of theory and practice. An indication of how much women felt the need to make more sense of it all was the proliferation of women's study groups from about 1972. No intellectual baddies zoomed into the field and left us 'ordinary' small group 'real' feminists gasping at their 'heavy' theories. The growing awareness of the complexity of women's oppression, our own contra-dictory reactions to change, and the deep entrenchment of women's inferiority made many of us feel the need to understand more clearly how it all arose, and what long-term strategies and tactics might best be developed to move towards liberation ...

But somehow between then and now the theories did become 'heavy' enough to lose contact with many women and with their basic impulse of political engagement at every level: that basic feeling that we could connect, through all the contradictions, with all women's lives. This belief got blurred. Theories and analyses began to explain the differences between women, which increasingly we had been experiencing, but instead of leading to more fruitful connections with women where their lives *did* or could intersect (and with an awareness and commitment to act against the different oppressions which many women experience) they seemed to separate us more. To many women sisterhood became an empty slogan.

Obviously all was not lost ... feminism is here and alive and in many ways kicking. It seems to me that now, more than ever before, we have to make that personal, political connection with women not yet convinced or touched directly by feminism; yet we flounder, and doubt ourselves. The 'new' angry women of 1981-82 who may or may not be connected in some way with WAVAW (Women Against Violence Against Women); the women espousing political lesbianism; women involved in anti-Tory or single-issue campaigns; those involved in women's studies or other feminist 'jobs for the girls' – none of these necessarily share the premise that the personal is political in the same way that early feminists did. Consciousness raising (CR) is something which perhaps the majority of feminists around now have not gone through, and although CR and sisterhood are certainly not magic formulae, they do appear to lead towards a confidence to engage with contradictions instead of assertions. Assertion politics (you must, you should, it *all* boils down to ...) too often ignores the rich history of work on the ideological level which did (with many faults and failures) break through the stranglehold of bourgeois/ male-dominated ideology. Newer concerns of feminism such as heterosexism and male violence are important to feminism, as is the present economic crisis which hits women so hard. But any feminist politics or theories which even vaguely mimic tired-out forms are not using to best advantage our history and knowledge. The economism of Wages for Housework is simply more crude that that of groups who maintain that a lack of waged work makes women concerned with issues of sexuality. The reformism of concentrating primarily on parliamentary struggles, the way in which the Labour Party features as a political priority for so many feminists, tends to side-step revolutionary feminist politics. And the ultra-leftism of being told to will yourself into an 'advanced' position – be that political lesbianism, or telling women that all men are rapists, thereby lifting the clouds from their eyes so they 'see' the truth and repudiate all men as the agents of their oppression – doesn't *use* what we've learned through the last ten or more years about the way struggle and contradiction can move us in fits and starts forwards.

Yet, the time is as ripe as ever – only the veneer has been reinforced. Happiness with our 'lot' is not running at a high tide any more than it was in the late sixties. Women are still exploited. The confusion and anger are there – even if in economic crisis women themselves try to shove their unhappiness into second place. We know that male-dominated fucking, whether it's a *Cosmo* variety or the old thrusting and banging, makes women miserable; that kids and isolated housing drive women mad; that combining shitty capitalist waged work, with unwaged work in the home, with caring for and being responsible for raising children, with all the assumptions of heterosexuality, drives many women crazy. Even as they try harder to cope! And it should all be in the *frontline* ... surely we know that! Shouldn't we attempt to reach that point in the majority of women where contradictions reside and help them to develop; help develop a wider and wider feminist world view and a sharper and sharper courage to believe and act on the possibility of change?

What is worth recapturing from our early years is exactly how profoundly ideological the original tenets of our movement were and how profoundly they led to political engagement and action. Can we afford to let Erin Pizzey declare in a *Sunday Times* article (13 December 1981): 'Why is it that there is no effective broad-based women's move-ment in Britain – a movement which could be a huge and effective force in engineering social change for women, yet not be hostile to men?' Can we afford to let her put forward such a 'heart-felt' plea and at the same time, after having been 'accused' of being a lesbian, report that 'My first feeling was of unbearably painful hurt. I heard my voice calmly telling anyone who was listening that I wasn't a lesbian: I was a happily married woman with children and grandchildren ... I felt myself cringe with shame and embarrassment as I babbled inanely. I put down the phone and went to our room and was unable to cry.'

Women like Erin Prizzey, who represents herself as a 'real' feminist; women like Shirley Williams, who comes across as a reasonable, working woman; women the media see as charmingly eccentric and hard working but certainly not loony feminists, are often as effective in undermining the women's liberation movement as denouncements from the hard right. There is nothing intrinsically revolutionary about advocating equal pay, childcare facilities, or abortion rights, especially when the institutions, power imbalances and social relations of class, sex, race remain unchallenged. Our task is surely to advocate rights, *and* struggle to build and maintain a revolutionary vision with many political offensives. Part of that is what we started off with. 'Such consciousness changing is as absolutely fundamental a form of progress toward a better society as any material or organizational gains – in fact, probably more fundamental, *since* consciousness must be the basis of political struggle' (Gordon, 1981).

I'm *not* advocating a return to the late 1960s, nor nostalgic evocations; we were confused if energetic beginners at politics – but driven by what felt like absolute necessity, we cut through some of the encrusted bullshit of traditional and/or male-dominated forms of politics. In our exploration of our own experiences, how we were socialized, and formed, of all oppressed people's struggles, we found a way of talking about consciousness which led to a collective appreciation of women's oppression and the need for revolutionary change and action.

Notes

In this article I quoted from some of the earliest publications of the London women's liberation movement. These include pamphlets and magazines – *Harpies Bizarre, Bird*, and the long-running *Shrew. The London Newsletter*, begun in 1969, is now published weekly from A Women's Place. I have not quoted from internal newsletters and where possible I have tried to check the quotations here with the women concerned.

1. We were, at the time, all heterosexual in my small group. Well, as far as I know we were. None of us articulated anti-lesbianism in the group ... we didn't need to as we kept the issue collectively locked away. Who knows what we thought about individually. My imagination was hooked, although it was years before ...

References

Belden, Jack (1970) *China Shakes the World*. New York: Monthly Review Press.

Fanon, Frantz (1965) *The Wretched of the Earth*. London: MacGibbon & Kee.

Fanon, Frantz (1967) *Black Skin, White Masks*. New York: Grove Press.

Feminist Practice (1979) *Notes from the Tenth Year*. London: In Theory Press.

Gordon Linda (1981) 'The Politics of Sexual Harassment'. *Radical America* Vol.15 No.4.

Hinton, William (1966) *Fanshen: A Documentary of Revolution in a Chinese Village*. New York: Monthly Review Press.

My Old Man Said Follow the Vanguard

– FROM *VERY HEAVEN*, 1988

It's beginning to feel odd and unsettling – all this looking back, reflecting on the past. It makes it into an object to be examined, one which is finished off, looked at through barricades of years gone by. Then me today is severed from me yesterday or else I'm a walking, talking relic. Positioning myself in the 1960s goes against my emotional grain – not, mind you, that I don't get off on memories, on recording events and feelings. It's just that now, at the end of the eighties, it seems that instead of telling people we made history at the beginning of the women's liberation movement, I'm being told that I'm part of history.

I'm forty-six-years-old and can remember fiercely and passionately saying to myself in 1969 that women's liberation was my life, would remain my life until I died. I might not be so fierce or passionate, the agenda is certainly different, but I still believe that I'll be involved in something more than a personal feminism until I die. Women's liberation is what enabled me to make sense of the world, enabled me to live with incomplete or contradictory answers, gave me an intellectual and emotional curiosity, sustained me and led me to develop faltering courage in myself and ultimately opened the door to lesbianism for me. The women's liberation movement, my participation in it, has been the means by which I've wiggled and wormed my way unevenly through the privileges, assumptions and constraints of my class, race and sex so that I sometimes live with what feels like a knowing engagement with politics.

The sixties were very much a bridging time, taking up of new identities and roles which had obvious connections to my life as a young girl and teenager in the fifties. In 1960 I turned nineteen and completed my first year of college. Neither I nor any of my friends took much notice of leaving the fifties. Perhaps you don't note dates so much at that age – you're so much *in* them that the transition from one decade to the next has no defined meaning. At the same time I felt that the fifties were mine, mine to feel attached to, formed by, trapped in – my youth. Elvis singing

'Heartbreak Hotel', The Penguins' 'Earth Angel', the fashions, the Korean War, pacifism, the fear and undercurrent I didn't really understand which was part of liberal/left politics, an unformed moral sense of the unjustness of prejudice ... growing up liberal, white. Even now I get a *frisson* of irritation and amusement when fashion decrees the fifties are back – how could they want to bring that back, and anyway they've got it *all* wrong. As far as gender went, I didn't feel consciously rebellious about sex inequalities. I was preoccupied with the horror and injustice of killing, war, much affected by the Holocaust and fears of the atom bomb. Racial prejudice seemed cruel and wrong, I was naïvely righteous about it with no real conception of my own problematic place in the scheme of things.

I had no analysis of why bad things happened in the world, or for that matter between people, except that they were wrong. I was reduced to frustrated, humiliated tears more than once while engaged in a tough argument with young sailors stationed at the submarine base not too far from my parents' rural Connecticut home. There on the sandy summer beach, what would start out as a flirtation would end in impotent misery – I couldn't explain what I believed more than to defend it as morally right. Once at college there were encounters with more sophisticated cynical young men and women, who spouted cold war 'facts and figures' effectively against my 'soft' feelings. I was exposed and small and enraged – but I was never persuaded to drop my beliefs.

I almost made it into the sixties a virgin. But I'd been picked up and enthusiastically fucked by an 'older man' while visiting New York City for the first time during the week after graduating from high school. Classically, that first fuck was a huge let down. Dizzy and wet with desire, I'd abandoned my fears only to discover that I wasn't even sure 'it' had happened. A huge chasm opened up between my desires and my sexual practice. One which widened in the more permissive environment and times I found myself in at college in the early sixties.

As far as men or boys went we were a dismissive little bunch of heterosexual girls – but true to our times we put out for them even as we gossiped nastily behind their backs. We nicknamed one Greenwich Village man who dated a number of us 'Squirrel Monkey' because he crawled all over nibbling, and Ellen told us about her date, who when they were 'parking' late at night unzipped his fly and invited her to feel. 'Put that thing away', was her outraged command and the phrase entered our joking sexual vocabulary.

But we put out, either because we wanted to be in love or because it was too much trouble to say no. As opposed to sexual exploits, we didn't talk much about sexual pleasure at all. I remember the bemused and confused response which greeted the revelation that Judith 'came' almost as soon as her boyfriend entered her. I'm amazed now when I think of the sexual acrobatics I performed back then with no pleasurable outcome – I could move my hips for hours, take it on all fours, fuck fast and furious, be on top, be stimulated by hand or mouth, grudgingly suck someone off and never a glimmer of the pleasure I felt in anticipation or in fantasy.

It was all a mystery to me – once after fucking for ages with my 'older man', who wasn't at all a wham-bam-thank-you-ma'am type, I felt my hands and feet tingling and asked my sophisticated lover if it could be an orgasm. He was quite sweet really and opined that I'd hyperventilated. The frustrating part of all this – and it involved about ten men over three years – was that I kept on desiring something, kept on getting wet and wanting it until it happened. And through it all I never used birth control.

In 1961 I came to London in search of a junior year abroad. I lived with two American college friends and never found a college that would accept me. The year was a significant one: chaotic, a little bit wild and for me a step away from my previous and predictable life.

I was away from my homeland, my parents, living independently from institutional structures, rules and provisions. I threw myself into dance classes at Madame de Vos' ballet studio in Notting Hill Gate where my modern training stuck out a mile. Martha Graham was practically unknown and London Contemporary Dance a long way off. I had no ballet training and in class would reduce myself to self-flagellating tears of frustration. But Madame de Vos liked me and together we'd watch advanced classes from the upstairs balcony where she would criticize certain rigidities in British training which left dancers unable to move their backs freely.

Otherwise I hung around coffee bars of the LSE graduate lounge where my friends and I had made acquaintances. There I met a young man I fell head over heels in love with and right before my return to the States, I had my first ever orgasm with him. But before coming for the first time, I came in contact with people whose political perspectives and cultures were completely different from mine. They spoke to my concerns and confidently answered many of the arguments I'd engaged in so ineffectively in the USA. Socialism wasn't a dirty word. Here I encountered class for the first time. As is still true for the majority of Americans, I had no knowledge of class as either an historical heritage or as part of a political analysis. I'd never been taught anything about the rich and varied American class struggles of the nineteenth and twentieth centuries. My grandfather had been a 'poor boy' who 'worked his way up'. To talk about class smacked of communism and even for many liberals and/or poor people that was anathema. The young man I fell in love with was a socialist, a Marxist even. His father was in the Communist Party and his whole family was poor, radical and working class.

After that year in London I spent a year back in the USA longing to get back to London and I made it clear to my parents that come hell or high water, that's where I was going. For once I felt completely confident that I wanted to throw my lot in with someone else – there were no questions or hesitations. I knew that John didn't believe in marriage, I didn't think I did, but I managed to convince myself and him that we should – for my parents' sake. I doubt that was the whole story. I think I wanted to get married, even if I flippantly said to my best friend in the USA 'Oh, you can always get divorced', shortly before taking the marriage plunge.

After college finished for the year, I got the first Icelandic flight to London I could and winged my way back to freedom and love.

The sixties for me was leaving my parents' home in order to set up one with my husband. I'd been away at school and college for years but 'home' was still with the family, and with the exception of my year in London when I lived with two friends, I'd never been remotely near to living on my own. I would be forty-one years old before I did so. The sixties' years were about separating myself from the USA and everything I couldn't get to grips with there – and an important part of that was the benign but controlling influence of my parents. It was a time to develop my independence and to take shaky steps towards a politics which wasn't based primarily on moral outrage. For me, it happened within a marriage which challenged many of the middle-class assumptions and patterns of my parents' and contemporaries' marriages. We were not part of 'swinging London': although I thought about the constraints of mono-gamy from time to time, in day-to-day terms it simply wasn't an issue. We were both monogamous and with the exception of one or two little fantasies about particular men, I never fancied or slept with another man.

Although I didn't find monogamous marriage sexually restrictive, still off and on I felt the terrible absence of my friends. I'd always had close and constant girlfriends – boyfriends and lovers might come and go, but we girls were loyal and committed to each other. I met my best friend when I was six and had a number of other women friends from high school. But come marriage or 'living together' and we went our separate ways. There was nothing I knew then which might have enabled me to conceptualize this mutual and accepted abandonment.

During the year I was back in the USA, away from but in love with John, I had an illegal abortion. A few minutes passively participating in a lonely, drunken, joyless fuck led to a secret, dazed Puerto Rican abortion on Valentine's eve. There was absolutely no question in my mind about that abortion. I 'knew' I was pregnant immediately but I never though of the foetus as a baby. My search for an abortion and for the money to pay for it left me exhausted – the underground of illegal abortions was a nightmare. I was lucky to find a proper, if squalid, money spinning clinic;

friends were not so fortunate and endured abortions in abandoned New York city tenements, lying on newspaper on the floor with a bottle of whisky to dull the pain, being left alone to struggle to the street when it was over and make their way home. Others made assignments with male voices on the phone, directed to highway exit telephone booths where they were then sent on to a second pickup point to finally pay for the chemicals they were to drink. These were supposed to bring on a miscarriage which would have to be finished off in a hospital where the woman was warned she would risk arrest if she breathed a word of how she happened to be miscarrying.

In my search I was supported and helped by my close women friends at college. One day a friend borrowed a car and four of us set off for upstate New York where someone had heard there was a well-known abortionist. Arriving in the little town, we somehow managed to make our way to the address, only to find that the man was 'away'. His assistant proceeded to examine me in what I realized half-way through was a purely sexual way. He had no intention of giving me an abortion. Deflated, disgusted and frantic, I was at least surrounded by the care and concern of my friends. The Puerto Rican connection came through a New York man I had dated but had no desire to sleep with. The night before flying there I spent in the city with him. I was doing what I desperately wanted to do but was in a state of blanked-out emotions. That night, the bastard who was 'helping' me fucked me, and I went through it as if in a dream; it seemed part of the payment I had to make.

My search for an abortion and for the money went on side by side with the necessity of maintaining a normal façade and carrying on as usual. I took exams, performed in a series of dance recitals and gave nothing away. My girlfriends took me through it all and a room-mate's mother spontaneously lent me the bulk of the money I needed. Six months later when I sent her the first repayment, she wrote back to tell me that she didn't want the money back, that she had had an abortion as a young women and understood my situation. If the time came when I was older and had more money, she hoped I would help another young women out. These were the sorts of friends I was leaving, but with hugs and promises to write, and with thoughts only of England, I flew off.

I was terrified of telling John about my abortion – away from my true love for a year and look what happens! I was afraid he would reject me – not so much for the abortion but because I slept with someone else. He was hurt and I hated that, but he accepted it and never used it against me.

In London we lived on John's grant, supplemented by his occasional supply teaching and some gifts from my parents. I didn't worry about working as long as we were getting by. I wanted to dance but there was no way I could earn a living at it. Teaching was not on as I didn't have a degree. John was accustomed to being poor and I experienced living without the middle-class comforts of American life as liberating. I was part of a generation of Americans who were questioning a conservative consumer-oriented society, so living without a fridge, vacuum cleaner, TV or central heating didn't bother me a bit. (Now I can see the inverted class dimensions of the ease with which I accepted less than I had been used to, but I'm still glad I went that way.) We spent what money we had on going to films at the National Film Theatre, plays at the Royal Court and occasional meals at Jimmy's or our local Indian restaurant. I didn't drink or at that point smoke. We were childless. We revelled in our tiny basement flat. Certainly my middle-class background informed the relief I experienced stepping out of those particular class expectations.

After two years' married life in Camden Town, when I took up dance classes at Madame de Vos' again, typed my husband's Ph.D. thesis, tried to learn how to cook, and socialized mainly with John's friends, we decided to spend a year in the USA so I could finish my college degree.

We ended up staying for two years in New York City. Being back in the USA, married and living in a small rent-controlled flat in Greenwich Village during the mid-sixties turned out to be an exciting and different experience for both of us. John got his first teaching job at the New School for Social Research, at that time a left haven in American academia, and he stepped right into the middle of New Left activism and renewed interest in Marxism. Many of his students, not much younger than he was, were involved in Students for a Democratic Society (SDS) and a number of them became close and lasting friends. Being involved in left-wing politics at that point meant anti-Vietnam war work, community politics and the challenge of Black Power.

This was mostly John's terrain. I cared deeply about the issues, and my ideas were influenced, particularly about racism, but I didn't feel part of the student world and wasn't sure where I fitted in. Many of my friends had been involved in the civil rights movement during the two years I was in England and I had followed it in the news and radical press. Back in the States, I personally experienced the strength of the anti-war movement, the necessity to stand up and be counted right there in the 'belly of the monster'. Anti-war demonstrations in New York City drew in such a huge cross-section of pacifists, radicals and militant Black people, plus many previously uninvolved 'ordinary citizens' that it took my breath away, and more than once I was moved to tears. But I continued to go along to demonstrations as an individual, still carrying with me a very American reluctance to subsume an idealized individuality into any notion of a collective.

I didn't agonize over any of this too much. I was busy commuting daily to college, dancing and just getting a buzz out of living in the city.

When friends came over at night, the conversation would be of politics: class, Marxism, the war, organizing, SDS, racism, consumerism, American capitalism. I wasn't bored at all, but I tended to feel that I was listening-in and I knew that the men, no matter how nice, weren't particularly interested in my or the other women's lives. I remember one conversation between two of us women about the side effects of the Pill – did it give us headaches or weight gain? We carried on for a while with the men making little additions to the conversation. I remember it well because it was unusual for women to dominate the conversation with 'women talk'. However there was no undercurrent of resentment and we certainly didn't complain. When John and I got together with my school and college friends, the women dominated the conversation as much as the men. It wasn't that the women I knew had nothing to say, only that we, as much as the men, tended to accept that some areas of conversation and concern were more the men's. No one ever articulated this and therefore it was never a topic of speculation or debate.

The second year in New York City both John and I worked and for the first time had money to spare. We ate bagels with cream cheese, onion and smoked salmon at a 6th Avenue luncheonette, frequented a tiny Italian restaurant south of Houston Street in what is now trendy Soho but was then an old Italian neighbourhood. We attended dance concerts around the City, saw all the radical theatre going, bought the Sunday *New York Times* late on Saturday nights, nipping home to pull out the fold-up bed and settle in for a luxurious read. I bought dozens of cheap earrings at the Jewel Box on 8th Street and blew my first pay cheque on a fur bedspread. We saw Bo Diddley and other musicians at local venues and with a group of SDS friends travelled up town to the big 'Be In' in Central Park. I never thought of myself as a hippy and now I have to laugh when my boys call me one. I stayed away from long print skirts and ran a mile at the idea of 'love beads', being much more attracted to an earlier bohemian image.

Living in the city for two years had a profound effect on John: he was welcomed into left intellectual groupings, and felt less an interloper in the looser American academic scene than in the more rigidly class-stratified British one. The vitality and dedication with which people on the left were engaging with politics excited him; his Marxism and class-consciousness made him a valuable part of these groups.

For me the years were significant for other reasons. I enjoyed the easy socializing with old and new friends and immersed myself in the city's culture, seeing it all anew after living in London for two years. I'd never lived in the States as an 'adult', nor had I lived before in an American city. I'd finished my degree successfully, getting more out of that final year as a 'mature' student than ever before. I had a job and time to take dance classes at the Merce Cunningham Studio which I loved. As happy and productive as that time was, it was a temporary sojourn; we both wanted to return to London.

In the early spring of 1967 when we'd already decided to return to London that summer, John suggested we have a baby and I thought, 'Hey, why not?' I never doubted I'd have kids some day and we'd already been married for four years. I didn't dwell much on what it would mean. I assumed I would be okay as a mother. After all, from the age of eleven I'd enjoyed an ace reputation as a babysitter, I'd been a successful nursery teacher – I loved kids. Anyway, ever since high school everyone told me I'd be a great mother.

In early summer 1967 we packed bits of furniture and belongings in wooden crates and clutching carrier bags with kitchen utensils poking out the top we flew back to London, me just pregnant. My pregnancy was spent in Stoke Newington in London where we finally found a flat. No more cheap central London basement flats we could afford. Until I was about six or seven months pregnant, I trekked across London to go to dance classes. One day Madame de Vos took me aside and explained apologetically that I would have to stop classes. A rather large pregnant woman leaping around was making the others students nervous. A few years earlier a teacher of mine had taught an energetic class the day before she gave birth. Ah well, this was England and I stopped. I felt more and more lonely and isolated. I didn't know anyone where I lived, transportation was poor and no one dropped by. I felt acutely, for the first time since I married, the absence of friends. I wobbled a bit.

John had found a university teaching job and was involved in teacher/student politics. I went on anti-Vietnam war demonstrations, keeping well to the side at Grosvenor Square, accompanied John to political meetings, and started natural birth classes at Charing Cross Hospital. I practised my breathing exercises religiously. My mother had been knocked out when giving birth to all three of her children and I had decided that I wanted to be fully awake and 'in control'. The teacher advised women to open their mouths wide in the final stages of delivery, as the vagina would follow suit. She had given this advice to her own daughter before her wedding night and was sure that it helped! This titbit of information was imparted to us at a 'fathers' night' and a white South African communist, her husband, John and I sat at the back of the room like naughty schoolkids choking back our laughter.

I didn't laugh much in labour. I was late and huge. One morning I got out of the bed which took up most of the room. I stood naked in front of the full-length mirror on the wardrobe, looked at myself and shrieked. Literally overnight my belly was rippled with stretch marks. Baby was out-growing the womb. A few days later I went into hospital with high blood pressure and for days lay around miserably while different doctors decided first to induce, then to wait, then to induce, until I finally started of my own accord.

It went on and on and on. I was picked up and tossed into labour. I was out of control. I hung on to my breathing like a shipwrecked thing until the labour went into chaos. This was not anything like the books or the teacher said, where the anarchy of the transitional phase lasts a relatively short time. I was vomiting, hooked up to a drip, exhausted and thought I might die. After being knocked out with an injection for a few hours, I woke up only to have it all start again at the same stage. After more than thirty hours in labour they wheeled me into the delivery room – 'Time to push, mother'. This was not a great success and I ended up with deep forceps thrust in me in order to haul an over-nine-pound, traumatized baby into the world. I lay there, bloody, bowed and blank. All I wanted to do was sleep. (When he was about two, Tom claimed he could remember the struggle to be born.)

John fell in love hook, line and sinker the moment he held Tom. I went into a lengthy period of subdued shock. My breasts filled up to bursting with milk and I had to go on a monstrous milking machine to express the extra to feed ailing babies. I was the breast-feeding star of the ward. Sisters went from bed to bed coaxing reluctant nipples into recalcitrant babies' mouths. Women who were desperately keen to breast-feed had problems, women who didn't want to were bullied into it. My breasts squirted, my baby sucked heartily from the first.

But my cunt was a misery. I could hardly make it down the hall to the loo. I felt like my insides would burst out the minute I stood up; sitting down was agony and only possible on a foam rubber ring. I couldn't believe this was normal but everyone said it was. Months later in the USA a friend's doctor husband had a look because I was still in so much pain. He said I'd been sewed up badly and unevenly after the episiotomy.

Back in Stoke Newington I sat with my big, quiet, wide-eyed baby and stared at him wondering who I was, who he was. I sat for hours with him on the breast, I wiped up shit, pinned nappies on, lay on the floor trying to figure out where the muscles were which would allow me to attempt sit-ups and wondered. I was floundering badly but I think I must have looked all right. Pictures from my album show smiling or contemplative family life. There *was* pleasure and contentment, but through it all I felt displaced emotionally. I wasn't sure what anything meant. I'd joined the grown-up world of mothers and yet I felt more unsure and lonely than ever before. I could perform all the techniques of motherhood competently, I was riveted by the baby, but I had an awful feeling that being a mother didn't fit me well. I was a failure in what I assumed would come most naturally. I had seen myself at best as happy and flexible, not dependent on a baby to give my life meaning, welcoming it rather as a new dimension of responsibility and pleasure. That the experience was different from what I'd imagined it would be wouldn't necessarily have been depressing as I quite liked being taken by surprise, startled and then coming to grips with new feelings and circumstances. No, this was something different and much more fundamentally fearful and guilt-inspiring.

I heard about women's liberation the first summer I was a mother and paid it no special heed. It was 1968, students were in revolt, the Chinese Cultural Revolution was in full tilt, we were told there'd been a sexual revolution. I myself had participated in CND marches and anti-war demonstrations. I'd had an abortion, moved continents, married, finished a degree, worked and had a baby. As the decade moved to a close I came undone. I regretted none of it, but could see no coherency in my life. I was married and now had another man's name; I had a baby and was therefore a mother. I'd been taught to value myself as an individual at the same time that selfishness was castigated. I'd been encouraged to get a liberal education and broaden my horizons, but with no particular goal in mind other than being a better human being. My personal feelings of outrage at injustice had been nurtured but I couldn't find a way into sustained activity for meaningful change. I was ripe for women's liberation but had to make the connection for myself.

In 1969 I went along to a small women's group in Tufnell Park. Twenty years later I'm still involved, in a very different way, in women's liberation, although it's not even called that any more. I had another baby in March 1970, a week after attending the first women's liberation conference at Ruskin College in Oxford. I went with John and Tom. All the women I knew were heterosexual and many had small children. We all believed that women's liberation would create better relationships between men and women. I still believe that's ultimately true, but what none of us could contemplate at that moment was how profoundly it might shake up our own relationships with men.

Is it mainly men of my generation who are nostalgic about the sixties? Certainly for me, it's the seventies which signal change, growth and understanding of things. It was in the seventies that I became part of a movement which made sense of the world in a way which also gave me agency. I can wax nostalgic about aspects of sixties' culture and be moved all over again by the struggles which other oppressed groups waged. I can see the connections and acknowledge my debt to those. But it's the world-wide revolt of women in the seventies which ushered me so firmly into a politics which encompassed the public and the personal, with all the attendant pleasures and pains which that implies.

From 1969

– FROM '68, '78, '88

It was my husband who told me about a small group of women, mainly Americans, who were meeting in Tufnell Park. Perhaps I should go? Did I finally ring someone or did one of the women get in touch with me? I can't remember; but early in 1969 I found myself sitting somewhat self-consciously in a living room, talking with other women about isolation, feelings of inadequacy, ambivalences towards motherhood, and hearing sympathetic voices confirming, identifying and expanding. I know, even if I can no longer touch its electricity, that I left with a wonderful feeling, a spinning head and a churning stomach.

I didn't rush out into the night with the course of a new life shaking the old. I didn't fling open the door at home to announce changes to be made there. My relationship was a good one, I neither did all the housework, nor did my husband oppress me physically or emotionally. At that point it was a shaded shift in my perception of the world. I suddenly saw myself, my marriage and motherhood, in a critical light. I saw without fully articulating it that my (and many other women's) feelings of inadequacy, guilt, loneliness sprang in good part simply from being a woman. It was exhilarating and scary. Women's isolation from each other, their emotional and physical work on behalf of others, helped perpetuate the rotten society we lived in. These may seem like clichés now – they certainly didn't then.

But where did a good marriage fit the oppressive nature of marriage as an institution? I sensed huge personal contradictions to come, and was anxious even as I lunged forward. Would women's liberation demand changes of me and my marriage which I didn't want or couldn't take on? The implications of the liberation movement were vast and yet for our particular, mainly white, western urban variety of women, so incredibly personalized. For some women involvement in the movement relatively quickly provided the courage to exit from miserable oppressive relationships with men or prolonged domestic battles. What took *me* literally years to get a grasp of was my own level of unease at the separate compartments I had to maintain in my life. My pleasure at being with women – talking, planning, eating, organizing, writing, studying – a togetherness which was based initially on a deep loathing of the assumptions and abuses of male power and the framework of 'naturalness' it resided in – jarred with the individualized equality my husband and I enjoyed. The violence and 'otherness' of the dominant (and different) worlds of men which produced such rage in me insinuated itself into my privatized nuclear family, where I was the only woman.

1969–78: A Calendar of Action

From the few initial, mainly localized, small groups, within a year there had grown a movement of thousands of women. In London the Women's Liberation Workshop brought together the mushrooming groups, primarily through the weekly newsletter which I took from the first copy in 1969 till the last in 1985.

Being part of one group threw up possibilities (or demands) for other projects. There was so much to do and everything appeared to be linked. I can no longer separate out the perfect chronology of events which I took part in, when I think of the me who lived through the last twenty years. But I was active on some level throughout that time.

Spring 1969: My first meeting at Tufnell Park; Women's Workshops at Essex University Festival of Revolution; Women's Liberation attend the big equal pay rally in Trafalgar Square after leafleting the Underground from 5.30a.m.; Sticker campaign against negative images of women, stickers huge and homemade and very difficult to slap on quickly; Tufnell Park group goes to Ideal Home Exhibition with questionnaire and statement about manipulation by advertisers; Group starts making a short film, 'Women, Are You Happy With Your Life?'

Autumn 1969: First regular get-togethers of London women's liberation, discuss whether we can 'use' the media to get our message across. Dominant opinion is that the media will distort whatever we have to say and we should spurn them, developing alternative modes of communication. Some women disagree and do go on TV and radio. First Miss World protest: *Mis-Fit Refuses to Conform, Mis-Conception Demands Free Abortion for all Women, Mis-Placed Demands a Chance to Get Out of the House.*

Early 1970: Meetings to work out a statement of aims and purpose for the Women's Liberation Workshop, the umbrella organization for small groups and individual women in London; First Women's Liberation conference at Ruskin College – Men attend, are involved in a film of the event and run the crêche. I go with John and Tom who is almost two years old. I'm very pregnant and give birth to second son about ten days later.

Summer 1970: Write article on my post-natal depression for *Shrew*, the magazine rotated between groups in the Workshop. This issue produced by women centred in a communal house in Grosvenor Avenue, Islington, some of whom go on to produce the short-lived, libertarian and lively *Women's Newspaper*; Dialectics of revolution at the Round House – Women take to stage to protest men totally dominating the event.

1969/70: A group in North London leaflets against the Vietnam War every week, plays volley ball on Hampstead Heath with the Vietcong flag flying on the net pole, sets up Hole in the Wall community centre in a few rooms above a shop near where I live. We have mixed meetings (men and women) to discuss childcare. Rudi and Gretchen Dutschke are living in London and join meetings, we read translations of German SDS papers, particularly one by Helke Sanders on men, childcare and women.

Autumn 1970: Second Miss World protest – five women arrested, four go on to stand trial, lots of media coverage, full page in the *Observer*. *Winter*: London open meetings to formulate Demands of the WLM in time for the first big International Women's Day march in London. Arguments about nature of transitional demands, histories of left groups etc., but four demands decided on – Equal Pay Now, Equal Education and Opportunities, Free Contraception and Abortion on Demand, Free 24-hour Nurseries.

March 8th 1971: Large march, snowing, hundreds of placards with the demands, women's street theatre, leaflets, big media impact. Women's Liberation Workshop shoots up to over eighty groups in a year.

From 1971: Talks to secondary school girls and boys, and all sorts of groups both sympathetic and antagonistic.

Autumn 1971: National women's liberation conference at Skegness. International Socialists and miners holding conferences at the same time and holiday camp puts on strip show. The WL conference is primarily organized by two Maoist sectarian groups but it backfires for them – women chase men off the stage, lesbians hitherto more or less invisible raise hell and demand a voice.

1972: Study groups for women – psychoanalytic Family Study group, then a number of Marxist study groups; I join Women in Ireland group, *Red Rag* starts up, and *Spare Rib* the following year. I join *Red Rag* after the first issue which was produced by Communist Party women; Community organizing. I know women setting up Essex Road Women's Centre in shopfront underneath a feminist's flat (now Cheer's Wine Bar).

A number of us in Camden and Islington decide to set up different, grass roots women's centre on site in Maiden Lane with tenants' association, old age pensioners, free school, and first incarnation of Greek Theatro Technis. Leaflet local estates, set up pregnancy testing service, run jumble sales. Good links with the tenants but limited success in drawing other local women in to rather depressing collection of old, run-down railway buildings. Free school kids hate us and destroy our tiny room repeatedly.

Still, from about 1972 until 1974/5 all sorts of things appeared possible. Study and the beginnings of analysis felt utterly connected to the 'doing' of women's liberation, necessary to what seemed more and more likely to be a long hard slog. Community-based organizing around birth control, childcare and consciousness-raising meant that the personal was still political, that women's subjective experiences were still central to the action.

Somewhere along the line, 'small groups' became 'consciousness-raising groups', and still later 'women's liberation' became 'feminism'. Feminism has outlasted women's liberation, perhaps because it is the easiest label to apply individually. Feminists can fit, even if uncomfortably, into boardrooms and academia. Feminism doesn't suggest a political movement.

Sisterhood was powerful – for some. Those who defined it, felt it while caught in their own movements of struggle with men and society. It's hard for me to grab hold of the 'we' in this. I don't want to deny or disown my part. But for me and others, there was a recognition that all was not right in the women's liberation movement which led us in the early seventies to Marxist study groups in an effort to understand class divides.

I was profoundly affected by Mao's notion of contradiction. It spoke to me on a gut level. Ideological struggle came to the forefront of my political vision in the seventies and I still see it, undoubtedly differently, as a key to political change.

But there's no doubt that for all the talk, many of us white middle-class women just didn't grab hold of the most basic bit of the conversation and taste it. We could explain difference, acknowledge it, but continuously round the corner was the need to move out of the centre of our self-defined circle, to question the circle's parameters. Even the idea that room should be made in it for others missed the point: other women needed to set their own agendas, had their own specific, complex histories.

But I am glad that I was part of that particular historical moment almost twenty years ago. I think of other white middle-class women when I say that, who avoided or rejected feminism, *not* because of its very real problems in relation to the complexities of race, class, sexuality and age, but because of its radical challenge to men. The inadequacies of the early movement may ironically have been part of its life-spring as well. The anger of women who were excluded or absent may eventually be seen as part of a longer process of definition and political agency. Nothing is inevitable – neither success nor failure.

1974: I go to China on a Society for Anglo-Chinese Understanding tour and come back full of excitement for the Cultural Revolution. Become active in SACU, working with men for the first time in five years. Particularly keen on enabling more working-class people to go to China, and one workers' tour includes members of Camden Tenants' Association. For a year I am part of a Marxist study group with four older local working-class people, and two middle-class women. A spin-off from my Chinese experience is the name I use now, inspired by 'liberation names' to replace my husband's surname.

1974: Start teaching in Holloway Prison – first dance, then women's health and women's studies. From then on, I remain focused on women's health issues in one way or another, and teach at Holloway for the next ten years.

1972–78: Attend every national and London Women's Liberation conference, always riveted, sometimes confused, adrenalin flowing. Conferences seem like vast yearly consciousness-raising exercises around specific issues – wages for housework, lesbianism, internationalism and imperialism, racism, battered women, rape, abortion – and increasingly around the different tendencies defining themselves within feminism. There is no concept of different *feminisms* yet and it is as if we are all struggling over a patch of contested ground.

1976: Women's liberation movement spins off a subsidiary women's health movement, starting early seventies with small groups learning vaginal self-examination. Now conferences to share information, devise alternative health projects, organize campaigns to fight within the NHS, and increasingly to defend it against hospital closures. Join Women Against Racism and Fascism.

1978: Take a Health Education Diploma at South Bank Poly.

1979: I begin a five-year stint on the *Spare Rib* collective, the first time I've been involved in a journal since leaving *Red Rag* in 1976. Some of the most stressful, chaotic, painful times I've ever been through, but I fall in love with the process of putting a magazine together. Wake up in the morning with *SR* and go to bed at night with it. All the issues and projects I've been part of in one way or another show up in the magazine. And I feel driven, sometimes against my will, sometimes late in the day, to say what I see even if my heart sinks and my stomach heaves as I say it.

1978–88: Growing Up Backwards

By 1978 the first batches of my friends were dropping away from the women's liberation movement but not from feminism, either worn out with the bickering, fed up with meetings, explaining things again and again, alienated by one or another grouping of different women who were appearing all over the place, or perhaps wanting to move on to other time-consuming work. Or simply to fall away and live a quiet life. A significant number of women were getting jobs in which they could be, or fight to be, feminists – in education, trade unions, women's centres. Some, having gained new confidence through feminism, were deciding to train for new careers or entering previously male-dominated areas of work.

I don't understand the generation gap. I maintain peer group friends but get to know much younger women. Throughout the seventies I feel more and more able: more energy, skills, ideas. More confidence, It's the WLM which enables me – why should I want to leave that?

Growing up backwards. I can try things out – teaching in Holloway Prison, going for a diploma in health education. I never had a career to be thwarted in, so everything I learn and discover through feminism is an awakening, a new possibility, a plus in life.

By 1979 there were a lot more visible lesbians around, and a not insignificant number of heterosexual women, particularly those who had been inside the movement for a while, felt silenced and criticized. Classic manifestations occurred when I was working on *Spare Rib* at that time. The magazine was accused of excluding heterosexual women's lives and experiences yet even a casual adding up of 'lesbian' material in the magazine revealed how little space it was actually allotted. It was lesbianism in itself which created an uncomfortable challenge.

Myself, I'd been fantasizing about lesbianism for a long time, but was convinced that it wouldn't happen to me. I had seen some friends come out, and read all the lesbian pamphlets and newspapers from the States I could get my hands on. I was angered and attracted by a lot of it. Any women can? Sure. As far as I could see a lot of the American literature featured pictures or drawings of young white, slim, free women, who seemed to spend a lot of time with their long straight, clean hair blowing romantically in the wind. Where were the images of women as objects of lesbian desire who had stretch marks, flabby tummies, little kids demanding crisps, or even male partners they loved and hadn't simply been enduring until their repressed lesbianism was allowed to flower?

Being with women was always a pleasure to me, but any discussion about making a political choice to be a lesbian left me cold. I supported lesbian demands within the women's liberation movement but not because I saw myself there. Now it's not surprising to me that I fell madly in love with a woman completely outside of feminism who had been a lesbian since she was thirteen and was part of a much older lesbian subculture. Making love with a woman was a revelation to me; my fantasies had been all about being swept off my feet and being made love to. What I discovered were the acute and breathtaking pleasures of making love to a woman.

> I fall madly in love with younger women. I play 'mother' when I've refused to 'mother' my own children in traditional terms. I want

passionate sex, fun and intensity. I fall for the girls who I think offer that and find out they need to be looked after. I walk around dreaming of my object of desire, I suffer through violence and dramas, acting 'grown up' but not getting out – I get something from it. I return regularly each week to the ongoing domestic life of my family – a refuge which drives me nuts. My kids make me mad. I'm the screaming witch bitch there. Back to my lover who manipulates and demands, and I service.

All along my ambivalence about motherhood continued. I rarely found another woman who shared the frightening rages and frustrations which I felt with my little boys. I identified more with non-feminist women who went to pieces over nothing than with my sisters who had children in the movement, who always seemed more together about things than I did. I knew that even if the 'problem' was social, it expressed itself through something deeply disturbing and unresolved in myself.

Into the eighties – two more relationships, still living with husband and kids. When my third relationship founders, on the surface because of her infidelity, I go to pieces, sobbing in the toilet at *Spare Rib*, curled up in a ball on the floor at home.

'What's the matter, Mummy?'

I'm propelled into moving out of my domestic set up. The disjunction between the parts of my life, the constraints of playing out relationships only on my lovers' home grounds, are impossible. I'm out into a temporary, short-life flat, on my own for the first time in my life, still howling in agony over my relationship. But there's a silver lining. I'm in love with my tiny place. I luxuriate in being alone. I talk to myself. I eat in bed.

And continue regular visits to my kids and husband.

My husband never joined a men's group or knew anything about them. His political and personal integrity, and a kind of stoic attitude to life, meant that he had the ability to empathize with my changes while expressing his own sorrow. He chose to be the mainstay in the children's lives. He scrubbed and cooked and cleaned and took them to the One O'Clock Club, the zoo, cinema and plays; he liaised with the schools, spoke to the teachers, took them juice in the night. Only a mother's role – as many women know full well – but one I didn't want, couldn't do with any grace. One which filled me with resentment. He isn't a saint, but if he hadn't been who he is, could I have left my young children, with pain but little guilt? And would I still be welcomed back, the lesbian who lives alone, to visit and do their washing and mine in their machine?

(I'm standing in a single changing room in a lingerie shop in Manhattan, eighteen-years-old, trying on bras, flat-chested and cornered. The sales woman whips open the curtain and seeing me in a 36AA bra which still crumples, tells me she has the answer. Leaves and reappears with a padded construction, stays for the trying on and crows with approval once it's hooked into place. I'm caught, buy it and wear it back to college, sweating and near tears. I recount my shopping trial to my three room-mates. I don't want a bra. I wish I had bigger breasts but this is no solution. It's not me. If a boy thinks I have bigger tits with my clothes on, how will he react when he sees (or feels) the truth. My room-mates commiserate and one suggests we get rid of it then and there. She gets out the scissors and with increasing wildness and laughter we proceed to snip it into strips, bits, ripping out the foam rubber. Finally we burn the remains in a waste paper basket. A stink but satisfying. It's 1959. Who's heard of a bra burner?)

I can't remember when I stopped wearing a bra of any kind, but I'm sure it was post women's liberation. I'd always been interested in clothes and fashion since about age fourteen, but nothing that took a lot of time and effort – a mild bohemianism. After having a second baby I felt overcome with personal sluttishness. A lot of the time I wore an old army jacket, jeans or trousers, and big sweaters because it was easier to breast-feed. I pulled my long hair back with a rubber band because it was so often in need of washing. I didn't have the time or the wish to 'look good' and it was a relief that within the women's liberation movement no one expected you to be trying.

The overwhelmingly heterosexual movement also incorporated a critique of fashion. Women wanted to be accepted as they were; they wanted to dress for themselves, not to attract men. The fashion business was there to feed upon women's insecurities, declaring last season's fashions obsolete and making a fortune in the process. Well, fuck that. We would wear what we wanted, which for many women then was loose, trousered, functional, recycled or cheap. To talk about clothing or make-up as creative expressions, as some feminists continued to do, struck most of us as a poor justification. I remember one friend in a fury when another feminist appeared at a mixed party with a low cut dress on. I don't believe she was envious or puritanical in her reaction – she saw it as a betrayal of all we'd fought for – and against.

My interest in clothes resurfaced at about the time my children were both in school, but it wasn't until I started having sexual relationships with women that reformism really hit. Dressing up in a way that you knew another women found attractive didn't feel the same as within the confines of heterosexuality. All the clothing and style signals, I now experienced as if in an unidentical twin world, a subculture of opposition. Dressing up before could have been interpreted as for men, which spoiled the pleasure. Dressing up for myself and for other women's eyes was delightful, sometimes wicked and always pleasurable.

In 1985 I joined the newly opened London Lesbian and Gay Centre, and soon found myself in the midst of an almighty row about whether gay and lesbian sado-masochist groups could meet in the centre. After much discussion, the small group of lesbians came down in favour. Thinking through the storm that followed brought me to a place of relative certainty which I don't think I'd ever felt about any decision before.

Between feminists it's still horrible to think of women hating each other, not speaking. Hating me, me hating them. It's hard to acknowledge my own anger. But my lesbianism has been the thing that's finally given me the courage I wasn't sure I had. I can still tremble, but I'm much more able to speak out about troubling and unpopular things if I believe they should be heard. My lesbianism has made me less fearful of being disliked by others, including other lesbians.

My Quaker background has sometimes led me into a mediator position. That way I'm in less danger of personal rejection, of course. But I'm also enabled to see the changes in the women's liberation movement without feeling pushed outside.

In 1984 I left the *Spare Rib* collective, wanting to stay forever but tired out. Two years later I came back, not as part of the collective, to co-ordinate a monthly health page which I packed in this spring, tired out again. In the meanwhile I took up an invitation from the quarterly *Feminist Review* collective in 1985, amazed and secretly flattered to be asked, as I am not an academic. In 1986 I started work at Sheba Feminist Publishers, and am still there now.

A small racially-mixed collective – prioritizing writing by Black, working-class or lesbian women, and first-time writers – we manage to sort out most of our personal problems in a way which doesn't totally take over our publishing work. After all the mixed-up bitterness between women on *Spare Rib*, after its well-intentioned but ultimately flawed attempts at creating a racially-mixed collective, I was still left with the knowledge that I found working in all-white collectives limited. I do work in other groups with all-white women, but see it as a defeat, if only a temporary one.

The women I've worked with, been friends or lovers with, cut across the decades from '68 to '88. I find it amusing and beyond my experience when I hear women of my age, dedicated feminists, declare themselves outside of the movement or excluded from it. I don't see myself as some sort of wiser elder mother. I see myself as learning, swimming with more resilience and fewer illusions. I work with younger women often – I don't deny our age differences but frankly they're not that important. I work primarily with lesbians – that, whatever our age, does seem to give us something in common. We're all intrigued and in love with the possibility of passion between women and, in the present climate of Section 28 of the Local Government Act which seeks to silence homosexuality and make it more unacceptable than ever, with maintaining our courage and will to fight.

I identify with the oppression of all women; for me lesbianism is not necessarily political. But living in this society as a lesbian, while it has shot me up to the stars, has grounded my sensibilities firmly. I'm unwilling to waste time by keeping my mouth shut when I know what I think. And as long as I have something I'm eager to say, then I'll stick around with other women in feminist collectives and projects and hopefully live to see a popular resurgence of resistance to the conservatism of the eighties.

Nothing stays the same. The specific historical moment which gave rise to the WLM has passed, but the time for feminism continues. The underlying causes remain, although they may be subject to shifts and changes. I've chosen to ride with subsequent waves, because this move-ment is where I still want to be, where I experience extremes of pleasure, passion, possibility and a collective identity with women. Sometimes it comes apart and seems lost, but I don't much fancy any other alternative.

The WLM was the beginning of something I'd lived without before. I developed myself in it, found my place in a foreign country through it, became a lesbian through it, separated from my roles as wife and mother, understood and was part of a politics which spoke to me, of me, about others, about others and me. I feel lucky to have been where I was, who I was in the late sixties. I can see its flaws, but I could never wish the movement had passed me by.

Recipes and Reflections

– FROM *TURNING THE TABLES*, 1988

Food reverberates with different meanings and sensations at different points in my life. As a young girl at home with my younger brothers and mother and father, it came superimposed by the ritual of the evening meal, by the ideology of the white liberal middle-class 'family together' imperative. There, the pleasure of eating came second to the 'right' social interactions. Learning how to cook then (as I see it now) was learning how to service this event and was almost devoid of any immediate sense of taste, smell and the physical pleasure of eating. I resisted the 'chore' of learning how to cook *for* the family. This is how I remember it today; my memories play tricks on me and I trick my memories into new shapes and forms ...

Other contradicting memories are already crowding into my head – it wasn't all meatloaf, potato and vegetable (which in any case I regularly ate up, not simply out of duty, but in quite happy acceptance). Now I'm remembering the delights of fresh corn on the cob, local maple syrup on thick pancakes and waffles, tart/sweet home-made grape jelly my mother made from the wild grapes which grew locally in the rural chicken-farming Connecticut of my childhood.

I resisted learning to cook though; not so much because it was 'women's work' which I wanted to avoid – no cloudy pre-feminist figur-ations danced in my tomboy's head. It was, I think, more a tiny rebellion of the child against the rules and regulations of 'family life' as I knew them, and a direct refusal to be 'taught' by my mother in a situation where I felt trapped in her critical gaze.

My pleasure in food developed as an individualized experience, an exploration which took place on an uneven road to independence. Before cooking came eating: I discovered, secretly, that the rules of moderation so revered by my parents could be broken. Toast could accommodate huge dollops of margarine – not just the thin spread I'd first been presented with as a toddler and then taught how to create myself. Cream cheese, salami, peanut butter, honey, could all be, if not indulged in too often, eaten on their own, in spoonfuls, not just spread thinly between two slices of Pepperidge Farm Bread.

I ate the ordinary, relatively bland and 'nutritionally sound' food of my parents' table while slowly developing a delight in the extremes of sweet and savoury in my bedroom or in solitary no-one-else-at-home times in the kitchen. I never binged secretly on totally forbidden foods; never rejected the food my mother and father cooked – I simply branched out broke the unspoken rules, discovered that that was easy and gave me pleasure.

When I got married to an Englishman, I suddenly took on the cook's role. Nobody had to say it, I bought it. Modern young woman of the early sixties and all, I still didn't have the political means to coherently question my unquestioning acceptance that eventually, women cooked. Inevitably I'd been given *The Joy of Cooking* as a wedding present. I followed the recipes religiously – head bobbing back and forth from the chosen recipe to the work at hand. But most of the time I relied on my mother's traditional fare – meatloaf, hamburgers, frozen green beans, rice, baked potatoes. It all came full circle!

Only slowly did I begin to loosen the grip of that tradition which I'd rebelled against as a child and young woman. My husband was not a conventional man and in any case his attitude to food was quite different from mine. Having grown up in a working-class family during the war, his childhood was dominated first by scarcity and later by a continual sense that what food *was* in the house had been obtained (often through credit) to eat *that* day. Saving and moderation, therefore, were the choices of those who *had* something to save or to be moderate about. I began to see food and its preparation as shaped by different circumstances, choices and possibilities. I started to get politics.

In the twenty or so years between then and now, I've continued along a bumpy, contradictory road in my relationship to food and cooking. I've gone through the years of guilt and expediency when my children were young, when fishfingers dominated and I secretly tried to introduce wheatgerm into their hamburgers.

Somewhere along the line, for too complicated reasons to go into here, my husband chose to take over the cooking almost completely. Somewhere else along the line, I stopped being guilty about not cooking and more or less accepted that eating when I wanted, how I wanted was okay. I started revelling in occasional solitary meals, made up of all sorts of bits and pieces – reclaiming my childhood joys.

Later, I moved away from my family and for the first time in my life, started living on my own. It's really since then that I've started exploring and enjoying cooking – for myself and for women friends and lovers. I do find real pleasure in letting whatever sort of taste I most desire drift into my mind – the taste of coriander, the comfort of a cheese sauce, the texture of lightly cooked vegetables with a squeeze of lemon juice, the spicy flavours in stir-fried noodles; licking the plate clean after fried eggs and toast; droozling ginger in syrup over Greek yoghurt; garlic and pasta; Mr Patak's Brinjal Pickles, taramasalata, brie, ripe peaches; the unnervingly sweet corn on the cob you can get at 'out of season' times in London; tomato/onion/mayonnaise sandwiches; Dutch mustard loaded onto bits of Italian salami; cold, creamy courgette soup; cream cheese and smoked salmon on bagels from the bagel shop in Ridley Road; Chinese-style seaweed, baked potatoes heaped with butter, Greek yoghurt, grated cheese, salt and pepper, *all at once*; fresh grilled fish, scallops when in season and within reach of my purse; prawns eaten any way except in cocktail … I could go on and on.

I walk into the supermarket, or look in my food cupboard, my mind opens, my eyes gaze. I see what fits my desire and just 'know' what I want to put together to eat. It hardly ever fails.

After all this drooling over food, my recipes are extremely simple, fast and mostly to do with the common courgette.

GRATED COURGETTES

Take any number of courgettes – 1 medium/large size is enough for two people if it's to accompany other dishes. But use as many as you want. Firm, fresh courgettes are best but it works with older, tattier ones as well. Cut into 2 or 3 segments after washing and drying.

Grate using an ordinary cheese grater – it goes extremely fast. If you want to be thorough leave the grated mass of courgettes to drain on kitchen towels or whatever for $\frac{1}{2}$ hour or so. If you don't have the time don't worry. You'll just get a wetter result.

Heat a frying pan and put about 1 tbs of butter or marg in the pan to melt and start to bubble (You can use a smaller amount to cook this dish or lots if you like buttery things.)

Dump in the courgettes which should spread out and not be too thickly piled up. Stir them around, pause, stir again, pause a bit, stir. In all it shouldn't take more than between 2–3 minutes. Don't overcook!

The colour of the vegetable is gorgeous – pale and dark green, and I have no idea why, but it tastes 100 times fresher and more delightful than sliced courgettes cooked in the same butter and frying pan.

I've tried cooking shredded courgettes and carrots together, which was okay, but better was popping a knob of creamy garlic cheese in right before serving.

BASIC COURGETTE SOUP – COLD OR HOT

2 medium courgettes – washed and cut into chunks

2 medium onions – cut into chunky slices

1 pint chicken or vegetable stock

4 oz or so of plain yoghurt

Salt and freshly ground pepper to taste

Chopped chives to sprinkle

Heat up the stock to boiling (use a stock cube if you want). Dump in the vegetables and simmer till the courgettes can be easily pierced with a fork. Puree the vegetables and stock in a blender, adding the yoghurt and salt and pepper to taste. If serving cold, chill.

Variations

1. Substitute 6 carrots for the courgettes for carrot soup.

2. Add a red pepper (cut up) to the courgettes and stock when cooking – you get lovely red specks throughout the soup when it's pureed up.

3. Add some cayenne pepper to 'heat' it up.

4. Vary the amounts of vegetables and liquid for thick or thin soup.

All great with garlic bread.

CRAB MEAT AND BREADCRUMBS

Use as much crabmeat as you can afford or need – from fishmongers or frozen from the supermarket. Picking your own crabs is tedious and to be undertaken only when and if you have lots of time, lots of crabs and are well relaxed. Doing it with friends is best.

Crumble up some stale bread – the amount according to how much crab meat you have, or how many people you have to stretch the dish to. I usually use about 2 slices of crumbly wholemeal bread.

Melt some butter in a frying pan. Fry the breadcrumbs till they're golden brown (now that's a real cookbook phrase for you). Add the crab and stir. Don't overcook. 2 – 3 minutes should be plenty. The essence of frying up seafood like crab, prawns, scallops, etc. is to cook thoroughly *but* minimally. Otherwise they toughen up.

Add seasoning to taste, which are: a dash of Worcestershire sauce, lemon juice, cayenne pepper or a small amount of fresh chillis, salt. My preference in this dish is lightly hot – let the crab taste shine through.

Menopause Waltz

– FROM *A CERTAIN AGE*, 1993

It wasn't as if she woke up one day and it was gone. Not at all. There were literally years of taking leave, and it was never straightforward. Even now, at fifty-one, when she hadn't seen a drop of red on her knickers for three or four years, its effects lingered: a hot flush here and there; a low-down ache in her gut which took her by surprise before she remembered it wouldn't come again. Over thirty years of bleeding, and then the wind-down and final dribble. She realized there was no way to tell a meno-pausal tale without a menstrual story.

She had never been one of those women who loved their periods. As a child – and she had been only nine when it started: intially excited, rushing into her parents' bedroom in the early morning of its first appearance – her mother's spontaneous reaction dampened things considerably: 'Oh dear, I am sorry. You're so young.' Still, looking back, she was pretty sure that even if her mother had swept her up in pride, gushing, 'Now you are a woman,' she would have seen the truth before long.

When her periods started coming regularly, from about the age of ten, she experienced a monthly cycle which often included at least one day of heavy, hot, aching cramps, and a week of bleeding into bulky disposable towels which had to be saved in paper bags in her closet and then taken out to the incinerator and burned. She meticulously tied up each used towel and wrapped it in miles of toilet paper – these tight, bloody knots took hours to burn, her cross to bear. What fun was it, and how could she be pleased about the fact that every month she inevitably bled through, at least once, on to her knickers, and had to soak them in cold water, rub salt on to them, scrub them, and still have light tan stains left in the crotch? In her teen years, on her heaviest days, she was known to stuff two – or, in desperation, even three – Kotex down her knickers, or into the special rubber-crotched pants her mother bought her.

Sometimes the cramps were agony. Her mother was of the get-up-and-go school. She rarely communicated any sisterly commiseration, which possibly meant she didn't experience the kind of pain her daughter did. She had a little green-and-white-striped terrycloth-covered electric pad which the girl would go to bed with, holding it to her tummy, fantasizing about a long wooden spoon, wrapped round with cool, wet cotton, which dipped into her and scooped out the dark pool of clotty liquid that lay like poison in her belly. When something was planned by her parents, and she had already spent a half-hour or so curled up with the hot pad, her mother would call her, telling her to get ready to go out, claiming that if she would just get up and start to do something it would feel better. As a result, more than once, she lay in misery, brutish and rolling rhythmically, in the back of the station wagon, while her parents and brothers swam or picnicked.

` No, she knew it was not a good thing, although she quickly understood it was the way of things. Her mother was modern in the 1950s sense of the word. She never suggested that there was anything about menstruation to be proud of, but then she never called it the curse either. No, it was something to get used to, to try to ignore as much as possible. Keep busy. Be active. That would take your mind off any little discomfort.

Somewhere along the line, the girl became obsessively concerned that her father or her brothers – or any man, for that matter – might guess that she had her period. Nothing was to be said by her mother. But she could never quite trust her to guard this secret. She wanted her mother to understand without having to tell her. But her mother was careless about her feelings and often seemed oblivious to her distress as she dropped hints that the girl was acting oddly because she had her period. Agonies of burning shame and embarrassment. In high school she worried every single month about bleeding through on to the back of her skirt. She worried about smelling. She worried about starting somewhere without access to a Kotex. All these things happened.

The truth was that after so many years of bleeding every month, she did get used to it. Life went on. She was generally a happy girl, with lots of friends and a good sense of humour. She was blessed with a good 1950s American-style diet, a lot of fresh country air, plenty of excercise, and an urge towards nonconformity. Fucking didn't happen until she was eighteen, so for most of her teenage years she kissed and petted and rolled around with boys fully, or at least partially, dressed. No worries about contraception then, or waiting with baited breath for a period to arrive, but what did you do about a boy feeling the heavy wodge of Kotex as you pressed your clothed bodies together?

Fucking brought new menstrual worries – more concerned with how you told someone you had your period when they wanted to root around down there than with the possibility of getting pregnant. One time she didn't say anything, and he, an older man, removed her pants and her Kotex, and proceeded to fuck her without realizing that she still had a tampon in. She never said a word, but it was hard getting hold of it after it had been banged up inside. Tampons had become possible only after experiencing intercourse. Before that she hadn't been able to get one in, practically fainting in the toilet stall at school with the effort of unsuccessfully poking and pushing about.

Somewhere along the way she picked up that her period pains would improve after she got married. Then, as she got older, she understood that meant after she had a baby. Fortunately, periods did not play a role in her decision to get married or have babies, although she did end up doing both. She fell in love with a British boy and became an American living abroad. She also spent six years on the Pill, which got rid of cramps, got rid of heavy bleeding, prevented conception, but made her feel bloated and strange.

After two babies, living in London, she threw away the Pill for good, tried the coil, which created blood baths from hell, and finally got sterilized. Pregnancy had brought the first disruption of her regular periods. As she settled back to normal it was clear that her cycle was changing, as was the world. Women's liberation arrived in the late 1960s, hot from its American successes. She was captivated, enchanted, transfixed. She was in the midst of her drudge years – all lank long hair, sleepless baby-filled nights and identity crisis. Now, with other women, she discussed many things, including women's bloody cycles. She could see clearly how menstruation's meaning, and even some of the ways it was experienced, arose from what they began to call conditioning. It fascinated her; menstrual stories revealed so much about how girls became women, about fear and loathing, about the female body, about sexuality, about difference.

But she could never make the existential leap into totally accepting and adoring her periods. Embarrassment and shame might be the result of conditioning, but bleeding would happen, happy or sad. She cringed at the new matriarchists who wanted to reclaim menstruation, celebrate it and even – oh my God – dabble in it, adorn their faces with it, drip it across city pavements and country fields. Symbolic or literal, either way it didn't sit well, it didn't strike a note of recognition. It was ridiculous. Menstrual blood was sticky on the thighs if it flowed unplugged. It smelled – sorry, but it did – if it was left on a pad in the warmth. Of course she wanted to change attitudes to menstruation – the attitude of girls who would bleed, her own, men's and society's. But she wanted nothing to do with locating women's possibilities and powers so firmly in their biology.

She fell in love with a woman, and with lesbian sex. So besotted with making love to women was she that even their blood didn't stand in her way. Now, all these years later, she took her mother's advice and plunged in, keeping busy, letting passion transcend any worry, licking and tasting, and finding it not at all displeasing. To think that the man in her life had told her for so long that it didn't matter to him if she was bleeding and she never really believed him, and certainly never talked about her periods with him.

Periods became a small part of her woman-orientated life. Lovers shared the intimacies of bodies and wondered if, by living together, their cycles were synchronizing, like nuns' did. Fucking with a bleeding lover was one thing; sharing all these details made her go queasy. She might be compelled by her own bloody discharge, but that didn't mean she felt the same way about her girlfriend's. Why did lesbians have to talk about bleeding all the time? It seemed that every time you got together someone was menstruating, feeling pre-menstrual, having period pains, or suffering from something related to it. Every serious lover she had had terrible period problems, and she expected (and fully expected herself) to be commiserating and sympathetic. In fact she was much better at telling and listening to menstrual stories than at coping with blood clots themselves.

In her late thirties her cycles were changing again. This time, after about six months, she realized something different was beginning: her period was more irregular, and the cycle was getting shorter and shorter. She wondered to herself if this was part of a changing pattern leading to the menopause. Could it be? Wasn't it kind of early? No one else her age brought up the subject. The more she read about the menstrual cycle, the more she realized that there was no clearly defined thing called the menopause. It seemed rare for anyone to be pre-menstrual one moment and post-menopausal the next. The fact was that this process might take years and years to complete.

In the early 1980s she attended an international women's health conference in Switzerland. She went to a workshop on the menopause run by one of the original American *Our Bodies Ourselves* collective members, who eloquently approached the subject with a fan in her hand. She came away from that workshop imagining legions of hot flushing women, willing to whip out their fans in offices, parks, on the streets, in cinemas, recklessly declaring to the world their bloody crisis, perhaps even delighting in it. She fantasized herself as such a woman, and found pleasure in it. But it still felt a long way off.

By the time she was forty-three she began to experience the odd hot flush. What a peculiar sensation! The first time it happened was in public on her own. She felt like a little girl, dying to tell someone, turn to the next person she saw and say, 'My God, you know what's happening to me?' The sweat poured down between her breasts, and her face blushed steamily. And then it was gone, a matter of a thirty-second hormonal eruption. And it wasn't really bad. In fact she decided that it was a little like New York City summer heat: the more you fought against it, the worse it became. The only thing to do was to surrender yourself to it totally, let it flow through you. She began to imagine herself as the menopausal lady, taking London by storm with an outspoken acknowledgement of her condition. During the day her more modest acts were limited to flinging the windows of the office open, joking that it was another hot flush and she simply had to have air! She bought a beautiful blue Chinese fan, but at the appropriate moment it wasn't always easy to find at the bottom of her work-filled bag.

She was living on her own by now, leaving boys, home, and best-friend husband to sleep like a baby in a tiny, courtyard-facing, noisy, short-life flat in King's Cross. She was besotted with her small estate and, after the first shock of being on her own, enamoured of that condition. Her life felt filled with possibility and a good amount of pleasure. She found her forties her most fulfilling decade yet. At the same time, she had some pretty spectacular relationship failures which left her curled in a ball on the floor sobbing through the nights, but in the end she recovered. Once, when the loss and betrayal and grief turned the world grey for a couple of months, she felt compelled to find a shrink, something she had never thought would be necessary or right for her. It was, and it worked, and she changed a tiny bit.

After six months or so of hot flushing, just as she was really getting serious about it all, the daytime flushes went, disappeared, vanished. The nighttime soaks remained – usually not extreme, but sometimes occurring up to ten or twelve times a night. The first time it had happened, with her lover lying there beside her, she felt embarrassed, but the woman was intrigued and interested. She was – as all her lovers had been – younger, and certainly not menopausal. They discovered that sex and flushes often went together, and that a good session of snogging could bring a little one on. Her girlfriend got blasé and was prone to say things like 'Having a little flush then, Susie?' which, while comforting, was occasionally irritating.

She told everyone she was menopausal, including her mother, who denied it. 'No,' said her mother, 'you aren't.' In a perfect continuation of their relationship, she found herself defensively arguing yes, it was happening to her, as if perhaps she was the one who had made a mistake. Then she decided to let it pass. Other people believed her, although they usually told her she was too young or went glazed in the eyes and pretended their attention was demanded elsewhere.

She wrote a secret poem called 'Menopause Waltz' in which her ambivalences were expressed. She didn't dread the loss of her bloody cycle, but she did worry about getting a dried-up cunt. That, more than anything else, nagged and made her apprehensive. It was hard to admit, because somehow it seemed self-obsessed and vaguely unimportant. But in fact, here she was, relatively late in life, getting off on slick vaginal secretions, sliding-sweet, sexy-wet. Her own and others'. Feeling sexual meant getting wet; getting wet meant fingers could open her up, and wanting more. Wanting more meant asking for it harder, and more and more. Getting sucked and licked was the best thing ever for fantastic orgasms, but fucking with a woman was different and amazing. Even if you were in a fantasy at home on your own, it was nice to reach down and push in and feel how warm and smooth and wet you were. Was this going to be lost? The descriptions were not reassuring: thinning vaginal walls, atrophied vaginas, dry, possibly sore, cunts. Dreadful. It didn't seem to be happening at all during the menopausal process, but what about later?

It was double-edged, starting the menopause early. It worried her when people told her she looked too young to be menopausal, because although she was a bit flattered, she then wondered what people would think when, inevitably, she did look old. Having never been particularly attached to her periods but being a worry-wort, she also puzzled that perhaps she was being a bit offhand about their loss. It was true that the few years of change had made her more interested in the real bloody discharge, more attentive to its smell, look and texture. When it was truly gone, would she have some sort of psychic crisis? Claiming that personally it had nothing substantial to do with feeling complete as a woman might be a huge denial. God, sometimes she wished she hadn't dabbled in psychoanalytic chit-chat.

She kept a menstrual chart through all of her forties and that was how she finally figured out it was gone for good and that she was post-menopausal. It was quite a shock to realize that more than two years had gone by since her last period, because she still thought of herself as being in some sort of process. She remembered the series of dreams – they must have happened in the first year of an absence of blood. Each time she was sitting on the toilet; each time she reached down, tissue in hand, and came up with red-stained paper. Each time she woke up feeling incredibly sad and then as consciousness returned, incredibly relieved.

There were no tampons in her flat; she had thrown away the last of them and expected her lover to provide her own. She rarely thought about periods. It felt entirely natural not to have them, no fuss, no pain, no stains, no smell of warm blood, no lower gut ache or loosening of the bowels. Goodbye to all that.

She still had hot flushes at least a couple of times a week. She still felt the ebb and flow of bodily changes which seemed to be steered by hormonal patterns. Her emotions had never been at the total beck and call of her physiological processes, but they were still gratifyingly inconsistent, surprising and pleasurable. But this happened without the inconvenience of one whole bloody week a month taken up with periods. It was fantastic when she realized how absolutely freeing it was.

At the same time she also realized that she felt considerably distanced and uncaring about other women's periods. She did try to be polite and interested when the conversation turned to who was having what sort of period. She made the right noises when a woman friend or lover complained of bad pains or something associated with menstruation. But really it was like trying to hark back to the Dark Ages. Of course it wasn't their fault. She certainly wasn't suggesting, if only to herself, that they should all go out and get hysterectomies. No, she wouldn't even have joked that way. It was more feeling sorry for them, but also feeling as if she'd done her time, it had had its moments and served its purpose, but now she was leaving it behind.

Her current and steadiest ever lover, still in her thirties and regular as clockwork, was not one of her complaining companions. But she suspected that even she noticed her lack of interest. More difficult was the recognition that she wasn't really keen to fuck with her beloved when she was bleeding. In her thirties and much of her forties, she had spent a lot of time as a women's health activist and writer, talking with women about overcoming their self-disgust, their dislike of their own and other women's monthly bleeding. Oh, she could hear the times she had said, 'It's not dirty. There is nothing wrong with having sex when you are menstruating. You may find you feel randy then.' She had gently prodded women to engage with their partners' dislike of or ambivalence about their blood, and tell them if they were interested in sex at that time. In the past her own husband had communicated to her that he was not turned off at all by her bleeding and would engage in any sexual acts that she wanted during that time. She realized now that he had been more accepting than she was.

Back in the seventies and early eighties she had been aware of feminist critiques of hormone replacement therapy. She had been part of the women's health movement, taught women's health in Holloway Prison, gained a diploma in Health Education, and finally ended up at *Spare Rib* magazine, where she was responsible for most of the health articles for the five years she stayed on the collective. She wasn't a hardliner about health care; if the menopause drove you nuts and made you miserable and HRT helped, she wasn't going to come on all judgemental. But she did think it was strange that after all the criticisms, all the exposés of how profit-driven and blandly disinterested in women drug companies were, anyone could merrily leap on the HRT bandwagon. Then there were the revolting paeans to the magical effects HRT had on women's ability to stay youthful and beautiful, with smooth faces and elastic cunts. When possible dangers associated with HRT began to come to light, it didn't surprise her at all.

Memories are short, time flies by, and drug companies are loath to give up. By the end of the eighties HRT was making a comeback, only now osteoporosis was the buzz word, striking terror in women's hearts. Suddenly every woman she knew was nervous about brittle bones, wondering if they too would end up cracking hips, developing dowager's humps, breaking wrists. Surely HRT was the answer – and, not only that, it dampened hot flushes and made women feel happy! Several of her contemporaries who were not even menopausal asked her if she was on HRT when she talked about her menopause. When she answered 'no', they asked, 'Why not?' To which she replied, 'Why?'

Why should she if she didn't find the flushes impossible, wasn't depressed, felt energetic and didn't believe HRT was the only way to stay fit and healthy? Thinking it over, she decided the subtext was almost always a fear of growing old, looking older. Strange that feminists, so confident in their more youthful twenties and thirties about the ephemeral nature of 'attractiveness', and its male-defined meanings, began to waver and lose confidence in their forties and fifties. Sad and understandable, but maddening. She wasn't immune – especially alone, at night. The more women she heard extolling the wonders of HRT with breathy sideways remarks about how good they felt – glowing skin, springy cunts – the more she wondered gloomily if she was making some sort of silly stand. Would she regret it in ten years' time? Then she would catch herself and think how ridiculous, she didn't look any different from the women who took HRT, she didn't need to medicalize her perfectly normal changes, she didn't have to bury the signals of change in her life. She had always celebrated change. Why stop now? She had no more reason to trust drug companies today than she had ten years ago. The difference now was that she didn't have a group of peers meeting together regularly to talk about their lives, committed to discovering the social roots of their private fears and confusions. She wasn't really hankering after those old days, but it helped to remember them.

In the last year or so, as she became more and more post-menopausal, she noticed more signs of ageing in herself. Were they connected to being post-menopausal, or were they happening because she was – older? Did it really matter? Her cunt was a little less wet. By this time she was deeply involved in AIDS work, running workshops and writing a lot for women about sex, sexuality, and safer sex. Familiarity with safer-sex techniques meant getting relaxed about lubricants. Lubes and latex go together like a horse and carriage. Her ex-lover in San Francisco sent her a plastic bottle of Probe, a water-based lube. It was wonderful. No more greasy gunk. What had seemed an admission of defeat, of sometimes needing help, of loss of spontaneity, was transformed into matter-of-factness and pleasure.

She thought, finally, that the menopause was a wonderful thing. It gave women a clear hint of their mortality, and if they were receptive, it gave them a chance to reflect on their life. For her it was a signpost of change, and signalled that she had completed the longest period of her life. She read Germaine Greer on the menopause, and wished that many other women could tell their tales as widely. For her the change was not about accepting a loss of sexual engagement, nor did she believe that lesbians necessarily experienced menopause in the same way as Greer claimed heterosexual women did. But she agreed wholeheartedly with her that any wishful desire for 'no change' was desperately sad and horrible.

She felt differently passionate, differently engaged, differently but happily a woman, now that she was free of menstruation. She could still be blue and get depresssed, but those were not conditions which typified her life. She could be deeply serious and self-sufficient at times, and laugh till her sides ached with a bunch of girlfriends at others. She could be pleased with her memories, filled with love for her grown-up children, and still fizz with expectation at a new idea for work or relaxation. She wept and raged at the grotesque levels of suffering and exploitation in the world, but she still considered herself committed to being part of changing that. She was sometimes confused and troubled by the end-of-the-century political scene, but she was confident in a way she had never been when she was younger. She was still the queen of second-hand shopping and still intended to get fit, but she fully understood that some possibilities were in the past for her. Each decade of her life had spun itself out at the time as the best. She saw no reason to think the next few wouldn't continue the tradition. Now if only she could shed those extra post-menopausal pounds ...

PART TWO

Contradictions Claimed

Early in my involvement in women's liberation, way back in the 1970s, alongside my enthusiasm, I experienced hazy feelings of disquiet as I sat in my local small women's group, or lay in bed endlessly rolling all these new ideas around in my head. The forceful ideas which were to change my life seemed so true, so persuasive, so obvious. What a relief to see the pieces fit into a pattern largely determined by male-dominated, capitalist society. The more we dug into women's lives, our own and others, the more we saw patterns, explanations. Those were hopeful days: we could challenge and change those conditions and thus change our own lives.

I didn't doubt the bold outlines of our uneven but vibrant analysis. But the patch of haze remained, often intensifying when our small women's group tried to extrapolate a generality from the collection of articulated individual histories and experiences. Outside the small group, in large and more public meetings, that uneasiness was stronger. Not all the time but enough to make me jittery at points. A dozen or so women meeting weekly in a living-room led to openness and trust. Secrets could be divulged, time could be spent on visions of a better future for women.

In larger meetings where strangers or little-known women came together it was different. Imagine a meeting room in a scruffy centre. Within a free-ranging discussion the subject of marriage comes up. A fierce and passionate woman denounces it. Marriage – an institution which oppressed and exploited all women, operated for all men's benefit. A woman new to women's liberation tentatively defends 'her' man, plaintively claiming he's different. The response? Palpable derision – did this saint do the housework, cook, look after the children? Had she kept her own name? No one addressed heterosexual desire; that would open a whole other can of worms. But I knew that many of the women who most vociferously denounced 'marriage' were either in one themselves or living quite cosily with a man. I knew some of the most adamantly anti-male women's liberationists had steamy sex lives with men. Wasn't silence about all this a contradiction and a hypocrisy?

I had been part of an expanding women's liberation movement in Britain from its inception. I too believed that marriage continued to imply ownership, even if this was as much symbolic as real. But I too knew that my husband was 'different'. However, in the flush of collective revelation there was no room for nuance nor any acceptable consciousness of differing realities contained within an over-reaching analysis. I contented myself with telling the 'truth' whenever 'men never ...' or 'men always ...' stock assertions came up. Some men might not, or could, but in fact my husband cooked, took care of the babies, never used physical violence, and was incapable of rape. Believing this didn't mean that lazy bastards, violent thugs or businessmen, or condescending lefties didn't exist in appallingly large numbers. Did *all* men have to fit into these monolithic moulds in order to prove these sexist attitudes and behaviours persisted? Was our analysis of institutionalized sexism and male power dependent on denying that individual men might struggle through the contradictions? Something was a bit off tune.

When I started reading about the Chinese revolution and ventured into Mao's writing I was struck by his notion of contradiction. I thought it was fucking brilliant. I could keep my women's liberation analysis and deal with the inconsistencies in my own life and others through a political understanding of the nature of contradictions. It made wonderful political and personal sense to me. Change seemed more realistic if the messy bits could be openly acknowledged and explored. Relations between different social forces, such as class, race, sex and gender could be read with much more subtlety. I haven't read Mao in years so I don't really know if what I appropriated and shaped to my own needs was 'correctly' Maoist. Who cares. When I first came into contact with postmodernism sometime in the mid-1980s I thought they were reinventing wheels all over the place.

Most of the essays and articles in this book are attentive in one way or another to contradictions. Being opposed to either/or thinking or binary divisions and being sensitive to what influences these tempting, trapping ways of framing things has helped me untangle difficult questions. It isn't a case of never taking a stand or even claiming that there are no truths. I am neither a down-the-line cultural relativist, nor drawn to totalizing truths.

In 'Capping the Cervix' written at the beginning of the 1980s I looked at the history and fate of cervical caps as a method of non-invasive, woman-controlled contraception. To put it in a context, I had to consider attitudes towards sexuality and the contradictions contained in the sexually 'liberating' 1960s. I was a teenager in the 1950s and had lived through an abortion and had used just about every form of birth control available after I started having penetrative sex with men. I tried to understand why we young adventurous women of the late 1950s and early sixties opened our arms to the Pill and frequently failed in the use of older forms of birth control which required a small degree of skill and lots of determination.

At the time there was a strong push within feminism to critique and reject the primacy of the Pill. Today that will has weakened. Yet today, as breast cancer activism seeks to secure more research and agitates for meaningful prevention measures, the Pill still looms as one of many possible sources of breast cancer. In the end, all the insistent demands for a non-toxic, woman-controlled method of contraception have turned up very little – such a method wouldn't make a pharmaceutical fortune.

At *Spare Rib* I coordinated the health articles. Premenstrual tension (PMT) was in the news in the early 1980s because it was being used for the first time as a defence in criminal cases. Again, a contradictory situation arose. To use it as a defence it was necessary to claim biological origins for women's wacky or destructive behaviour. I critiqued the behaviour-determining role of hormones at the same time that I acknowledged the debilitating effects of PMT in many women's lives. Within the constraints of a monthly magazine, the short PMT article attempted to politicize a mainstream news story.

In 1982 I went on a health and social service tour to Cuba. I didn't go expecting to find heaven on earth. But I did find a fascinating society struggling to maintain itself in the face of American hostility and economic sanctions. At the time it was considered bad form among some circles of British and American socialist feminists to publish anything negative about certain socialist countries. I guess it depended on which ones your particular group or party supported at the time; if you were non-aligned you were not supposed to impose your western biases and cultural views onto a third-world country.

I was hyper-aware of the dangers of reading onto Cuba the concerns and solutions relevant to my own society and I certainly wanted to make it clear that I supported Cuba's struggle to exist in a hostile world. But I could not for the life of me see how Cuba's official and informal homophobia was off critical limits. I undertook situating my criticisms within a framework of support. The only letters which came into the magazine in the following months were from socialist-feminist lesbians who denounced me for imposing my concerns on a socialist society which needed total support. Pushing totalizing claims of truth, shoving contradictions, problems or failures under the carpet creates disillusionment and cynicism in the end. More difficult perhaps but far more creative and long-lasting to explore these.

Susan Ardill and I posed questions in our 1990 article 'Butch/Femme Obsession'. Although we had had many engrossing talks and much gossip about butch/femme we had reached a plateau of saturation by 1989. Is it a kind of perversity which never allows us to let things lie? Anyway, we were initially propelled into writing by the proliferation of butch/femme as just another style choice on the one hand, and on the other by a romanticization of butch/femme as timeless and precious lesbian identities. We say at the beginning of that piece, 'Now that butch/femme has finally achieved respectability and is sweeping sections of the visible British urban lesbian cultures, we find ourselves reacting against it. These days it all seems like hot air and style. Last gasp of the 1980s or new wave for the nineties, it hardly seems to matter – there's something shallow going on.'

Six years later, it looks as if something shallow *and* something completely different are going on. The advent of lesbian chic, the elevation of famous 'role models' like kd lang, and the adoption of a sort of post punk SM, masculinity among young (or not so young) women, some of them lesbian, and the arrival of a bastardized notion of gender as performance, all feed into current butch/femme styles. There *is* something ephemeral going on.

But many of our questions about the deeper meanings and implications of butch/femme remain under-theorized, although Joan Nestle's collection, *The Persistent Desire*, goes some way to fleshing the questions out more fully. Many of our political questions remain too. Although some feminist critics of butch/femme still carry on with their denunciations, there's a slight shift in the scenarios they describe. Now some critics collapse butch/femme and SM into each other. Although it is patently clear to me that not all butch/femme lesbians are into SM or vice versa, they get lumped together, equally bad or one and the same ...

There are significant numbers of women around now who see butch/femme as the defining aspect of their lesbianism, woman who would be hard-pressed to say that the word lesbian designates their sexual identity, preferring butch or femme. Some are convinced they would be lost without their butch or femme identity. But others who have delighted in *playing* with femme have been struck when a lover wants 'the perfect femme' and they have no interest in conforming to a prescribed 'role'.

Myself, I'm still ambivalent. Sometimes I am conscious of being femme, some days I dress very girly (a contradiction in terms for a fifty-four-year-old?), other days I don't give a hoot, others I feel positively tomboyish, and just as often I don't think about femme at all. Femme would not be among my most cherished self definitions nor is my lover's butchness the thing I prize most, although contrarily I am still in the grip of the erotic charge our 'difference' causes and which I believe has a great deal to do with butch/femme.

AIDS entered my life in the early 1980s when a good friend who was nursing in San Francisco wrote about gay friends of hers who were getting ill with a mystery disease. By the mid-1980s Susan Ardill and I were keen to write about the meaning of AIDS for women. 'AIDS and Women – Building a Feminist Framework' was the second of our articles which appeared in *Spare Rib* in 1987. After delineating every single sexual activity we could imagine and addressing the concerns of heterosexuals, bisexuals and lesbians, in part two, reprinted here, we began to theorize about AIDS and women. It seems amazing today that these articles on women and

AIDS were probably the first to appear in a British newsstand magazine.

The work Susan and I did together for these articles formed the basis, the jumping-off point for much of my future work around HIV/AIDS. Although there are significant changes I would make if I were writing these pieces today, I also think we got off on the right foot. Reading it now I can see the connections to later writing on lesbians and HIV I did with Pratibha Parmar (included in Part Four). In 1987 Susan and I write, 'AIDS gives us all permission to talk sex, talk desire, talk "dirty", talk fear, talk confusion, talk fantasy.' In 1992 Pratibha and I take that 'permission' and extend it into a necessary framework for lesbians to understand and evaluate the place of AIDS and HIV transmission in their lives.

In 1990 an interview I conducted with American AIDS and gay activist Cindy Patton ('Mapping: Lesbians, AIDS and Sexuality') was published in *Feminist Review*. Cindy wrote one of the earliest (and most engaging) books analysing the emerging AIDS crisis, *Sex and Germs: The Politics of AIDS*. I was captivated by Cindy's activism and intellect – as well as her girl-about-town lesbianism. Even then I was a lesbian safer-sex doubter while Cindy was a keen promoter. We continued to disagree although I was enthusiastic about her idea that everyone should learn the techniques – crash courses on the application of latex – and then make personal adjustments and evaluations with that knowledge firmly in place.

When the special lesbian issue of *Feminist Review* came out with the interview in it nothing much happened. But it must have been circulating slowly because I began to hear rumours that I condoned child sexual abuse. Whoa. Where is this coming from? I realized there were women around who didn't like my politics one little bit, but had it sunk to this? It didn't take much to appreciate that the accusations were based on a (mis)reading of 'Mapping'. It was the only time I had spoken about child sexual abuse.

Three years before 'Mapping', Susan Ardill and I had dissected the politics of vociferous anti-porn and SM lesbian feminists in 'Upsetting an Applecart'. Anger over that article still simmered. 'Mapping', which took on in a different way some of the same feminist politics Susan and I had taken aim at previously, also included a discussion of memory and child sexual abuse which Cindy and I both contributed to. In the five years since its publication that brief conversation has been used a number of times as the basis of attacks on both of us.

'Mapping' explores contradictions in the breathtakingly bumpy terrain of HIV/AIDS. Cindy delivered free wheeling, generously open and usefully provocative opinions. It was exactly what I hoped for. The negative responses to our interview engaged with a minute part of what was said. They exhibit all the features I find most use*less*: misreading, labelling, no truck with ambivalence or ambiguity, certainly not with contradictions. A stubborn, weathered optimism gives me hope that the ongoing, exploratory work of other feminists around sex and gender will thrive and challenge inflexibility.

Capping the Cervix – Understanding Our Sexuality
– FROM *SPARE RIB* 105, APRIL 1981

The 1960s and 1970s were heydays for the pill and IUD. By the mid-1970s 'old-fashioned' barrier methods which women used had all but disappeared as popular choices. My own history bridged the year or so between the accepted use of older devices and the adoption of the new methods. In 1961, deciding I needed birth control meant being fitted with a diaphragm. I was never comfortable using or even thinking about my 'device', and not surprisingly got pregnant with it sitting in my bag, next to the bed. After an illegal abortion, I went straight on to the pill, determined never to get unwillingly pregnant again. I saw myself as unable to cope with something like the diaphragm. The pill was a 'god' send.

It seems to me that various developments came together in the early 1960s to ensure the uncritical widespread acceptance and use of the pill. The application of western technological and scientific knowledge to the 'problem' of birth control was of central importance. The motivation for new discoveries in this field did not come from women's demands, as there was no popular women's movement in the 1950s. The motivation came from the confidence of a male-dominated, profit-orientated belief in the power of science and technology to advance and protect the 'free world'. In the 1950s USA government officials and agencies, politicians and financiers came together in support of population control ideas and methods. The book *Population Bomb*, which presented a picture of the world as a ticking time-bomb which, if set off, would result in a population explosion causing war and communism, illustrated America's conservative concern with the politics of population.

The pill and the IUD were always tied up with American population control programmes and were used on women in Third World countries and on Black and poor women inside the USA. At the same time powerful drug companies and doctors pushed the pill, and many women wanted it. Seemingly they had made a 'choice'. Why did so many of these women reject barrier methods of birth control and take up the pill and, to a lesser extent, the IUD?

During the late 1950s the hold of traditional sex morals was breaking down. Sex, divorce, motherhood, the family, youth, were all beginning to be seen as problems. No coherent alternative morality emerged, but the cohesion of the old one was weakening. In growing numbers women were being pressed with a changing triad of ideas, practices and institutions around sex, reproduction and marriage. The shakiness of the 'holy' trinity meant that each aspect jarred but didn't separate from the others. We neither had the practical methods nor the challenging ideas which would enable us to struggle to make breaks between whom we slept with and when, how we felt about it, if and when we'd have children and who'd care for them, and if and what we thought about marriage.

Our lives were changing, but were filled with confusion and ambivalence, not the least about sleeping with men and using birth control. Many of us who 'did it' still usually did so because of pressure and/or highly romantic expectations, and often continued to out of optimism and/or resignation. At the same time, we tended to be ill at ease with our bodies and lacked the most basic body knowledge. The 'myth of the vaginal orgasm' was untoppled but some of us knew more about sex from historical novelettes than from any prevailing psychological or physiological theories. We also knew at some level about birth control and often said we didn't want to get pregnant, but lots of us didn't use birth control. All this ambivalence and confusion about our bodies, men, reproduction, sex and marriage, affected negatively the possibility of controlling our own fertility.

Our use, misuse, or non-use of the then-available barrier methods of birth control (primarily the diaphragm, various creams or pessaries, the cervical cap in Britain and Europe, or demands for a male lover to use a condom) were reflected in the contradictions I've described. Women also were receiving increasingly strident messages from men that if they didn't 'put out' they were frigid, teases, old-fashioned, or just hadn't discovered how great it was to fuck! Women had not defined their own needs, but they were, as always, terrified of unwanted pregnancies.

So it wasn't surprising that when the pill came along, most heterosexual women welcomed it with open arms. The only difficulty was to get over the fear that if you took the pill and were unmarried you were announcing to every man who came along your 'availability'. On the other hand, the pill was easy to take, you didn't have to be familiar with your body, and it offered the surest way of avoiding pregnancy. We could *let* sex happen to us, while the successful use of barrier methods demanded much more than passivity.

The pill, at least initially, didn't challenge this at all; sex was about 'doing it', but not about resolving in a pro-woman way the contradictions we faced in sexual relations with men. The pill permitted a separation between sex and reproduction, but in favour of male penetration.

However, contained within the so-called sexual revolution and the popularity of the pill was an eventual feminist critique and struggle.

It is true that women were not given any counter-information about the pill which might have affected their use of it. But even if we had had the known information about possible risks, would we, at that time in history, have rejected the pill in favour of the older barrier methods? In order to understand the complexity of how we felt about ourselves in relationship to birth control, we have to look at the different influences on women. Of course the profit motives of the drug and IUD companies were an integral part of what shaped our patterns of 'choice', as were our naive beliefs in the progressive and neutral nature of western science and technology.

It is the drug and pharmacuetical companies and their 'tame' scientists who, more than anyone else, must bear the responsibility for the widespread use of the pill and IUD. Given women's oppression, our internalized self-hatred, and the lack of a collective challenge to our subordination to men, it's not hard to see why many of us were easily persuaded that we were being modern and rational in our use of the pill.

Twenty years after its introduction, the pill's ascendancy as one of the most common forms of birth control in the west is over. In the years since the pill was introduced, extensive research has shown just how dangerous hormones can be for women. Serious short-term effects came to light to reveal far more than the initial talk of 'weight gains', 'headaches', and 'nausea'. Thrombosis and possible links with cancer began to look very real and members of the medical profession itself regarded the pill as a danger to women.

From the late 1960s, the growing impact of feminism, especially in relation to the demystification of doctors, drugs, and the whole idea of medicine as a form of social control and as a part of sexual, race and class divisions, meant that more women were looking critically at what the medical profession was telling them to do. For example, many women were disturbed by medical intervention in pregnancy and childbirth. Why had events which had previously been seen as healthy occasions been defined by the medical profession as illnesses to be managed? More women were open to the idea of using forms of contraception which they controlled and which had fewer, if any, side-effects.

Consciousness-raising and feminist analysis of our sexuality were both a start to the long task of resolving some of the ambivalence and confusion we had felt about ourselves throughout the late 1950s and 1960s – feelings I've suggested led to our uncritical use of the pill in the first place – and to our abandonment of the 'messy', 'unreliable' barrier methods. The development of women's health groups and the prolifer-ation of feminist health courses and literature helped women to learn about and like their bodies, to gather together information, and discuss the links between sexuality and birth control. The autonomy of the women's movement made it possible and necessary to assert the wholeness of women apart from men – and the nature of our needs and desires both in relationship to men and to one another. As more women became lesbians, I think it brought home even more sharply to heterosexual women that they were taking risks with their bodies *for* the men they related to, and they felt angry at the casual assumption that it was okay for women to pump pills into themselves for years on end.

So in this country, and even more in the USA, a significant number of women were scared and angry enough about the risks they were taking with the pill and the IUD to decide that any advantages of those methods were far outweighed by the risks. The alternative which many women turned to was initially the diaphragm. Then in 1977 Barbara Seaman published a popular and influential book in the USA called *Women and the Crisis in Sex Hormones*. One short chapter was called 'Gone but not forgotten: the cervical cap'. Most people date the upsurge in interest in the cap from the publication of this book. Today in the USA there are 30,000 to 40,000 women who have been fitted with caps from a variety of mainly alternative clinics and institutions.

All of this throws up some interesting questions for us as feminists. We can't go around claiming that the older forms of barrier contraceptives represent some golden past of woman-controlled fertility. Technological advances in themselves are not bad and I would welcome new forms of birth control which were proved safe and effective – surely something not out of the reach of a woman-centred science and technology. Also we still have to ask whether the impact of feminism and self-help has significantly changed women's attitudes towards their bodies and towards birth control, compared with twenty years ago.

Now government agencies in the USA have restricted health clinics from fitting caps, in the name of possible unknown risks. There is no point in simply saying they've got it *all* wrong – even if we oppose the restrictions. It's a matter of the politics of the approach. In the USA we see that it is traditional, government-approved groups and institutions which will set up studies of the cap and evaluate information. The very structure which feminist-informed health care sprang up in opposition to will sit in judgement on a method of birth control which *feminists* introduced as an *alternative* to mainline medical choices.

The head of the National Institute of Child Health and Human Development, which will sponsor a three-year government (Food and Drug Administration)-approved study, responded to the anger of feminist health activists at the restrictions on the cap: 'The people who are complaining are the same ones who yelled at the FDA for not requiring more studies on tampons. Either they want the FDA to protect them or they don't.' It's exactly this sterile notion of 'either/or' which reveals the limitations of the FDA position. Yes, feminists are saying that tampons came under scrutiny only after serious health problems arose. The difference is that it's huge multinational companies who produce and market tampons, and make immense fortunes out of menstruation. They had, and have, no intrinsic motive to monitor or investigate their own produce unless they're forced to.

On the other hand, women's health clinics tend to have no profit motivation in fitting cervical caps; they're motivated by feminist politics and perspectives. If problems with the cap became apparent why would they want to cover them up? It's not feminist health workers who've been shoving pills down women's throats over the past twenty years, or injecting women with Depo-Provera.

Here in Britain we welcome any studies which throw more light on the effectiveness or possible health risks of the cervical cap, but we also want to take into account the known benefits *for* a heterosexual woman of using a device which pumps *no* extra hormones into her body, which can be left in place for a longer period of time than a diaphragm and therefore can possibly be more conducive to a pleasurable sexual life, and which, in common with the diaphragm, may offer protection from infections brought to the cervix by other sources – primarily the penis.

A feminist approach to birth control would have to take into account the present range of options women have, the context in which those choices are made and what possible future developments we want to see. How do we most effectively present counter-information? How do we assess information from different sources? How can we make informed decisions and measure effectively the relative risks of various forms of birth control?

One thing for certain is that we must counter arguments based on 'either/or' thinking. We may want the cap to be available without claiming that it is perfect. The politics of demanding the right to try a cervical cap from Family Planning Association Clinics involves challenging the medical profession's preference for pushing the easiest and fastest-taught method, and its keenness for drugs and technology. After all, we must insist that birth control, like other health care, exists for us, not we for it.

Thanks to Diane St Clair and Marianne Godfrey for helping me to get this article together.

PMT

– FROM *SPARE RIB* 116, MARCH 1982

The recent flurry of media interest in premenstrual tension (PMT), after it was successfully used in court to explain and excuse serious crimes, has died out as fast as it originally appeared. It might be argued that any public discussion of the menstrual cycle was a good thing, given the shame, secrecy and ignorance which still surround the subject. Certainly women who suffer badly from PMT will welcome, on some levels, a validation of their condition – too often seen simply as a psychological problem or just as women's lot … 'grin and bear it, dear'.

Unfortunately, but not surprisingly, the court findings, and the research and arguments they were based on are too easily used against women even as they were used for women to get them off criminal charges. What will linger much more as 'general knowledge' are half-truths about the menstrual cycle which will maintain and fuel biologically determined views of women's instability and inability to act responsibly in the world – views which blame PMT for women's uncharacteristic' behaviour in the family at 'certain times' of the month. 'In the pre-menstrual phase women may be irritable, angry and emotionally labile. During the postmenstrual phase, however, they float through life, wafted along on a tide of hormones, euphoric, placid and tolerant, womanly in every way and easy to live with.'[1]

Katharina Dalton's (whose findings and views on PMT were used in the court cases) husband put it 'nicely' in the foreword to her book *The Menstrual Cycle*. 'These findings [show] the extent to which the cyclical changes in the levels of a woman's hormones are responsible for her unpredictable changes of personality.' And further, 'Every woman is at the mercy of the constantly recurring ebb and flow of her hormones.'

Dr Dalton is now the popularly accepted 'expert' on PMT. Her views are reproduced as gospel in women's magazines, newspapers, and increasingly in the literature of organizations such as the Royal Society for the Prevention of Accidents, whose latest leaflets on the dangers of PMT all feature a fractured women's symbol. They are reflected in the material of the medically- and establishment-oriented Women's Health Concern (a charity among whose supporters are drug companies) which describes itself as being known as 'the national sorting house for women's health problems'.

Dalton locates the primary cause of PMT in hormonal imbalance and recommends treatment with progesterone. But there are questions and criticisms about Dalton's research and her treatment. As feminists we have to come to grips with a contradictory situation: Dalton, a woman doctor, pays attention to women's menstrual cycles. She says it is a 'real' condition – not a neurotic one. She has set up a clinic to help women suffering from PMT. It's obviously her life's work *but* … her most widely adopted point about PMT is that during their premenstrual period women commit irrational, nasty, evil, criminal, accidental acts. She uses her statistics to prove that women batter babies, commit suicide and crimes, disrupt their home life, and miss work more during this time.

There are a number of points it's useful to make in any discussion of PMT. One of them is to do with the politics of scientific and statistical evidence. There is nothing neutral about science. Facts depend on the questions asked, how they are posed in relationship to other things, and what the researcher expects to find. All the recent scaremongering about increases in female suicides, accidents, crimes of violence and depression, hardly ever makes the point that men commit suicide more than women, commit more crimes of violence, and are involved in more fatal accidents than women. And some of the media's descriptions of how women behave in the family when suffering from PMT read like cries of anger at impossible relationships with men, children and frustration with the drudgeries of housework, rather than 'irrational' behaviour.

Our premenstrual increase in emotional and behavioural determinants doesn't come anywhere near the violent havoc men cause in the world. The argument that women can't be trusted in positions of power and responsibility becomes ludicrous when one looks at the state of a male-dominated world now. And nowhere do we read that women should not be allowed to partake in the responsible work of having and raising babies and small children because of PMT.

Strangely absent from any arguments about PMT is any recognition that men are subject to cyclical patterns of hormones which affect their emotions and responses and which are apparently less predictable than our patterns. Although this is generally recognized among researchers, it is ignored by men themselves; most would hotly deny that they had cycles.

Dr Anthony Clare, a critic of Katharina Dalton and the school of hormone imbalances, raises doubts about her treatment: 'One of the few double-blind studies of progesterone in premenstrual depression failed to establish its superiority over placebo [dummy], while an American study claimed to show an improvement using doses of progesterone of between 1 to 5 mg, doses so small that they must be considered homeopathic.'[2] And in a letter to *The Times* late last year he said, 'No consistent biochemical or hormonal abnormality has been discovered. There is considerable controversy over the likely cause and most appropriate treatment. Some even doubt the existence of the condition.'

Feminist and other critics state quite frankly (and have done for the last ten years or more) that far too little is known by anyone about the female hormonal system to draw more than hit or miss conclusions about what causes PMT, what PMT causes, or about treatment with hormones. And there are serious questions about the political conclusions which are drawn from Dalton's work and treatment. Conclusions which *fail* to see women as social beings in an exploitative, sexist and male-dominated society, or see women as ultimately determined by their biology ... their 'raging' hormones ... which need to be controlled and stabilized.

All research does indicate that retention of fluid is one of the main problems women have premenstrually. As long ago as the mid-1950s I was told to avoid salty foods and reduce fluid intake before my periods as a way of lessening period pains. Now some people believe this may help PMT too. Other self-help suggestions include taking vitamin B6 (pyridoxine), especially in the week before a period is due; calcium (always in conjunction with magnesium) and Vitamin D. Another possibility is food rich in potassium. Certain herbal teas are considered useful and exercise, particularly yoga, seems to help some women. All this may be difficult for many women to put into practice, but it would be worth attempting – perhaps a little at a time.

Unless we look at the whole of our life – the way in which mind, body and society interact – we can find ourselves lulled into a mainly doctor-orientated, drug-centered view of health. As long ago as 1946, an American researcher into PMT said that the most common causes of its symptoms were nutritional deficiencies or poisoning from toxic substances in work environments. He was against giving hormone treatment, being sure that hormone-like drugs worsened the underlying cause, because they 'actually increase the body's nutritional requirements and strain the organs of the body which filter out poisons'.[3]

We know that PMT is real, that many women are affected in varying degrees, and that whether it is physiological *or* psychological *or* an interaction of both, it exists as a problem and must be taken seriously. The causes of PMT are probably many and varied – it is *not* a disease. But why shouldn't we take the *positive* things about our menstrual cycle seriously as well? What if we were allowed to fully develop the positive aspects of experiencing a flux and flow of ups and downs – to be more in touch with our cycle and the changes it brings? To rid ourselves of shame or disgust about our menstrual blood? An American feminist book on menstruation says, 'To reject and eliminate the body processes, to let our moods be dampened through progesterone or estrogen or testosterone, is in part to agree with those who hold that womanhood is an inferior state of being.'[4]

Notes

1 *Pulse*, 29 November 1980.
2 *Modern Medicine*, January 1979.
3 Morton Biskind, quoted in *How to Stay Out of the Gynecologists Office*, Federation of Feminist Women's Health Centers, 1981.
4 *The Curse – A Cultural History of Menstruation*, Janice Delany, Mary Jane Lupton and Emily Toth, Mentor Books, 1974.

How Cuba Doesn't Cope with Sexuality

– FROM *SPARE RIB* 125, DECEMBER 1982

As feminists, we believe that sexuality, the possibility and struggle for choice around sexual preference *and* questions about sexual practice, are completely relevant to any questions of revolution. We know that they are central to women's liberation. In Britain there are fewer and fewer groupings of feminists who would deny the crucial importance of class, race, imperialism, age, disability, and on and on, to any understanding and commitment to women's liberation. But this growing awareness of the complexity of women's different situations worldwide should not negate long-term feminist concerns with those areas of oppression which are specific to women and which were only recognized through the emergence of autonomous women's movements during the last fifteen years. Women had to say for themselves, initially from their own experience, that the family, childbirth, childcare, housework, abortion, violence against women in the 'home' and on the streets, and sexuality were all valid political areas for women's struggles. They were, in fact, key to women's liberation.

The way in which heterosexuality is understood and practised in male-dominated society cannot be neatly separated from male dominance. If we accept that little girls learn, among other things, how to be submissive women (or to rebel against submission), then it is not too difficult to see that we also learn to 'choose' heterosexuality (or to unlearn that 'choice' and rebel against it). Far from being 'free', the choice is largely determined for us from the day we're born. The notion of free choice implies celibacy or lesbianism are offered equally, on neutral territory, and also falsely implies that women simply and rationally decide about their sexuality.

Not surprisingly, unresolved contradictions about sexuality exist in Cuba. British feminists' questions about heterosexuality and lesbianism in Cuba are not necessarily being imposed crudely from outside. These are concerns for women everywhere. Heterosexuality is uncritically accepted as natural in Cuba and homosexuality – already a reality in Cuba – is obsessively feared and loathed by the majority as unnatural. While not believing for a moment that in Cuba the power of men over women has been left unscathed by the revolution, unfortunately it does not automatically follow that all inequality quickly or slowly falls away after a revolution. Socialism must go way beyond the 'liberal' tolerance of a so-called 'deviating' minority, and analyse critically the framework which makes male dominated heterosexuality *part* of what maintains male domination.

Cuban Attitudes to Family Violence
In Cuba, the heterosexual family is considered the basic unit of society. Cuba's socialism makes its ideal family *and* the way in which people actually live, very different from what we know in Britain. The Cuban family tends to be much more connected to the collective life of the community, less isolated. The country's commitment to the working class means that health care, housing, education and work affect family relations differently than in Britain. Cuba is still an economically poor nation and this also has its effects on domestic life. Housing is often old and cramped, consumer goods are sometimes scarce.

If asked about male violence, Cuban women are quick to point out that there is virtually no rape in Cuba. However, on the streets, verbal approaches are made all the time – a kind of loud hissing noise is most common. Obviously this is unasked for and assumed by most as a male 'right', *but* there is no fear that it will go any further. Cuban women show *no* hesitation in walking alone, anywhere or at any time. However, to leap from that reality, to assertions that rape is not a problem in Cuba or that violence against women is infrequent and not condoned, brushes aside much of what may go on inside the home. This is publicly ignored and remains 'private' and personal. In Britain, until recently, violence – either rape and/or beating – within the home was viewed by everyone as something quite separate from what happened to women on the streets. Now, though women's refuges and incest survivors' groups, the violence of 'happy families' has been revealed.

Fidel's Statement on Homosexuals
In 1971, at the Congress on Education and Culture, Fidel referred specifically to homosexuals in his speech and this statement was included in the declaration of the Congress. It seems worth quoting it in full:

> The social pathological character of homosexual deviations was recognized. It was resolved that all manifestations of homosexual devi-

ations are to be firmly rejected and prevented from spreading. It was pointed out, however, that a study, investigation, and analysis of this complex problem should always determine the measures to be adopted.

It was decided that homosexuality should not be considered a central problem or a fundamental one in our society, but rather its attention and solution are necessary.

A study was made of the origin and evolution of this phenomenon and of its present-day scope and anti-social character. An in-depth analysis was made of the preventative and educational measures that are to be put into effect against existing focuses, including the control and relocation of isolated cases and degrees of deterioration.

On the basis of these considerations, it was resolved that it would be convenient to adopt the following measures:

a) Extension of the co-educational system: recognition of its importance in the formation of children and the young.

b) Appropriate sexual education for parents, teachers and pupils. This work must not be treated as a special subject but as one falling into the general teaching syllabus, such as biology, physiology, etc.

c) Stimulation of proper approach to sex. A campaign of information should be put into effect among adolescents and young people which would contribute to the acquisition of scientific knowledge of sex and the eradication of prejudices and doubts which in some cases result in the placing of too much importance on sex.

d) Promotion of discussion among the youth in those cases where it becomes necessary to delve into the human aspect of sex relations. It was resolved that for notorious homosexuals to have influence in the formation of our youth is not to be tolerated on the basis of their 'artistic merits'. Consequently, a study is called for to determine how best to tackle the problems of the presence of homosexuals in the various institutions of our cultural sector. It was proposed that a study should be made to find a way of applying measures with a view to transferring to other organizations those who, as homosexuals, should not have any direct influence on our youth through artistic and cultural activities.

It was resolved that those whose morals do not correspond to the prestige of our revolution should be barred from any groups of performers representing our country abroad. Finally, it was agreed to demand that severe penalties be applied to those who corrupt the morals of minors, depraved repeat offenders and irredeemable anti-social elements. Cultural institutions cannot serve as a platform for false intellectuals who try to make snobbery, extravagant conduct, homosexuality and other social aberrations into expressions of revolutionary spirit and art, isolated from the masses and the spirit of the revolution.

Why Lesbians Left Cuba in the '80s Exodus

Nine years later, in the spring of 1980, thousands of homosexuals including lesbians, left Cuba. (Estimates vary between 3,000 to 10,000.) For many, the primary reason for wanting to leave was the impossibility of living openly as homosexuals in Cuba. They were reviled, along with 'criminals', 'scum', 'traitors', and the 'unidentified' who also left, as the remnants of Cuban anti-social elements. An official Cuban pamphlet about the 'exodus', published in 1980 says, 'Even though in our country homosexuals are not persecuted or harassed, there are quite a few of them involved in the Peruvian embassy, aside from all those involved in gambling and drugs, who find it difficult to satisfy their vices here.' (Cuba's Position 1980). The rest of the pamphlet never mentions homosexuals but is imbued with the sentiments expressed here: 'Good riddance to the parasites! Good riddance to the anti-social elements! Good riddance to the lumpen! Good riddance to the criminals! Good riddance to the scum!' Yes, perhaps for all those named elements, 'good riddance!' but what about the homosexuals?

In Cuba the law which is used to harass and imprison homosexuals is called the law of 'dangerousness' or in Spanish, '*peligrosidad*'. This is a vaguely worded statute which can give up to four to six years for various offences to do with drunkenness, prostitution, gambling and so on, but is used also against homosexuals.

Several women I met in Cuba said that 'people' didn't focus much on lesbianism because popular imagination couldn't really 'see' women as sexual partners. However, a lesbian said in a 1981 interview in New York, 'In Cuba, life is hard, but the Revolution brought free medical care, schools. But a dog is worth more than a homosexual in Cuba. If they had let me live my life as a lesbian in peace, I never would have left Cuba, never!'

'Communism in theory is good, but in practice it's bad. Fidel is wonderful for children. For the education of children, building schools. He has done everything for children. Fidel has built hospitals. But then Fidel asked all the anti-social elements to leave Cuba. You get charged with "*peligrosidad*", "dangerousness". I am not against Fidel's principles of the Revolution, I am against being oppressed as a lesbian.' (Hilda Ruiz in *Big Apple Dyke News*, New York, July-Aug 1981).

Another lesbian now in the USA said in an interview, 'Here I have more freedom in regards to being a homosexual. Otherwise, I would prefer to be in Cuba, but I don't want to be in prison.' (*Connexions*, Fall 1981, No.2).

A few Cuban women we met on our trip said they personally had homosexual friends (nearly always professional men) who were accepted in Cuban society as long as they didn't 'flaunt' their homosexuality. There really wasn't a problem! And much has been made out of the fact that an

East German sex education book was published in Cuba a few years ago which suggested toleration towards homosexuals. But against these 'liberal' drops in the bucket, we see that during the 'exodus' an outpouring of extreme anti-homosexual sentiment on posters and in slogans, was allowed to go by without comment. And who could be surprised, if disappointed?

If there was *any* liberalization of official thought on homosexuality in Cuba, then at the time of the 'exodus' it would have been possible to make a progressive intervention. Perhaps an opening up of discussion in the media and through the mass organizations about homosexuality when the fear and loathing was at its most open and vulnerable?

The Revolution Hasn't Transformed Relationships

Although Cuban women are verbally sharp and aggressive in public, and in many ways exude confidence, heterosexuality is not miraculously transformed by Cuban socialism. In those areas defined as 'proper' areas of change, women may be playing a more aggressive, demanding role in relation to men, as 'benefits' their equality in socialism. Women speak out strongly in the work places, in the mass organizations, the neighbour-hoods and on the streets. In school, young women do very well but sexist behaviour still goes on unchallenged as do so many sexual divisions of labour. The fact is that men still hold most of the positions of power at most levels. And just as women have not moved into the real position of power in Cuba neither have Cuban men started doing so-called women's jobs (in the home or out at work) in any great numbers.

Neither the society as a whole nor women specifically have collectively scrutinized those aspects of patriarchy not under socialist challenge. Therefore sexuality and domestic life are relatively unpoliticized. Of course we can be impressed with the achievements of socialism and hate the capitalist exploitation which exists in our own society. However, it is exactly Cuba's socialism which suggests that all oppression and inequality must be questioned.

It's not just a question of weighing up different bits and pieces, or naming the contradictions … the easy physicality, the relative openness of those in authority to young people's sexuality (if heterosexual), the high divorce rate the growing number of women turning up at psychiatrists with what the profession refers to as 'frigidity', (we heard this from the director of a large psychiatric hospital outside Camaguey), the lack of any notion that women might not want or like sex with men unless they are sick and/or 'unnatural'.

The question remains – will any existing socialist revolution, unless forced to, ever tackle head on, and transform patriarchal power, including male-dominated heterosexuality and the framework in which that recreates itself? I've suggested that in Cuba the underbelly of this question is the Cuban national obsession against homosexuality, which stems, in turn, from a particular form of male-dominated heterosexuality.

Will the Cuban Revolution Continue For Women?

I believe that the material basis for struggles around sexuality exist now in Cuba, both in terms of external conditions and of the possibilities for changes in consciousness. Cracks exist – 'problems' present themselves, for instance, in the current Cuban concern about women's frigidity, and in unchallenged hatred of homosexuals. On the other hand, control of reproduction via freely available birth control is a reality – one which is backed up by abortion. Socialist consciousness about sexuality after more than twenty years can't be simply hinged on the hangovers of the past, or of reactionary tradition. Much defensive play is made by Cubans willing to discuss homosexuality, of the fact that male homosexual prostitution in pre-revolutionary Cuba forms the basis for present-day popular revulsion. But female prostitution and vice involving girls in those years didn't lead to a rejection of heterosexuality. It did lead to a recognition of the need to change at least certain aspects of the relationship between men and women.

Any criticism of the Cuban attitude and position on homosexuality should be placed in the context of our own society, where 'tolerance' exists at best as long as homosexuality doesn't challenge any of the repressive exploitative norms of that society.

My view of Cuba is not of an unmoving static entity. The involvement that many Cuban people feel in their country's development is obviously way beyond and of a different order than we experience here. A visitor can't fail to note how many Cubans radiate pride, confidence and commitment to their revolution. And many male homosexuals and lesbians have chosen to stay 'with the revolution' even though their sexuality must remain closeted. I don't believe the Cuban revolution stands or falls on its failure so *far* to grapple with homosexuality and sexual politics. A Mexican statement published in 1980 after the exodus ends by saying, 'We socialist, antisexist lesbians and gay men should not lend ourselves to the anti-social manipulations practised by capitalist imperialism. On the contrary, at the same time that we denounce homophobia and other sexist vestiges of the Cuban government, we firmly defend and support the Cuban people in its revolutionary process.'

References

Cuba, the Second Decade, eds J Griffiths and P Griffiths, Writers and Readers Books.
Gays Under the Cuban Revolution, Allen Young, Grey Fox Press, San Francisco.
Feminist Review 2 and 3.

Aids and Women: Building a Feminist Framework

– WRITTEN WITH SUSAN ARDILL AND PUBLISHED IN *SPARE RIB*,
NO 178, MAY 1987

Testing

Many of the issues in which AIDS raises for us slide into each other. For instance when we begin to think about whether or not to test for the AIDS antibody, it brings up all sorts of uncomfortable thoughts. At present, testing for the antibody to HIV is the only way to be relatively certain someone has been infected with HIV. Very few women and heterosexual men are HIV positive in this country – yet, so don't panic. There are excellent reasons for not having it: antibody positive people have run into discrimination around housing, insurance, social security, dental and medical care, and work place harassment. There are also the psychological repercussions of having to live with the knowledge that you could develop AIDS. However, many women, particularly at this point, may have the urge to get the test in order to prove that they're clear and then stay safe. If you decide on testing, get it done under a false name and ensure you can get counselling before and, in the unlikely event you test HIV positive, after.

The Trouble with Labels

Attempting to balance out realistic and unrealistic responses to the different crises which AIDS engenders in each of us is not easy. As we said last month, we have been presented with the concept of 'at risk' groups in order to evaluate our sexual partners and ourselves. But this is not without its problems. For example, now that the media is slowly turning towards women and AIDS, New York is the centre of attention. In New York City AIDS is now the highest cause of death for women between the ages of 25-29 and it is suggested that by 1988 it will be the leading cause for all women of childbearing age in the city. Black women form a large percentage of these women. Ergo, Black women form an 'at risk' group. Here is a perfect example of a label masking the real conditions of poverty, racism and powerlessness, which create the situations bringing these women into contact with HIV. This label 'at risk', also carries implications that everyone in such a group is dangerous, for instance that every Black woman from New York City is likely to be HIV infectious. With any 'high risk' group, 'high risk' becomes confused with 'infected'. The *conditions* of oppression are equated with the *outcome* of oppression.

Of course we all belong to certain economic, social and cultural groups and have to deal with the consequences of this. The problem is that to be Black, working class, a woman, a homosexual or lesbian within the western societies we are talking about is to be disadvantaged or exploited and oppressed. In the USA 12 per cent of the population is Black and occupies the lowest rungs of the social ladder. The poorest suffer most from disease and chronic illness. Especially in inner cities, the combination of poverty and racism can result in a kind of despair with drugs offering a temporary high. This is a hard material reality. So the fact that 25 per cent of all Americans with AIDS are Black (many heterosexual and infected through IV drug use) clearly illustrates the way a society influences patterns of disease.

For lesbians, who still represent the 'safest' category in relation to their sexual practice, AIDS should not be a major threat. And yet many lesbians are frightened. In discussing this article with friends, we've been surprised at how many women, including lesbians, have at some point fucked with a bisexual or gay men; how many have slept with someone involved in IV drug use. Also it appears possible, if not probable, that women can pass it on to other women. In a letter to an American medical journal in December 1986, seven doctors described a case of woman-to-woman sexual transmission of HIV. One woman was an IV drug user and unknowingly HIV positive. She and her lover engaged in vaginal, anal and oral sex while the HIV-positive woman had her period. Both women had vaginal bleeding as a result of what the doctors called 'traumatic sexual activity'. The second women's other 'at risk' factors were negligible and she went on to acquire HIV.

Blaming Africa for AIDS

Different questions and priorities face people in many other countries, particularly in Central Africa where HIV primarily affects heterosexuals and the number of men, women, and children who are HIV-positive is high. We need information, coming from Africans themselves, not from western observers, which weighs up and analyses all the specific conditions in which HIV is found in those countries – does the ELISA test discriminate accurately between HIV antibodies and those developing from one or more of the viral diseases prevalent in Central Africa? Are there accurate comparisons of numbers of people who are HIV positive through the multiple use of needles and the use of unscreened blood in clinical and hospital settings, with numbers infected through heterosexual sex? No one knows the history of HIV. Blaming Africans for starting AIDS, or anyone else because of their geography, race, or sexuality, is ridiculous.

The classic desire to blame a disease on someone else comes into play here. Because AIDS is so often cast as a moral affliction, blaming it on gays and Africans is particularly appealing to a racist, homophobic country. This is particularly clear in the advice to British citizens not to sleep with Africans coming from countries with a high incidence of AIDS. So far we haven't seen written advice about avoiding people from Edinburgh or Los Angeles. The collapsing mechanism at play again – if you are African, you are at risk.

Ironically, Africa is used as an example of what the future could be for 'us', as well. There it gets heterosexuals! Watch your ways! At best this is couched in terms of compassion and concern, but too often it comes over in a patronizing and Eurocentric manner, as in the appalling series on AIDS and Africa which the *Guardian* carried earlier this year. Here and in most other coverage of Africa, prostitutes are blamed almost wholesale for the spread of AIDS. If prostitutes are not named directly, the implication is that large numbers of African women behave as if they were prostitutes!

Looking at Prostitution

This blaming of prostitutes fits in with a similar labelling in this country. We need to explore this area briefly because it is complicated and contradictory. Prostitutes here are not an 'at risk' group. Contrary to popular opinion and advice, prostitutes in general know better than non-prostitutes how to protect themselves from sexually transmitted diseases. It's good business and health sense. Yet women who turn to prostitution in total desperation, out of a need to finance, let's say drug addiction, may approach the job in a very different way and may do risky things or already be infected through their involvement in IV drug use.

As feminists, we want to explode the myth of the infectious prostitute. The women's movement needs to be ready to act in their defence if they are scapegoated in the future. But we also think it's important to point out that it isn't necessarily a 'them' and 'us' situation. There are probably women reading this article who have at some time in their life moved in and out of, at least, the edges of prostitution, but who may not define themselves as prostitutes. The issue is women's control over their sexuality and recognizing that the conditions in which many women live mean that prostitution is either a realistic work choice, or a necessity.

Who Needs to Change?

For heterosexual women and bisexual women, changing the way in which they relate to men and attempting to change the men they relate to raises possibilities and problems. The government's 'preventive' AIDS message is CONDOMS for 'everyone'. (The wholesale absence of lesbianism as a sexual practice in any AIDS material is most obvious in the government's obsession with the poor penis.) Yet many, particularly young men, are still blanking out when it comes to their own cum coming in a condom. Is this because they simply don't believe they're risky sexual partners, or because they don't want to cut down their sexual pleasure? Men have been selfish about sex for so long that some are still bound to resist their pleasure being curtailed in any way. The popular media is urging women to carry condoms; women are faced with taking responsibility yet again. This may be realistic but it shouldn't let men off the hook. Right now many heterosexuals may not be 'at risk' from AIDS but many heterosexual women *are* 'at risk' from unwanted pregnancies, cervical cancer and STDs through unprotected fucking. In relation to women's health generally then, a well-dressed penis wears rubber. The question remains about how confident and able women are to insist on male use of condoms.

Turning the Clock Back

AIDS touches off deeply buried fears or ignorance of sex. The negative aspect of the AIDS crisis – don't do this, avoid that, change or you may die – strikes at the heart of sexual acceptance and celebration. For women the acceptance of the body – for oneself, of the other – is such a breakthrough. Separating out sexual pleasure, procreation, and marriage was a huge step towards women seizing control of their lives.

This is what makes our fear now so heart-rending and what we, as feminists, must seize hold of and attempt to turn around. The physical aspect of women's sexuality is all about body fluids and blood. It's a diffusion of wetness, not at all the same as male ejaculation. Struggling to find our own bodies, our own secretions not only acceptable, but sources of pleasure has been one of feminism's general aims, and any success is delicately balanced. We still live in a culture which defines women's bodies as unclean and disgusting.

We must use our feminism to understand the 'meanings' of AIDS. Finally the government has been forced to break its own code of silence and denial about sexual diversity. Heterosexual fucking is being discussed in a way which by its very nature makes it 'a problem'. In a sense we are all being urged to be 'unnatural'. This government has put its own sexual ideological agenda 'at risk' in the AIDS campaign, gambling that ultimately it will establish its control over a lot more than AIDS. Will we let it win?

Sexually active heterosexuals should take seriously the possibility of coming into contact with HIV, and yet it seems to us that the notion of a whole nation practising 'safe sex', even if the overall risk is minimal, has to be questioned. The underbelly of the dominant 'safe sex' message is that the ideal Tory family (preferably white and middle class) is not only a moral good, it's the *only* place that individuals can experience unrestricted sexual passion. Promiscuity is equated with infection, monogamy with safety, when in fact 'promiscuous' sex can be safe, and monogamous relationships, if one partner happens to be HIV positive, could be dangerous.

Talking Sex and Sexuality

AIDS has opened up space and legitimized a feminist discussion on sexuality. AIDS gives us all permission, to talk sex, talk desire, talk 'dirty', talk fear, talk confusion, talk fantasy. It gives us the chance to talk about how we feel about men, how we feel about feelings, pressures to be sexual, pressures not to be sexual. It gives us a chance to talk about lesbianism, heterosexuality, bisexuality; about the links between sex and sexuality, class, gender, race, age and what is really 'normal' or 'natural' about any of it.

Part of OUR discussion on sex and sexuality should focus on what we see and experience as erotic. Dominant AIDS ideology calls for new forms of sexual practice, most often in the guise of 'safe sex'. We do accept that the possibility of coming in contact with HIV, no matter how tiny, must inform what we do and how we do it. Will this necessarily create the conditions for new erotic desires, sexualized parts of the body, and shifts in how we 'get off'? Can old sexual fantasies complement new sexual practices? We should give a specific example. If vaginal or anal fucking is dangerous when done with a penis in certain circumstances but penetration is still desired, does penetration by other means, such as dildos, take on a different meaning? Then the desire to be fucked is the primary desire, and the penis' pleasure must be satisfied during or after by means other than penetration.

We would like to caution ourselves here. In some discussions around AIDS and sexuality we see a tendency to reduce change to each individual's will power. AIDS within this moralistic framework, could be seen as ultimately a social and psychic good because people will be forced to change 'illness making' behaviour and thoughts into 'health making' ones. However, in our view, certain sexual acts, done in certain ways, are not in themselves 'bad'; they are simply and unfortunately ways in which a particular virus can be transmitted.

We would also maintain that desire has as much to do with unconscious processes which do not respond in any straightforward way to a purely 'rational' approach and that putting the onus to change on individuals is tantamount to blaming individuals for getting it in the first place. This individualizing defuses the possibilities of a political/collective response to AIDS.

Finding Answers through Feminism

Now when mainstream experts and the media go on non-stop about the death of the sexual revolution and the return of romance, it is time to reaffirm feminism's older concerns with redefining patriarchal ideas about sexuality and sexual practice. In this feminists are ideally situated; we have an analysis of gender, sex and sexual identity which already gives us a foothold in the struggle.

We can envisage a 'grass roots' revival of feminist organizing around AIDS in which groups of women get together in women's centres, in public meetings, wherever, to talk about AIDS, find out 'facts', and talk about sex. Specific groups of women might choose to meet and discuss the particular ways in which AIDS does and doesn't affect them.

The white domination of most AIDS organizing and the racism Black people may meet from those groups pose barriers to approaching or feeling at ease in them. Obviously there is more than one level to the discussion which Black women might want to have about AIDS and sexuality, and while racism must always be the concern of all feminists, that doesn't preclude the necessity and desirability of particular groups of women defining together their AIDS agenda.

We must demand that more emphasis be placed in research on the ways the AIDS virus is transmitted to women and from women, heterosexually, bisexually and in lesbian sex. However this is only a partial answer and should be viewed cautiously. Waiting for, or even demanding, answers from either official health education sources or the medical profession could trap us within their concepts of 'good', 'bad', 'normal', or abnormal. Long-established feminist critiques of the so-called neutrality of science and technology should not be ditched in the discussion of AIDS simply because we're desperate for information.

Developing a feminist framework in which to situate AIDS necessitates talking about a lot more than AIDS. As feminists we are uniquely prepared to intervene in our own and other people's panic and confusion. At the same time, holding on to and developing our pleasure and power as *women* reaffirms our visions of the future.

Butch/Femme Obsessions

– WRITTEN WITH SUSAN ARDILL AND PUBLISHED IN
FEMINIST REVIEW 34, SPRING 1990

Now that butch/femme has finally achieved respectability and is sweeping sections of the visible British urban lesbian cultures, we find ourselves reacting against it. These days it all seems like hot air and style. Last gasp of the 1980s or new wave for the nineties, it hardly seems to matter – there's something shallow going on.

What appears to be happening is a definition of who's butch and who's femme through trial by clothing, or haircuts, or make-up. All us tarted up femmes running around in cocktail dresses, and all them butches dressed *à la* Radclyffe Hall. Or black leather or whatever. A great big mess of dress style, top-bottom terminology – and what else?

Butch/femme now runs the risk of becoming as *de rigeur* for parts of the lesbian subculture as androgyny, short hair for all, and a clean scrubbed face was a decade ago. Also holding sway at the moment is a theoretical strand which emphasizes the fluidity of sexual identity, the impossibility of pinning it down. When it comes to the resurgence of butch/femme (or, perhaps more properly, the resurgence of femme) the 'fluidity' school seems to champion a celebratory approach, a refusal to consider any deeper, or problematic, elements. 'Gender play' is all the rage, but, in all this, where is a feminist consciousness and challenge to gender divisions and inequalities? We don't want to dichotomize the two, or suggest that one precludes the other. We just wonder how all this playing with appearances – in clothes *and* behaviour – impinges on our relationships and sense of our lesbian selves in the world.

While we don't believe for a moment that we're literally born butch or femme, we do think that what happens to us as babies, as little girls, can give us a lot to think about in relation to our later lives as lesbians, butch, femme or whatever. We suspect that butch/femme is a lot more than style or 'roles', which are what the current vogue seems to emphasize. Considering it all just a matter of choice, fun and flair might go some way however towards enabling lesbian desires to be brought into the open. At the same time, there now seems to be a consensus of avoidance around some of the serious issues involved.

We'd like to see a discussion begin which would consider the meanings of butch/femme in the context of the social and psychic construction of lesbianism, its relationship to masculinity and femininity. A massive project, of course – the whole subject is very tangled and confusing. In this article we can only ask some pointed questions and suggest other paths we would like to go down in the future.

We do think butch and femme exist in some form as a set of social behaviours, meanings and codes within many modern lesbian cultures, although these are not static across race, class and national boundaries. Underpinning this, for some lesbians, we think there may also exist some internal psychic structure, a way of organizing sexual desire, which maybe we can also describe as butch/femme (or perhaps we should be calling it something else?). But there is no necessarily simple or obvious link between these two spheres – internal and external. We don't think that every lesbian who is either butch or femme either acknowledges this or wants to be identified as such. We think that some lesbians around who call themselves butch or femme are the opposite of what they claim. We know that some lesbians believe they are neither butch nor femme and don't need those categories on any level. And it seems that there are butches in successful relationships with other butches and femmes with femmes. One of us thinks that at this point in the historical development of a lesbian identity/psyche, butch/femme may be part of the very infrastructure of lesbian desire. The other one thinks that it's all more tenuous, changing and slippery than that, and believes that other forces may be as powerful in defining lesbian desire.

A central question has to be whether butch/femme is liberating or constricting for lesbians. Are some elements of it inevitable in relationships between women? Is the new embrace of 'femmeness' subversive in the same way the clone look was for gay men a decade ago – so that femininity is no longer essentially a position in relation to men: you can be a lesbian *and* a 'real' woman.

The absence of any precise or agreed definition about what butch and femme are produces endless heated arguments among lesbians. One straightforward and fairly widespread view is that they are merely methods of dress and behaviour – roles, in other words. Another view is that butch/femme are metaphors for subject/object in lesbian relationships: that talking about ourselves or others as butch/femme essentially describes how we negotiate desire. Because lesbian experience is so untheorized and unsupported, even within radical or alternative cultures, any lesbian language of self-description and self-analysis has tended to remain underdeveloped. So these two words (and their equivalents in other cultures and contexts) have become dreadfully overburdened. They have to be infinitely elastic terms – living slang, taking on endless nuances of meaning.

What interests us – we use the words in both the senses above, and many more – is the relationship *between* the different meanings. If we describe someone as 'femming it up' (the way they dress) are we also assuming, implying or guessing that she takes certain emotional positions in her relationship or that she will behave in a particular way in bed? Does everything proceed along simple, predictable lines, even in disguised forms? Or is it all more contradictory, fluid?

Psychic Mysteries

We wonder what psychoanalysis has to offer us on these questions. Very little psychoanalytic theory has been produced which looks at *lesbianism* from a non-pathologizing viewpoint, let alone at butch and femme. Can we extrapolate from recent feminist analytic work on femininity? Or are heterosexual feminist theoreticians missing a very important boat by largely leaving lesbians out of their calculations? We're not on very sure ground when we discuss psychoanalysis, but there are some areas we'd love to see developed.

If difference is necessary for desire to exist, *what* difference? Are butch and femme ways of organizing certain differences between women and then eroticizing them? Is butch/femme a simple matter of masculine and feminine identifications? In a psychoanalytic account of the girl's 'achievement' of her proper feminine position, this attainment seems to go hand in hand with the establishment of the psychic conditions necessary for later female heterosexuality – so, how can psychoanalysis account for femme lesbians? Does an unconscious refusal to recognize their status as 'castrated' girls underly the butchness of some women? Are butches driven by the necessity to maintain that fantasy to themselves and others? Can femmes have the same fantasy, with a different outcome? Do butch lesbians hate women? What is a femme's relationship to a butch's masculine identification? What distinguishes a femme from a heterosexual woman – why does she desire a woman? (Or does she want to be *desired by* a woman?) Are there more femmes than butches in modern western societies and if so why? Are there (as we guess) butch heterosexual women, and what does that say about heterosexual relationships? Inevitably, where does bisexuality fit into it all? What impact does current feminism have on butch and femme psychic identities of today, if any?

All we can do here is ask these questions – we're nowhere near being able to provide comprehensive answers.

Social Meanings

At this point we return to considering lesbianism as a social identity, as socially constructed, and butch/femme in that light as well. In so doing we could approach it from many angles, but here we are content to throw in bits and pieces from different directions. Some of the questions echo ones we tried to articulate above, in thinking about the psychic sphere. The answers we could come up with have different resonances and meanings when the questions are asked in a social context.

We look at ourselves, and the lesbians we know, or observe, or are told about, many of whom we think of as butch or femme. This is what we wonder:

• Who wanted to be a boy? Who was a tomboy? Looking at stories of lesbian lives, there seems to be no correlation between having been a tomboy and whether or not a lesbian is butch or femme. Wanting to *be* a boy is a different kettle of fish.

• Does being a woman cause psychic distress to some women?
What are the different meanings of femme, femininity and being a

woman and how are their meanings culturally and historically specific?

• When it comes to sex, do butch and femme have something to do with who is the object for the other and who looks at who? If butches are often caught in the Catch 22 of wanting a femme as the object of their desire at the same time that they are compelled to merge with that object, to domesticate the situation, what does that signify? Does the butch in the woman want the objectification of the feminine in her lover, the woman in the butch the domestication of her relationship? (And the lesbian loses it all in the end because the two are mutually exclusive?)

• And what about the femme? Does she want to be the object of desire? Does she desire the butch only as her objectifier? Is she better placed to resist the merging? Is it the femme who can keep the butch at arm's length and prolong desire?

• Who pursues who?
Who fucks who? What with?
Here are some stabs in the dark: do butches tend to particularly like and initiate tribadism? Do butches want to penetrate? Are femmes more attached to penetration?
We know that some butches don't like to be penetrated at all, or even to have their genitals touched – why is this? (On the other hand, what about the famous butches 'on the streets', who are infamously femme 'between the sheets'?) Don't misunderstand: we are not suggesting that a 'real' femme never really is wet to fuck her lover, and we know that many butches live in hope that their femme lover will want to fuck them too.

• Is it possible that butches and femmes experience penetration and orgasm in different ways?
If femmes find the womanly *masculinity* or androgyny of the butch attractive, where then is the *exact* location of the femme's sexual desire for the butch? In other words, how does a femme actually desire the butch's breasts, her cunt, her womanness? Is the contradiction between butchness and femaleness the exciting ingredient for the femme?

• Some lesbians who take on aspects of a butch identity may do so to hold at bay a desire to be passive, submissive, to give up control. They may be frightened of these things. But these 'butches' may be scared by the overt nature of butch/femme too. Is lack of self-awareness integral to the butch persona? Conversely, are we implying that femmes are more self-aware? What are femmes frightened of?

• If it's all about looks, the look, the gaze, then what is it that we enjoy about looking like lesbians or having lovers who look lesbian and/or butch? (Has butch, up until recently, equalled lesbian?) Is it necessarily part of butch/femme that the femme *look* feminine and the butch masculine? What about those classically narcissistic lesbian couples who look like each other, dress like each other? Is the butch/femme component of their relationship played out in private?

- Who is emotionally fluid?

Who is strong and protective?

Who takes care of who? We know femmes who complain (or not) of being the ones who take responsibility for the emotional well-being of the relationship. Sometimes this seems to be mixed up with aspects of a parent/child dynamic, but at others, it seems more about self-consciousness and the classic 'femininity' of the femme. However, there are the persuasive voices of butches who maintain that they enable the femme to feel safe and to be the baby.

- We wonder what sort of parent/child, mother/daughter, father/daughter narratives butch/femme is giving voice to. One of us thinks that in these scenarios, femme definitely seems to occupy the infantilized position. Maybe this reveals both its charm and its potentially self-destructive nature. The other emphatically thinks it's often butches who are the babies.

Freeing or Freezing?

When lesbians used to talk about their own experiences of butch/femme, it was set in the past, about specific times in their histories, about having to take on certain social roles in order to make it. These days talk is about the here and now, and among many lesbians we know, chiefly about the pleasure and powerfulness of being femme – of being free to be seductive, looked after, adored, as well as adoring. The flip side of that of course is the cost in terms of real social power – in a relationship and in the wider world – if you are restricted to, or your emotional happiness depends upon, that way of being. Maybe femmes are in the ascendant now – but are we going to see a lot of sapped, insecure and above all resentful women around in ten years' time? Maybe sooner – we've recently heard anecdotes about women (young, feminist) being told to more or less stay in line in a relationship in the name of butch/femme positions.

Where do we end up? Over the last decade we've both embraced butch/ femme, sometimes overtly, sometimes secretly, found it made sense of strong drives, was fun, enhanced the excitement, was a useful tool for analysing what went on. It can also be a trap, a drain, a smokescreen, too rigid for what's really felt and experienced in our relationships. The opening out of the complexities of our sexual, social and psychic lives as lesbians should lead to opportunities for deeper understanding, not new confining orthodoxies. So we end up ambivalent as usual, and leave it at that. For now.

Note

We would like to thank Diane Hamer and Clara Connolly and the FR lesbian issue group for detailed comments and advice. Thanks from Susan to Alison and Wendy for arguing it out, and from Sue to Mitch.

Mapping: Lesbians, AIDS and Sexuality

– AN INTERVIEW WITH CINDY PATTON FROM *FEMINIST REVIEW* 34, SPRING 1990 'SPECIAL ISSUE – PERVERSE POLITICS: LESBIAN ISSUES'

In this wide-ranging interview, Cindy Patton explores some of the cultural determinants of lesbian sexuality which affect discussions about the meaning of AIDS to lesbians.

Cindy: I'd like to talk first about the history of safe sex – in particular about the lesbian safe sex discussion, and how it's developed. It was in San Francisco, in late 1985 or early 1986, that the SF AIDS Foundation decided to do what became the first brochure on safe sex for lesbians. When you read the brochure now it feels like a gay male brochure changed to fit the technicalities needed to correspond to lesbians, rather than written from the subject position of women. It caused quite a furore at the time.

In Boston, *Gay Community News* quickly ran a lesbians and AIDS article, and other periodicals carried their own pieces. It really was as if lesbians had suddenly been brought into a debate about safe sex which had evolved from gay male sensibilities. Gay men had had to go through a whole process of thinking, 'My community is changing, I'm going to have to make some changes'. That entire preliminary phase did not happen in the lesbian community – if you can use that phrase – a brochure just appeared. I think that was one of the reasons why it was so divisive at the time. It almost seems as if gay men as a community had an opportunity to process developments around AIDS and then suddenly AIDS workers thought, 'We should do something about the lesbians'.

There were two accusations immediately levelled. One was that men were making lesbians do something they really didn't need to do. The second was that lesbians who believed in safe sex were being hysterical.

Sue: Yes, there were articles in lesbian publications in this country questioning the relevance, or the political desirability for lesbians to take on AIDS in any way.

Cindy: I think how the discussion of AIDS is played out in various lesbian communities depends on how those communities have dealt with sexuality in the first place. In communities where race and class divisions are primary, safe sex issues tend to intensify racism and classism. In communities where divisions are around pornography, the debate on safer sex circulates around its status as 'pornographic'. It's as if a little sex-bomb gets dropped and its explosion throws up and makes visible existing divisions about sexuality, which are then available for – often angry – debate.

I didn't realize the depth and the dynamics of some of that to begin with. But what I did notice was that the first lesbian debates on AIDS often circulated around strangely esoteric questions about scientific data. Women would ask stranger things than I'd ever heard from a gay man, like, 'Has there ever been a study on having warts on your hand and what happens then if you stick your fingers in your lover's cunt?' There were certainly things to be said about lesbians and STDs (sexually transmitted diseases), but the emotions behind the questions and the extreme reactions they evoked had to do with issues which had not been resolved in the lesbian community. There are, for example, some real differences in how the gay male community has been able to progress and construct itself and its sexuality, as compared with lesbians, who remain comparatively invisible. This complicated the whole issue of lesbian safe sex.

Sue: Don't you think as well though, that women have, and have had in different cultural and historical moments, health conversations which are a lot more detailed than the ones men usually have? The discourse around health, in women's magazines, in feminist magazines, in books like *Our Bodies Ourselves*, may well mean that women are more likely to ask the sort of question which you found bizarre or extreme. I agree that the tendency to question the relevance of safe sex for lesbians, which I've expressed myself, as well as heard expressed by other lesbians, can mask a much deeper sense of fear, antagonism and confusion, but I also think women are differently placed in relation to questions around health and are much more likely to become riveted by details of the body and the transmission of infection.

Cindy: That's possible, but it didn't feel like that. What it really felt like was that even lesbians didn't know what it was that lesbians did in sex, so there was no way that we could come up with a formula for figuring out what lesbian safe sex was. In groups of gay men there was a more generally accepted idea of what the range of sexual practice might be; there seemed to be a kind of menu of gay male sex acts, and you could go through the menu and figure out what needed to get changed. With lesbians there never seemed to be a perceived baseline of what lesbian sexuality was. I felt completely at sea compared with the work I had done with gay men. Women were either fearful of saying anything – 'What if everyone thinks it's weird'? – or so convinced that whatever they did was normal that they would just pop out with bizarre questions.

I think that it does get down to the fact that lesbian sexuality exists in a kind of void. We haven't had the opportunity to talk about sexuality in groups and to articulate it as a collective within which different modalities are given time to emerge. It's only recently that we've talked, for example, about butch/femme or SM (sado-masochism) or other labelled activities, and even in those debates it's never quite clear what women are really doing. I think the prior question is, do lesbians really want to talk? As a community, do we want to have the kind of discussions or cultural space and activities which produce different shades of sexuality? In early American lesbian-feminist culture, lesbian sex was thought of as having the possibility of being completely egalitarian; it would be undifferentiated and oceanic. On one level it's tempting to say we just haven't had time to get our act together and develop more differentiated categories of lesbian sexuality, but in fact many lesbians of that particular theoretical persuasion would in any case be opposed to having discussions that would lead to the differentiation of lesbian sexuality. On another level – and this is a historical development – AIDS has in some ways deflected attention from debates about sexuality. Instead of pursuing discussions of lesbian sexuality, the lesbian community has tended to subsume those discussions under the heading of safe sex.

There are also some aspects of lesbian sexual practice which help to exclude the larger questions of lesbian sexuality from discussions of safe sex – things like lower partner turnover and engaging in activities which in general are less likely to transmit a whole range of pathogens. Very few lesbians know another lesbian who is HIV positive and even fewer have the experience of knowing someone who had contracted HIV from their female lover. So the debates feel theoretical, unlike the debates around gay men's sex issues.

I think once you realize there is a woman in the community who has contracted HIV from a partner it changes the whole debate. A really interesting example of this came from a physician friend of mine who had been pretty much of the 'This is going to freak lesbians out, we shouldn't get too het up about this, we were just getting to express ourselves and if we talk about safe sex it really makes women shut down' school of thought. Eventually she had a lesbian client who said, 'I have

HIV and I want to know what I have to do', and she started to lay out her whole theoretical argument and the woman said, 'Fine, but I have to go home to my lover tonight and I want to know what's safe and not safe.' My friend was put on the spot.

I think as lesbians emerge who are HIV positive, who feel like they can actually talk about their experience (which very few of those women feel able to do), it is going to become clear that there are still some very practical questions which remain unanswered.

'No Semen in the Anus or Vagina'

Sue: Does that mean that your recent safe sex slogan for everyone, 'No semen in the anus or vagina', still stands? When you come down to the questions a lesbian like that might have, that slogan doesn't give her much to go on.

Cindy: At the time I wrote that, what I was trying to do was break down, or help people break down, the idea that belonging to the category 'lesbian' meant that your sexual practices by definition did not transmit HIV. There is, for example, a relatively new study of heterosexuals which suggest a connection between vaginal fluids, yeast infections and HIV; so medical data does need to be re-examined in the light of alleged oral transmission or manual transmission between heterosexuals and between women. It's certainly true that lesbian sex involves a lower range of risk than any activities which get semen in your anus or vagina, but I still think there are some questions to be asked. For instance, if vaginal fluid is highly infected how much of it gets smeared and where does it go? You can't use the male model of a single 'glob' of semen that moves from point A to point B. That's not how lesbians practice sex; it tends to be a lot wetter and if they're women who get very wet than vaginal fluid tends to get smeared around various places – but this isn't an issue that's been factored into any of the studies. The assumption seems to be, 'What's the concentration in X amount of whatever fluid and how long does it sit in any one place?' In these kinds of calculations, lesbian sexuality simply isn't accounted for – nor, I suspect, is heterosexual oral sex. Studies of transmission are simply based on an intercourse model. In so far as they consider vaginal fluid, what they're interested in is how much of it might have seeped into the penis. They don't look at how much might have got on the hands or the face.

Sue: You've said to me quite emphatically that you tell everyone to practise safe sex. But haven't we just been talking about how difficult it is for lesbians to talk about their sexuality let alone approach lovers with the idea that you negotiate safe sex or even decide if that's necessary?

Cindy: I'm frequently being called in to talk about safe sex, which immediately sets me up into a pedagogic situation – and as an educator, you're often thrown into situations in which people want to be rather passively educated, though you feel fundamentally that for people to become liberated or to address an issue they need to look at it in a different manner. It's much more a matter of getting people to unframe the question they themselves have already framed.

I try hard now not to get sucked into situations where people ask, 'Should we or shouldn't we?' I don't understand what safe sex means to them. I don't understand what's at stake for them. The basic modality in which decisions are made about safe sex seems to involve making a list of certain types of people and asking, 'Am I one of the people it applies to?' So when I go to do an educational intervention, or whatever you want to call it, I try to get people uncentred from that and to understand that as responsible people this is an issue that they are obligated to engage with. They may come to a different set of decisions in the end than I would, but it is not morally correct to say, 'I'm exempt from this'. And this goes for lesbians as much as anyone else. Even though many lesbians will decide in the end that the techniques of safe sex are not something they need or want, there is something very callous about saying, 'I don't need to know about this, it doesn't concern me'. We are in the midst of a huge cultural upheaval around sexuality. At a time when so many people's lives are being ruined by getting AIDS and by the cultural backlash of the epidemic, to refuse to participate in a cultural event which is so politically charged, to decide it doesn't apply to you, is very strange and wrong.

Identities
Sue: What you say about semen and vaginas raises interesting questions about the way lesbian identities might change with shifts in our understanding of sexuality.

Cindy: The reason I came up with that little catch-phrase about not getting semen in vaginas or anuses was because there has been such a proliferation of safe sex guidelines. What I wanted to do was figure out a very simple way to give the one piece of information that had the critical logic and information. Maybe for another year I will use that particular catch-phrase. When people have danced around that one, if things have evolved than I'll try something else.

On the issue of changing understandings of sexuality, many women who came out as lesbians thought we weren't going to have to deal with bad old baggage about heterosexuality that we had never really resolved. For many lesbians, entering the 'Lesbian Nation' meant shedding the detritus from issues like pregnancy, or sexual abuse, or having a hard time dealing with men because they're hard to deal with; they didn't see that those unresolved conflicts would be retained as part of the psyche. The discussion of safe sex has brought them to the fore again. I hear a lot of interesting responses when I suggest to women that they should practise safe sex; you can feel them tracking back to unresolved issues about pregnancy, sexual abuse, menopause, feeling bad about their body in general. All of that then gets hung on to the issue of safe sex.

What is coming out for example in the US lesbian community is the issue of child sexual abuse. The statistics you see of sexual abuse of women and sexual abuse of gay people, about which there have been a number of studies lately, suggest that people in these two categories are particularly likely to have been sexually abused. What's happening with AIDS is that the discussions it gives rise to about safe sex have triggered much more wide-ranging discussion, of which the child sexual abuse debate is one example.

Sue: I think the debate on child sexual abuse has surfaced around different issues in Britain; it's tended to be discussed much more in the context of struggles around SM. What's emphasized in discussions of child sexual abuse is the pain, both psychic and physical, for the survivor. The fact that child sexual abuse is then unproblematically linked to adult SM often makes it impossible for SM even to be discussed, let alone admitted as a category of lesbian sexual desire and practice. There has been no room yet, as far as I am aware, to engage in an open discussion about why you might, as a survivor of child sexual abuse, choose to practise SM in your sexual relationship. The survivor who is into SM is seen as continuing her victimization, or maybe as suffering from the disease of false conscious-ness. Lesbians are seen as deluded if they think they're able to deal with the trauma of abuse within or through SM activity. Child sexual abuse is so fused to SM that they cannot be seen separately. I find this frustrating because I would really like to be able to have a discussion which looked non-judgementally at the emotional and cultural components of lesbian SM and admitted the possibilities that for individual lesbians SM had the potential to be both positive and negative.

Cindy: I think there has been a little more space in the US because the SM battle was waged a bit earlier on, in 1982 or 1981. You have to understand that in the US we love a testimonial format. We're much more involved in grounding our legitimacy in personal experience than British people seem to be. In the US it's much more common for people to say all sorts of personal things publicly, so very quickly a fairly large number of male and female SM practitioners emerged in the mid-eighties who talked about having been sexually abused as children. There has also been an interesting development in politically progressive SM culture more recently, particularly around these new studies which seem to indicate that gay people have been more sexually abused than other people. As a result, there's now a real 'claiming' of childhood sexual abuse by SM practitioners. Some say, 'Well. I work this out through my SM', and some say 'Well, SM and child sexual abuse are simply two distinct features of my life'; either way, there have certainly been attempts to 'reclaim' child sexual abuse.

The Power to Interpret

Sue: But do you find any of this problematic? There's certainly something about the current discussion on child sexual abuse which makes me itchy. I don't want to let abusers off the hook or suggest all over again that children lie, or wipe away the fact that millions of people, mainly girls, have been and continue to be sexually abused, mainly by men. But I do wonder if there hasn't been a strange disowning of the complexity and importance of fantasy; a misunderstanding of how fantasy can work in the construction of present reality and, as importantly, in the reconstruction of the past. It has become a feminist heresy to suggest that there may be an element of fantasy that is being claimed as a physical reality, particularly in recollections of child sexual abuse. The possibility of fantasy muddies the waters, puts men in a marginally less clear position and generally makes things more complicated – but surely ultimately it does no one a service to deny the importance of fantasy?

Cindy: The best way to answer that question is perhaps to talk a little about the psychoanalysis of child sexual abuse – though I certainly can't do a survey of psychoanalysts. The more responsible feminist therapists I know don't try to essentialize the perceptions their clients have – and that contrasts sharply with mainstream psychoanalysis. The US is a very pop psychoanalytic culture; it has had a heavy dose of very bad Freudian psychoanalysis. The dominant model is a mixture of Freudian psycho-analysis and American philosophical pragmatism; so in cases of child sexual abuse, it's simply assumed that the stories the adult tells have to be really true. That denies the child, or the adult recalling the child, the power to interpret – which is ultimately very damaging because in this framework sexual abuse has to be claimed as a real event which was enormously formative. The confusion comes from not distinguishing something which happened in space and time over which we had no control, with the story into which it was written which we do have some control over. So within feminism, for example, there is a tendency to encourage women to claim victimhood – which means that child sexual experiences are rewritten as narratives of victimization.

Sue: That's true; I have several recollections of childhood experiences with my father which could indicate the possibility of sexual abuse. However, I'm confident there was none. In one case I was sitting on my father's lap in a very crowded car when he got an erection. I was horrified and very embarrassed. From everything I know about my father, so was he, but neither of us could say anything. We were both trapped by the situation. Who knows what his unconscious feelings about his young daughter were, but that's not what we're talking about here. I think if I had a different kind of personality and history, that perhaps I could take that relatively harmless memory and a few others as clues that I might have been sexually abused by my father.

Cindy: What more sophisticated psychotherapists and self-narratives do is to look at larger family patterns around the events. Are there systematic events, or are there single events – or events that happen no more than a couple of times – which for the child may have some psychic similarity but aren't part of a larger pattern or process? So to be trapped in the car and have your father get a hard-on is one thing and it might be upsetting, but it doesn't necessarily become psychically structuring unless you're always being trapped by adults in one way or another.

I also think it's a mistake to focus too much on events which become sexualized, rather than looking at discipline and control in general. A child may be subjected to one instance of abuse but may experience twenty-five occasions when she can't have her room as she wants it – and that form of disciplinary control is just as much a part of what forms the child's sexuality as are more obviously 'sexual' events. I think the tendency is to focus too much on sexual abuse as an essential category rather than understanding that, though this is something that has a particular set of resonances in our culture, there may be other forms of abuse that deserve attention. It seems damaging to me to privilege sexual abuse over other sorts of psychic abuse control.

In the past, we had a very deterministic view of sexuality. You yourself talked just now about how it's generally been assumed that if you were sexually abused, that's why you would be into SM, *or*, if you were sexually abused, why you would never be into SM. There was assumed to be a finite set of fixed events in early childhood that determined one's sexuality. I think that there are events that occur throughout one's life that determine or inform sexuality but I think they're much less predictable and less determining. If fact, they're constantly open to reinterpretation. The trick is to have narrative control and poetic licence about your own sexuality. If we stick to a narrative that says, 'there was once heterosexuality, then we invented lesbian liberation and somehow we're always going forward towards a point at which we'll reach a perfect sexuality', then we're mistaken. I think a lot of times what comes next may be regression.

Sexual Mapping

Sue: Can you say some more about the relationships between narrative – the stories we tell about ourselves – and safe sex?

Cindy: A little aphorism I once wrote says, 'Sex actually begins and ends in the grocery store and what we do later with someone else is just a re-enactment of that memory.' Which is a rhetorical thing to say, but I think it's important to maintain. It's unclear to me that having sex with someone is any more than the parallel play of two different people's vastly different memories. Sometimes it is obviously more than that, but the substantive part of the decision-making and cognitive process involved in sex has to do with something else. So the idea that you can rationally discuss safe sex is inconsistent with what most people *are* in relation to their own sexuality. That's why I try to get people to identify for themselves what it is that makes sex hang together for them in the first place. It's only then that they can look at what they have to do to stop themselves getting diseases.

What you always have to be aware of is that safe sex is really different for different people. For example, I've recently discovered an interesting thing about gay men. I've generally worked on the principle that, 'You have to negotiate safe sex and then you do it', and for the vast majority of gay men I know, this is how it works. But I've started hearing stories from men who have been practising safe sex, who tell me about times they'd had sex and suddenly just haven't put the condom on. No decision was made, it wasn't as if one person didn't want to have safe sex; the whole perception was that it would be a safe sex event – but then all of a sudden it became something different.

Clearly there is some narrative structure in those men's lives which demands that unsafe sex be linked to very high levels of anxiety before they reach a point at which, when the condom doesn't go on, they just stop. In order for safe sex to work, phase one seems to be to normalize it so that it's okay to practise safe sex; but then we have to reconstruct anxiety at the threshold of unsafe sex so that people don't accidentally forget the condom just because the framework 'safe sex' feels normal. People say that's horrible, that sexuality should just be 'natural' and fun, but that denies an intrinsic sexual narrativity. Everyone has something that makes them anxious. We need to get the red flags to go up before unsafe sex.

Sue: Unsafe sex for many heterosexual women has always been tre-mendously anxiety-producing in terms of unwanted pregnancy, but it hasn't necessarily stopped them fucking.

Cindy: That's because phase one of normalization never took place, whereas with many gay men safe sex has become the norm.

Sue: How, in the context you've outlined, would lesbians be enabled to negotiate safe sex? We seem to be in such a double-edged situation, where lots of women know the guidelines but hardly anyone has integrated them into their daily lives. In a context where many lesbians haven't even tentatively mapped out collective sexual categories, it seems that what you describe as the normalization process – the opening up of sexual discussion – still has to be the baseline from which we start.

Cindy: I think you're right. Let me give an example of the absence of a mapping of sexual categories; it seems to me that it's rare for lesbians to base their relationship decisions on sexual compatibility. It's just assumed that two women can work it out, and that there is nothing in the sexual narrative of either partner that makes them incompatible.

I think two things are going on here. One is that we don't have a discourse which allows us to say that category X and category Q are going to be hard to match up. But I believe a deeper problem is that we don't take our sexuality seriously enough as a project, in the charming way gay men did in the seventies. We think of that period now as one of crass hedonism; but to take one's sexuality seriously surely *can* be a revolutionary act.

Lesbian feminists like to think we're the ones who put egalitarian sexuality on the map, but really gay men in some very profound ways did it just as much or even more. By the late 1970s or early 1980s, for example, it was very uncool for a man never to get fucked. He might have a preference for fucking, but to refuse to get fucked was to be very uptight and withholding. According to the studies being done now by people like Gayle Rubin in the US, it seems that in Gay Liberation, post-Stonewall days, with the influence of feminism, the progressive left and ideas of free love, there was an increase in ideas of sexual mutuality in the US urban gay cultures. There was an emphasis on 'democratic fucking', with both partners being able to fuck and to be fucked. The result was that younger gay men were socialized into fucking at an earlier point in their sexual development. Younger gay men were coming out into a culture where intercourse was the dominant practice. That's changing now, of course; my sense is that young gay men now inhabit environments where safe sex is the major topic of discussion, and they are being socialized into intercourse a lot later. Intercourse is becoming something you do when you're in a 'real' relationship. What I'm seeing is something like the return of an eighteenth-century romantic sexuality where you do bundling and cuddling and hand jobs – all those quaint pre-Victorian activities. When you decide to have intercourse you actually do it 'properly'. And having intercourse isn't simply the end point of foreplay; it is more like a personal development choice. There are gay men I've worked with in their early twenties who've never had intercourse. They think they'd like to try it out sometime but it neither seems to be a native desire nor an act that they've necessarily eroticized.

Sue: There must be many gay men who are frightened to have intercourse even with a condom. Does that mean that they're looking for other forms of anal penetration, such as using a dildo?

Cindy: Well, curiously no. People tend to essentialize the penis as the implement of penetration; but what I often say jokingly when I'm speaking on safe sex is that it has given many men an excuse not to get fucked. Friends have said to me, 'I never get fucked now with safe sex', and I say, 'Well, you never liked it before anyway.' There is a way in which the safe sex discussion has enabled men who didn't want to have anal sex to avoid it. To put it another way: I think what's happening is a process of de-essentializing anal stimulation as intercourse.

Sue: And yet I think for lesbians the safe sex discussion has the possibility of making desires for anal stimulation more possible to speak about and to do. It's ironic.

Race, Sexuality and AIDS
Sue: Can you say something about how you think about race in relation to the kinds of questions you've been raising about sexuality?

Cindy: In the States we've tended to treat race, gender and sexuality together (sometimes we've treated race and class together, but our class structure is so different that it is difficult to do class analysis in the way that you're able to do in Europe). The similarity between race and sexuality is that they are two cultural notions which seem to be represented in the body, rather than necessarily conceptualized at the level of language. They're also not necessarily structured around binary divisions. There are certainly always two poles – you have black and white, straight and gay – but they're more available to become part of a continuum than gender. Gender is always bipolar; even the problem-atization of gender produced by transsexuals or cross-dressers is so mini-mal that it never really rocks the gender boat. The bipolar categories of sexuality and race are not only more immediately unstable, they're also often merged at the level of metaphor. For example, both bisexuality and interracial sexuality get represented in similar ways as liminal sexualities. I'm doing some work now on the representation of 'miscegenation' in US films, and the person of colour, like the 'true homosexual', gets brutally killed in the end. In AIDS work the cultural anxieties around sexuality and raciality meet again in the liminal space with polarizing effects. To give an example: Black community groups in Boston are finally able to get government funding for AIDS work. Everybody is recognizing that, in the Black community in particular, and the Latino community in different ways, large numbers of men of colour who have AIDS are being identified as bisexual or gay. That's a really stunning and difficult cultural transition for those communities, in the sense that it involves acknowledging the category 'gay'; it means saying, 'We're going to take these members of our community who we've always known about, but whom in the past we've called the hairdresser or the preacher – and we'll call them gay.' Funding is in some sense contingent upon the application of essentially white, western categories of sexuality on to very culturally diverse communities.

Many of the people doing AIDS work in the Black community have traditionally lived between two roles: their leadership position in roles which have been traditional homosexual roles within Black culture; and their roles as Black people in a largely white, gay male community. In addition, the greater power of Black women meant more women in leadership positions, especially in health care, and thus a number of women who have female partners but who are not at all out as lesbians. But it's not as if they're in the closet either. People in the white gay community say, 'Why don't these women come out?', but what they don't understand is that 'gay' is not a stable and meaningful category in the communities of colour.

What's happening slowly is that some of the white educators who are a little more sensitive (and I hope I'm one of them), are no longer saying, 'You better conform to my categories', or 'Our community is not going to work with your community'; we're saying instead, 'What is AIDS doing for our ability to construct categories? What's the effect of the AIDS crisis on our ability to construct our identity?' In some cases, AIDS is creating a whole new domain of categories. There are a number of largely professional Black men's gay groups in Boston, for example, which are going through a very interesting consciousness-raising process in trying to deal with the issue of how to relate to Black men who are not of their socio-economic class, and who also don't necessarily identify as gay. Professional Black gay men have now begun to recognize the need to address the class issues highlighted by sexuality within the Black community. They're saying, 'We call ourselves gay and we're comfortable with that but we're professionals. What about these other Black men; are they, for example, really bisexual? Is their sexuality really about thinking, "I'm a Black man and that means that I can have sex with whoever I want?"'

Will Lesbians Talk?

Sue: I want finally to return to the question of future directions for a discussion of lesbian sexuality. Something you said before the interview started implied that women who were into SM or butch/femme were the ones who had taken on the issue of safe sex; what I'm curious about is whether that is really true and also how much the safe sex discussion for lesbians has been formed through gay erotic symbolism.

Cindy: What I was saying before about SM and butch/femme is that they are the corners of lesbian culture where the boundaries of erotic space and fantasy have been most consciously mapped. I think that SM lesbians picked up on safe sex because they have more interaction with the gay male SM community. That's partly an historical phenomenon having to do with the oppression of SM people. Women who have erotic charges from SM often come out in the context either of gay men's SM culture or at least of contact with gay men generally.

There is actually a fair amount of sociology done on SM as a career in the sense of an entry into a subculture where you're expected to learn rules and norms from someone who has been there longer. You progress through developmental stages in that culture, from being a novice to being someone who can be let loose on their own, to someone who can actually teach others. SM culture tends to be very much oriented around that career process. I think all of that is antithetical to what we know as lesbian sexuality and is much more common in gay men's culture. Joan Nestle has of course written about femmes becoming butches at a certain age, but I think what she's talking about is not so much a career, as the acquisition of a set of competences. It may be that certain sexual practices in our culture require expertise, or knowledge of your own body that takes time, or requires particular social experiences, to master. I don't want to be essentialist and say that this is a biological development, but it may be that there are cultural structures in place that make it easier to navigate sexuality in predetermined ways than to choose a different trajectory. One of the problems is the paucity of sexual imagery for lesbians; the available pervert or queer imagery has been gay male porn. Some lesbian porn made for men does have an edge to it that defies heterosexuality and so appeals to lesbian experience, but I think it's more common for lesbians to enter porn culture through gay male porn. Many of us have the experience or can tell stories about wandering through a *Playboy* which sparked our lesbian imagination, without having led us to become connoisseurs of that particular type of pornography. Looking at gay male porn doesn't have to be the beginning of a particular 'career path'; I think it's possible at this point politically and culturally for lesbians to start looking at gay male porn.

Sue: A recent *On Our Backs* has a spread on girls looking at boys doing it.

Cindy: There is clearly a fascination among some lesbians about what men do, which is an interesting turnabout. It may be that within lesbian/gay culture gay men's sexuality has moved to a position of prominence because of AIDS. There are a lot of changes happening in gay male sexuality, and it may be that this offers a vocabulary that lesbians can take on and try out. But there are other strategies: when I was working on *Bad Attitude* (a lesbian porn magazine coming out of Boston), for example, we tried really hard to get women to do their own work around their sexuality for the magazine. We used images that were produced by the women themselves, that were very much what women were doing sexually at grass-roots level, rather than what was acceptable. One image, I don't know if you recall it, was of very beautiful smallish, athletic breasts, with a nipple ring and a very very sharp stiletto between the nipple ring. It was an elegant, stunning photograph but some women were really offended, and thought it was abusive to women. It got more of a reaction than the very stylized stuff in *On Our Backs*. *Bad Attitude* was trying to speak out of a set of authentic subject positions and to give women space to talk about their sexuality and develop a language, not impose one. It would be nice to do some consciousness-raising involving, say, art therapy work, to begin to find a language of our own somehow, to map our sexualities.

Sue: I think that would be fun and risky – which can be a fruitful and explosive combination.

Background Reading

Carter, Erica and Watney, Simon (eds) (1989) *Taking Liberties: AIDS and Cultural Politics*. London: Serpent's Tail.
Richardson, Diane (1987) *Women and the AIDS Crisis*. London: Pandora.
Rieder, Ines and Ruppelt, Patricia (eds) (1989) *Matters of Life and Death: Women Speak About AIDS*. London: Virago.

PART THREE

Sitting on a Fence

Sitting on a fence can be an exciting pastime. Perched, half in comfort and half scared you'll tip over, not quite sure which way to look, but with unique vantage points, it has a lot going for it. Precarious yet creatively safe. But fence-sitting suffers a bad reputation – if you don't takes sides you're accused of woolly-mindedness. However, resisting calls to take sides in seconds gives a girl more chance to suss things out. Fence-sitting is supposedly what nice people do – too nervous to give offence to anyone, too cowardly to take the consequences of deciding one way or another, too boring to have a mind of their own. For me it affords time for listening, time for exploration, time for letting something unwind and reveal more than is there at first sight. It gives space for uncertainty.

Although I have jettisoned a fair amount of self-deprecation over the years and found it more and more possible to take sides and bear the consequences and the power that confers, I'm interested that all the pieces in this section were written recently. Even if I'm now more skilled at peeling off a cloying nice layer, it hasn't ended my pleasure in sitting.

'Girls Who Kiss Girls and Who Cares?' from *The Good, the Bad and the Gorgeous*, was not something I wanted to write. One of the book's editors had to bully me into doing it. She insisted I had my chic tendencies – after all I'd been wearing lipstick for years and anyway I'd been reading women's magazines and other print media before the days when it was 'politically acceptable'. What other serious feminist in the seventies and eighties ordered *Woman* and *Woman's Own* to be saved when she was on holiday, who else left these and the more glossy sort lying about for anyone to see when there was a weighty feminist meeting in their living room? Okay, okay, reader, I wrote it and I'm glad I did.

I've seen other think pieces on lesbian chic by now – and it's a phenomenon which has kept up the pace. 'Girls Who Love Girls – Hollywood's Sexy Swinging Secrets' screams Australia's *New Weekly* in June 1995; *Vanity Fair* can't let an issue go by without something dykish in it; even London's *Evening Standard* seems obsessed, enough so that in August 1995, Suzanne Moore is writing critically on the 'Wannabe Gay'.

What I was determined to do in 'Girls Who Kiss Girls' was knock sideways the perceived truth that lesbian life pre-chic was dour and dowdy. But I also wanted to claim that today what was being labelled that way had everything to do with feminist politics and little to do with hairy armpits and baggy dungarees. I wanted to demonstrate how nineties' visibility personified by the chic lesbian didn't emerge suddenly, fully formed, from nothing. And I wanted to untangle my feelings about visibility, chic, feminism, co-option, and the pleasures and vexations these all evinced. Sitting on a fence was the most advantageous place to be when doing this.

In 1993 I did a reading at Hares and Hyenas lesbian and gay bookshop in Melbourne as part of a queer series. Most of the other writers were quite explicitly and perhaps obviously queer – the young HIV-positive gay man reading a queer rant about AIDS, some pretty sexy stuff from others and a very postmodern lesbian reading from an experimental novel in progress. I had searched my writing, looking for pieces which indicated my queer self and hadn't found much. So I was reduced to writing something new which explained my very queer ambivalence about queer itself.

What's happened to queer since then? When I reread my writing from 1993 did it feel incredibly old-fashioned and out-of-date? What's happened to young queer as it approaches political middle age? I'm not sure, except that it has become standard for conference titles. Lesbian and Gay and Bisexual and Transsexual and Transgendered and Transvestite and Queer has now been shortened to the much simpler inclusive Queer. And that's the way I occasionally use it too – as a type of shorthand to indicate the electric fences are off and (hopefully) there's some creative confusion going on. When I want to make it clear very quickly that I am *not* talking about a particular sort of lesbian politics I might also use queer to register a disassociation as much as an affiliation.

But sometimes I use it scathingly, sarcastically, as a put down. Then I want to shelve queer as something meaningless or even *passé*. I react to the already calcified rhetoric of queer's 'transgression', so overused that it's unable to convey excitement, let alone naughtiness. At those times I want to reclaim the specificity of lesbian, dyke, gay reality. Still developing the art of fence-sitting, rubbing up and down on the horn of the dilemma.

In 1992 I joined a panel of Australian and North American academics and high-flying cultural critics to discuss 'political correctness'. The general consensus was that it was all an Australian media beat-up and had little reality in Australian life – let the Americans continue with their madness. I wasn't so sure. I was included on the panel as one of two 'activists', although I'm not certain whether my lesbianism was considered activism or if it was my work around HIV/AIDS which gave me the monicker.

What has happened with political correctness in Australia since 1992? It didn't die a quiet death at all. Media-driven or not, it now flourishes in academic, political and cultural discourses. In a recent case accusations of political correctness flew wildly. When Helen Garner published her book,

The First Stone – her for the meanings beneath the case of an Ormond College master whose reputation was rubbished by accusations that he had sexually assaulted two women students in his charge – the forces which gathered around the (anonymous) girls were continually accused of political correctness – a slightly veiled reference to their feminism. Although Garner herself did not originally make these accusations, because she sympathized with the man, she became a *cause célèbre* for disgruntled men in important places.

At the beginning of December 1994 GINA (Girls in New Alliance) organized a forum in Melbourne to explore the reality, myths and politics of transsexuality and to give space for questions lesbians and other queer people might want to air around the subject. GINA is tiny but muscular, an ongoing, loosely organized group of dykes who came into existence in order to strike a new note in Melbourne's lesbian subculture when lesbian life appeared falsely divided between those who clubbed and those who had politics. We weren't keen on some brands of lesbian feminism which were claiming the moral high ground, so GINA was born.

Our major form of activity has been presenting 'GINA forums' which bring current, contentious, or simply interesting subjects into open discussion. The forums have all been aimed at lesbians who want to exercise their brains outside academia and have attracted large numbers of younger or disaffected dykes, some bisexuals, as well as the curious, a few queer boys, and the odd heterosexual. Within a broadly sex-radical framework, we aim to open up space for generous exploration of ambivalences and uncertainties. We refuse to be placed on one side or another of a rigid divide which allows no room for critical questions except those on 'the other side' and does not take into account our own ambivalences around such areas as pornography, censorship, SM and transsexuality.

And yet, GINA is certainly not a neutral participant in a divided lesbian world. We entered the fray exactly because we were dissatisfied and fed up with the fundamentalist lesbian politics of certain Melbourne dykes. Perhaps our position is best described as upholding a different understanding of how much many people long for an involvement in lesbian life and politics which is not premised on rules and regulations, but on exploration.

One of our most successful forums happened when controversies about transsexuality and transgenderism were raising ruckus in different Australian circles of lesbians. The Lesbian Space Project in Sydney was coming to grief over the inclusion or exclusion of trannys from the proposed venture and earlier a lesbian 'confest' in Brisbane had ended in tears when several trannys were spotted among the 'woman born woman' dykes. Although there are home-grown Australian anti-trannys, I heard more than one person wonder why the blow-up happened? Certainly Sydney transsexual, Aidy Griffin, felt confident enough to wonder in print: 'It may be purely coincidental, but Janice Raymond, the American author of *The Transsexual Empire* just happened to be at the conference' ('Gender Agenda' in the *Sydney Star Observer*). (Raymond believes that male-to-female lesbian transsexuals want to enter lesbian feminist 'space' and take it over because, in essence, they are still men who cannot bear autonomous women.)

In general, Melbourne lesbians did not display the extreme hostility towards transsexuals which boiled over in Brisbane and Sydney. However, we knew from our own discussions that many lesbians were ambivalent about transsexuality. We had clarified a lot for ourselves by talking with transsexuals and reading a range of materials. (In fact, since the forum, one of the male-to-female lesbians who came to the forum has joined GINA.) We wanted to open this experience up to more people and to put forward a different view than the one currently claiming the ethical high ground in Australia, which demands that lesbian space should be defended purely for 'female born lesbians', 'women born women' (or in some cases, 'womyn born womyn'). Personally, I loathe these new words for women. They feel awkward and mechanistic; usually I suspect I won't much care for the politics or style of a woman who uses 'womon', 'wim-min' or whatever, or sticks the word 'born' in between the alternative woman word of their choice.

In the keen discussion which followed the presentations, it was clear that the majority present were pleased to be able to listen to and question the transsexuals on the panel and that other trannys in the audience welcomed the chance to speak in a respectful atmosphere about their own experiences and thoughts. Other women could voice their unsettled feelings without feeling guilty and perhaps we all changed our percep-tions a bit. All the transsexuals present agreed that the medicalization of transsexuality was a problem and they spoke with understanding but criticism about the way in which male-identified notions of masculinity and femininity are too often imposed on hopeful trannys and in some cases embraced by them. The forum was a successful exercise in creative fence-sitting which was of benefit to everyone.

Girls Who Kiss Girls and Who Cares?

– FROM *THE GOOD, THE BAD AND THE GORGEOUS*, 1994

A mature woman sits down at her computer and stares into space. A lesbian contemplates her place in different mainstream cultural representations. A fifty-something fashion freak peruses a magazine. A mature lesbian feminist experiences the world as pleasurable, painful, difficult and easy. A woman remembers her childhood after a night of dreams. All of these women are part of me. Swarms of words and thoughts buzz around busily. Identity versus diversity. Flux and flow opposed to inner truth. Lesbianism as a major political statement, or sex acts between women as part of a smorgasbord of trendy sexual possibilities. Politics versus pleasure. The politics of pleasure. Contested power or contested sites? Polarizations of imagination and fantasy with real people and practice. The appeal of the outlawed, the naughty. The idea of transgression as an advertising tool. Once the wickedness is recognized and aspired to by others is it really wicked? Reality in the 1990s or opportunism at the edge of the century?

I want to look at and try to fasten down ever so tentatively the way in which lesbianism has surfaced as a fashion item and as a part of what's naughty and trendy in the 1990s by being brazenly selective about the mainstream British, American and Australian magazines I look at. I see a series of shifting sexual contradictions taking place, well mixed-up with co-options, ruptures, spaces, possibilities and marketing techniques. I want to understand better what is going on! As an avid consumer of magazines (my popular culture of choice) and as a self-consciously political creature, I'm tantalized. However, before speculating a popular culture's eye view of lesbianism, I want to set the scene, sift through a few bits of history, look at some of the different players.

In the 1970s what *challenged* mainstream media were the militant demands of feminism, demands which rocked any easy older certainty about women's place in the world. Even if popular media reacted with hostility to women's liberation, react and write about it they did. What *titillated* the media during the same period was the imagined connections between women's liberation and lesbianism. After all, it was 'common knowledge' that women's liberationists hated men. What else could they be but a bunch of 'hairy dykes'? Their accusations conveniently framed an attack on the politics of early feminists.

After the movement's first shameful (and defensive) response that its adherents were 'ordinary women', attitudes changed in fits and starts as lesbianism was accepted (sometimes grudgingly) into a line-up of politicized identities *within* feminism and gay politics. By the early part of the 1980s the fear emanating from *within* feminism that its demands would be dismissed as the mad-hatter rantings of man-hating lesbians had abated, largely because lesbians had forced the issue into the political arena. However, the media have continued to spit out their ignorant loathing and stereotyping of lesbians. Today the so-called loony, ugly (read not stereotypically feminine) lesbian, increasingly designated as an arbiter of rigid political correctness, remains a figure of derision and hatred, especially whenever the *politics* of feminism or lesbian feminism become a contentious issue in the larger society.

However, at some point during the mid to late 1980s something shifted in popular media's representations of lesbianism. An erotically charged image of a completely different lesbian began to materialize, coinciding with the older caricatured portrayal. kd lang and Cindy Crawford's now famous 1993 *Vanity Fair* lesbian-fantasy-come-true cover and the eulogistic article inside was perhaps this trend's culmination. The development of this new dynamic is what I'm interested in here, particularly in the way it has shown up in magazines, although I will allow my glance to wander to the pages of newspapers from time to time. Where did these images come from? How have meanings about lesbianism changed and where are the interchanges between those meanings in popular culture and the lived lives of lesbians? Clearly the existence of lesbianism and its subcultural manifestations is a pre-condition for the lesbian images appearing in glossy and not so glossy magazines. But what came first? The chic lesbian in her natural habitat or the chic lesbian in the pages of the media?

I remember an early 1980s issue of *Tatler* magazine which featured a gorgeous sailor girl model on the cover. The fashion spread inside was all about sailor fashions for women, and some of the layouts were suggestive of an erotic tension between the female models. An accompanying article covered real-life lipstick lesbians, clubbing in London. In the 1980s, British magazines like *Tatler* flirted more than once with lesbianism in their fashion layouts, once camping up a 1980s version of the upper-class country-weekend set, complete with languishing lesbians à la Vita Sackville-West.

The point is that in the magazines' terms these were attractive and seductive images whose main purpose (outside of advertising and selling!) was neither straightforward pornographic arousal nor putdown. For the knowing reader of the time, however, magazines like *Tatler*, British *Elle* and *Vogue* appeared as if compelled to reflect a fascination with all things sexually strange – but – only if they were stylishly dressed. These included vaguely s&m images, direct from or influenced by Helmut Newton, and fashion spreads peopled by effete young men and languid ladies draped and intertwined together, but desiring who?

Women posing in these magazines were also wearing men's suits, playing with images of maleness and borrowing from an ongoing lesbian cross-dressing tradition. In the mid 1980s, when Princess Di turned up at a star-studded event in a tuxedo, she was ensuring the public's interest in and acceptance of these new, slightly ambiguous ways some heterosexual women were choosing to dress. Although lesbianism was not overtly named in most of the magazine fashion features of the mid 1980s, its presence flirted around the edges outrageously.

Of course there have been other ways in which lesbianism has been inserted into magazines or the news media during the past ten or fifteen years. This often has occurred through a media eye view of the political agendas and campaigns of lesbian and/or gay groups, and through struggles around HIV and AIDS, although the odd lesbian sex scandal might occasionally surface. (Story-oriented tabloids such as the *National Enquirer* often seem obsessed with the existence of lesbians and gay men. What a hoot it is to read their gasping stories on the shock/horror world of TV/screen/sport star gay sex, right alongside the more usual tales of monster babies and UFO sightings.) Lesbians, for instance, might appear in the media through stories on lesbian headteachers, gays in the military, lesbians having babies, domestic partnership campaigns, lesbian and gay pride celebrations, Clause 28 demonstrators' involvement in local or national government, or supporting gay men with AIDS.

However, these are more news-based stories; their presence serves to make homosexuality, both female and male, less hidden and more a part of popular discourse around sexual identity. But I would argue that this type of story does not have the effect of creating a desirable lesbian object, nor of appealing directly to the woman who lusts after women. As well, the effect of such stories does not necessarily challenge the derisive way in which the character of the strident, 'ugly' lesbian continues to be used to attack feminist and/or lesbian-feminist supposed excesses; in other words, their militancy and the articulation of lesbianism's challenge to male-defined heterosexuality.

Musing over the possible underpinnings of lesbian chic and the continuing contradiction posed to it by an older lesbian feminism, leads me to think about shake-ups which might have altered how lesbianism is currently perceived. The first thing that comes to mind is the continuing SF scenario of AIDS. What makes it different from other frightening diseases of the late twentieth century is its real and imagined connections to assumed forms of heterosexual and gay male sexual practices. It's the historical timing of HIV which creates its difference from previous diseases linked to sex; making its first appearance at a particular point of sexual flux, when there was a lot of old unfinished sexual business around, but also new and energetic things happening, including signifi-cant numbers of women asserting themselves with men, demandingly saying, 'I want my pleasure too.' As well, more lesbians were branching out, tentatively exploring a more open approach to sex, kicking over the careful traces which previously had been maintained in a hostile yet perving world.

Since the 1970s, feminists have been actively criticizing and attacking popular women's magazines for their refusal to budge on the assumed heterosexuality of their readers, a heterosexuality which positioned the woman as eternally wanting to please her man, the man she was so lucky to have caught. Sex-obsessed magazines of the 1970s and the early 1980s like *Cosmopolitan* ran never-ending stories (and still do) on how to catch, keep and please a man sexually. Although many women's magazines had moved towards incorporating aspects of feminism by the late 1970s, especially around notions of equality, heterosexuality still ruled the roost. It was the unexpected, the wild card of AIDS, which I suggest served to prise open the magazines' covers slightly and allowed sexual diversity to seize some space within their pages. AIDS forced a recognition that sexual diversity existed and it did it relatively quickly. However, this sideways recognition did not mean that news-stand magazines took on the radical political position which posed lesbianism as a challenge to assumed or compulsory heterosexuality.

AIDS' imprint on various sexual discourses has been immense, recasting the debates and sexual politics of the 1960s, 1970s and 1980s in its light. It is commonplace to refer to the way in which AIDS has forced a more public and mainstream recognition of gay male sexuality in countries where homosexuals were the first and hardest hit by the virus. At the same time, a concurrent but more oblique recognition of gay male desire has crept in. In a narrative filled with ironies, one is the way in which gay men, now associated in mainstream culture with AIDS and death, at the same time have surfaced more openly as sexual, sexy people. Whether it is drag queens in Sydney's Mardi Gras, fabulously muscled bodies at the club or gym, or fashion freaks in the more bohemian parts of town, it's clear that gay men conjure up more than the ravages of AIDS.

One spin-off of this opened space has been the different way in which lesbianism is also signified. As first, lesbians are implicated in the AIDS tragedy by virtue of their perverse same-sex desire and practice. They are perceived as a 'danger' because they too are homosexual. Later, and in ways too complicated and varied to go into here, lesbian and gay coalition politics around a range of issues, including AIDS but perhaps more accurately described as 'gay and lesbian rights', assures the linkage between the two in the media and the public. Lesbians have grown in confidence and visibility in proportion to how strongly they've pushed for recognition and equality in the wider society, *and* expanded the boundaries of their own developing social networks and cultural representations.

The initial aspect of the heightened awareness of gays and lesbians in the media continues today but is not the *only* way AIDS has affected the attitudes displayed in the media. A decade later, different layers of lesbian and gay identities and lives have permeated, mixed it up with other cultural developments and produced for instance, AIDS activists, queer theory and queers, and 'outing' as a significant event in some countries – all of which have been covered in the media. There is a more general recognition, as famous people announce their HIV status or become ill with AIDS, that homosexuals really are 'everywhere' and that these deviant men have sisters. 'We are everywhere!' the rallying cry of the 1970s gay and lesbian activist, becomes a bizarre and poignant reality within the context of AIDS in the 1980s and 1990s for both gay men and lesbians, when they are *seen* to be everywhere.

But AIDS is only part of the explanation of why images of real-life lesbians like kd lang and the fantasy lesbians acted out by models in magazines have emerged as desirable objects on their own terms, while different images of lesbians continue to serve as the target for denunciations whenever any form of radical feminist politics is floated. Even the term 'lipstick lesbian' indirectly signals that there is another lesbian who overtly shuns make-up in the name of a political rejection of male-dominated notions of femininity. Yet in previous eras of lesbian style, lipstick was accepted. One has only to think of the French salon of Natalie Barney or the more recent western traditions of butch and femme.

A recent American anthology edited by Joan Nestle, *The Persistent Desire*, focused on butch/femme historically and in the present. Many of the older writers in it refer angrily to the rules and regulations of the women's movement of the 1970s which they say denied their experiences and desires. However, since the mid 1980s, many younger lesbians have been eager to rediscover and play with aspects of butch/femme. These women look upon the 1970s as *passé* and rigidly politically correct. Initially they materialized at the end of the 1970s on the lesbian and/or gay scenes of cities like London, New York, San Francisco and Sydney, attending women's balls dressed in tuxedos and ball gowns, well before Princess Di ever dreamt of cross-dressing.

I bring up those dim and seemingly superseded days of the 1970s, ones which the neo-butch/femme *aficionados* of the 1990s now regard so grimly, because they do have a bearing on how lesbianism is now being touted (or ridiculed) in the media. In fact, the pastiche of retro styles and culture which many younger lesbians and gay men have favoured in the past five years or so are in sync with a more generalized cultural appreciation of those styles by other groups of young people, young designers – straight or gay. The currently favoured butch/femme look and flavour is located in a reinvention of the styles of the 1940s, 1950s and 1960s. These neo-butch/femme styles of urban western life are titillating *and* complementary to current straight fashions, styles and attitudes which many magazines are covering and creating a wider interest in.

Reflecting on the ephemeral nature of what is 'in style' and what is not, what is retro and what is considered *passé*, and what meanings are attached to stylistic manifestations, it comes as a small but pleasant irony that grunge (no matter how briefly) brought back into fashion for a whole new generation of rebellious kids the flannel shirts and knitted hats of the pantomime 1970s lesbian feminist. That the girls of this wave of grunge style came back as anarchistic waifs, not tough feminists or dykes, gently reveals how skewed much of the current rejection of 1970s feminism's look is, superficially identifying a style of clothing with politics. As Courtney Love, singer with Hole, says in a July 1993 issue of *i-D*, 'The problem with Riot Grrrl is that a "girl" is seen as pretty, childlike and innocent while a "woman" is a hairy lesbian.'

I want to scrutinize a bit more the caricature lesbian whipping girl, the one who serves as the repository of mainstream hatred and fear of feminism's 'excesses'. Besides the flannel shirt (which in fact has been an androgynous item for many decades) she is often portrayed as an old fashioned bull-dagger butch. She is 'mannish' but not at all stylish and at the same time she is definitely a woman. Therefore she has to be ugly – in other words, butch. Interestingly, the *real* lesbian politics (which as she figures in the media, the diesel dyke butch caricature is *supposed* to represent) often contain angry denunciations of butch/femme relation-ships – even if delivered by a flannel-shirted adherent. In this inter-pretation, butch/femme is consigned to reactionary, heterosexually influenced role-playing. The 1970s lesbian feminist was likely to be blanketly anti-fashion *and* anti-butch/femme, although as other com-mentators have remarked, the idealized androgyny of the time made everyone look vaguely butch.

The popular media which use the stereotype to attack the radical politics they want to discredit have no understanding of the complex history of butch/femme, let alone the way it was rejected by 1970s lesbian feminists. Even ostensibly sympathetic articles about lesbianism appear compelled to say what today's lesbian chic is not: 'The stereotyped butch dyke who can't get a man and worse still, can't apply lipstick or use a razor, is a tired old image being pushed to the backburner' (Bernie Sheehan, 'Lesbian Chic', *Australian Women's Forum*, September 1993).

One of the ways in which the media used to signal their distress about confusing sexual identities, was to repeat *ad infinitum* the question 'Is it a boy or a girl?' Apparently this was supposed to result in general hysteria and a comforting return to 'normality'. It bedevilled earlier 'gender bending' from the 1960s long-haired hippy right up to Boy George in the early 1980s, but nowadays it seems largely to have disappeared. Who gives a fuck? is the general tone of things. However, *who* these indeterminate creatures literally fuck is of interest. Today, through the melded influences of gay, lesbian, feminist and AIDS organizing, an expanded repertoire of named or suggested sex acts can more easily be called into play, making it possible to more openly refer to sexual behaviours rather than being stuck in gender-bending obsessions.

At the same time, there is the possibility that these newly discovered people are simply sexually confusing creatures who challenge the gender expectations of dominant heterosexual culture *and* those of more traditional deviants, both lesbian and gay. Whether male or female, they may appear aggressively feminine, futuristic or ridiculously masculine. The sex acts they may or may not be capable of desiring or carrying out with each other then become irrelevant when compared to their 'we're here' presence in the pages of various magazines. The repertoire of sex acts and sexual personae made more generally available, are often written about through an excited exploration of transsexuals (or transgendered people), or specific sexual predilections like rubber or sadomasochism.

A December 1992 article by John Godfrey in *The Face* called 'The New Camp' maintains that there is a rise of stars and celebrities whose sexual identity is neither straight nor gay, but camp. 'Because the New Camp is where the old Camp has broken the taste barrier (good not bad), where dressing up is about glamour not gender, and looking good (i.e. the body beautiful) has nothing to do with sexuality.' And in 'Love the one you whip', Lee Tulloch describes fashion's move into fetishism.

'Fetishism is all the rage, as are its subcultures of S&M, B&D, D&S and Fem Dom' (*Mode*, Feb/Mar 1993). Illustrating the article are examples of stars and models in appropriate poses. There's Cindy Crawford in a *Vogue* fashion shot by Helmut Newton in which she wears a plastic bathing suit, and lies stiffly beside a pool in a position suggestive of bondage and masochism while model Helena Christensen stands above her in designer dominatrix gear pawing at Cindy's spread-out hair with her elegant shoe. (Cindy, it seems, has an ongoing fondness for kinkiness of the lesbian sort.) These forays into sexual diversity, portrayed as riveting and fascinating to a more sedate readership, exist alongside more serious, didactic features on sex in the time of AIDS, which endlessly list different sexual acts and their attendant risks. In these articles the focus is completely on 'naming' and transgression and no one ever mentions that people who live out their lives 'transgressively' may have trouble in the world – trouble with jobs, family or trouble with violence.

A lush and trendy art magazine in Australia (Pippa Leary, *black & white*, Summer 1992/93) carries an article in its first issue called 'Gender Agenda' about transgenderism, in which the author points out:

> In the world of pop music, the androgynous make-up of the Bowies and Annie Lennox has been replaced by the surgical make-over of the Jackson clan and Cher. A quick glance at the fashion photography of *Vogue*, or the Stephen Meisel portraits of Madonna, reveals that ambiguity is the state of play in the sexuality stakes.

Drawing on the buzz names of Foucault and Irigaray, transsexuals in this article are always male-to-female created bodies which the writer claims are now the ideal female model type.

Straight, gay or queer, these articles are primarily about transgressive personae and acts. But equivalent focus on lesbianism as a newly-arrived hot ticket is not hard to find. Back in late 1989, Nicola Shulman in her wonderfully titled *Harpers & Queen* article, 'Bra-Crossed Lovers', was revealing the rise of lesbianism within the nearly hooray-Henry set: 'It is one of the most intriguing phenomena of the late eighties that smart women are turning in droves to lesbianism.' Weighted down with heavy-handed attempts at humour, Shulman manages to convince that lesbianism is in vogue, but that it is a passing style, 'Occupying a place in the nation's consciousness similar to that of, say, roller-disco dancing in 1976'. In fact, it's being taken up by girls who ultimately want a man. To attract said man they need a clean bill of health. Why lesbianism? It's safe – from AIDS!

Shulman's unpleasant article also includes a list of negative lesbian stereotypes which the current crop are not! 'Naturally, you do not wish to deal in cheap parody, so you have straightaway thrown out the idea that these are persons with Eton crops and monocles who drink stout from straight glasses and call each other Jim.' Shulman doesn't get it, doesn't get that in late 1989 it is already perfectly fashionable to have an Eton crop and *not* call each other Jim, or that lesbians could look like either of these images plus many others. And she can't help but compare the unpleasant feminist to the current batch of (temporarily) gay girls. 'Neither do you suppose for a moment they must be feminist guerrillas who trim their hair with the coarse plate of the cheese-grater'. Shulman can have a go at feminists, implying in one short sentence their absurd militancy (guerrillas) coupled with their wilful unattractiveness (hair cut with a cheese-grater).

In the Winter 1993 issue of the Australian *HQ Magazine*, in an article called 'The Gay Divorcee', Julie Clarke wrote: 'It used to go something like this: you fall in love, get married, have kids and settle down. But nowadays, there's an addendum some women are finding hard to resist: you get divorced and fall for another woman. For them, it's goodbye phallus and sandpaper kisses, hello soft skin and sensational sex.' Clarke posits an idealized lesbian desire for the woman's body in reaction to the brutishness of heterosexual sex. She is obviously writing sympathetically about why previously straight women might find lesbianism attractive and her interviewees extol the joys of lesbianism. But even she has to describe the negative stereotype in order to claim it is not necessarily true. She goes on, 'Sure there are lesbians who believe that the whole world is a phallocentric conspiracy to harm and insult lesbians who are the only intrepid survivors of a vanquished race … women. The straight world in turn sees them as humourless "sleeping bags with legs".'By denouncing the stereotype as one, she indicates that some lesbians believe the heterosexual world is out to get them, the ones who in turn are perceived as 'sleeping bags with legs'. The boring, daggy lesbian is the one associated with difficult, challenging politics.

Clarke finishes off with a recent Sydney Mardi Gras Parade scene:

> But when a pack of fifty beautiful bare-breasted women glowered, Harley Davidson roared – and the Dykes on Bikes took off up Oxford Street in Sydney's Darlinghurst one balmy Saturday night in February, the crowd watching the Gay and Lesbian Mardi Gras Parade, mainly het couples, were gobsmacked'. 'Hubba, hubba!' exclaimed a woman beside me in the crowd, married, two children, husband an engineer, 'Now I'm tempted!'

The young, beautiful, sexually daring (and baring) dykes on bikes can appeal in a more directly sexual way to the 'normal' heterosexual housewife. The persona of the lesbian overburdened with politics is not seductive for her; lesbianism as part of a newly discovered interest in diversity – of identities and sexual acts is.

In a June 1993 copy of the English paper, the *Evening Standard*, Isabell Wolff visits a new lesbian sauna in London, called Dykes Delight. 'Forget the old dungarees image, the latest lesbians are bright, chic and glamorous … Everywhere you look, the joys of dykedom are being vigorously and joyfully extolled.' The funny thing is that no one extolled the joys of dykedom more vigorously than the lesbian feminists of the 1970s. In fact, at the time there was a veritable surge of lesbian activity by previously heterosexual women. Lesbianism was the highest form of feminism in which pleasure and politics were joined in perfect harmony. Differences between lesbians were of secondary importance. But however much they sung it from the mountain top, the media didn't choose to hear.

Wolff goes on to opine:

> If prejudices against lesbians still exist, they are probably less frequently expressed since lesbians are, to put it crudely, a lot harder to spot these days. The androgynous, dungareed, cropped-headed dykes with shoulders like the back of a sofa are still around, but in far smaller numbers… No longer is lesbianism a byword for dour, physical unattractiveness.

To be fair, the writer does bring in some lesbian voices of scepticism about what all this attention really means, but the overall message is how cool it is to be a dyke, especially now that the boring old lesbians are in retreat. And what did those boring old farts represent besides unattractiveness? Unmistakably, it must be politics. At the end of Wolff's article, 'Jane' – she can't use her real name – claims she does not feel

oppressed. 'Jane' then goes on to catalogue the things she can't do openly
or in public because she's a lesbian but ends up saying:

> Women are no longer lesbian because they're feminist and man-hating.
> They are lesbians because that's their preference, and they no longer feel
> they have to dress in a frumpy way. What we're all saying is 'OK, I'm a
> lesbian, I'm good looking and I'm going to have lots of fun.'

I'm sad that 'Jane' can't see the absurdity of her statement. She's bought
the polarization which the media has grabbed onto and parrots it back to
them. She is standing right next to an insight which begs to be seen: she
can dress however she wants, still have fun *and* proclaim a fierce feminism.
Camille Paglia would love her. Paglia, who wrote *Sexual Personae – Art and
Decadence from Nefertiti to Emily Dickinson* and *Sex, Art and American Culture*,
and writes about Madonna as if she personally discovered her, endlessly
plays the media's favourite running dog in the campaign against
feminism and lesbianism. Like the ex-communist of the cold war period,
she claims she knows what she is talking about. Because she couches her
critique of feminism and lesbianism in academic and polemic discourses,
and because she purports to speak from the position lesbian, her attacks
seem more fresh and radical than the tired clichés she actually deploys.
Paglia cravenly allows herself to be used as a legitimizer, giving (supposedly) an 'intellectual' veneer to conservative discomfort with the *politics*
of feminism and lesbianism. Paglia is the media's current sweetheart,
quoted widely whenever anyone wants to have a go at lesbian feminism.
The irony is that Camille missed the lesbian-chic boat completely,
complaining only a few years ago that there were no hot lesbians to fuck.

Some confusing stuff is definitely going on in the print media, but
who gains from it and who get used or abused or finally fucked over is
another question. If lesbians collude mindlessly with the denunciations
and ugly stereotyping of an image of the lesbian feminist of the 1970s
(always the dungarees, the flannel shirt, the large – or shrewish – body,
the plain and politically stern visage) they are not just claiming pleasure
and their right to be a different *style* of lesbian – they are also feeding into
the larger societal forces which are out to denounce feminism's 'excesses'.
This denunciation (which includes nasty jokes) is about a construction of
feminism's excesses which are, it is suggested, largely the work of the
extremist lesbian. These 'excesses' include much of the radical political
agenda of feminism, including its analyses of the social, cultural and
economic. By excess, I mean feminism's and lesbian feminism's challenge
to femininity, to what it is to be womanly, to fashion, to the uses of
language, to notions of the naturalness of motherhood, to male
domination, to violence against women. In this discourse lesbianism itself
in its *lesbian-feminist* guise is often construed as an excess. Definitely to be

avoided; excessive not in the cool, surface-obsessed shock techniques of the late 1980s or early 1990s sexual challenges, but in its endless seriousness. This idea of excess exists within lesbianism itself but there it is often the excess of the butch/femme relationship or of lesbian sadomasochists which comes in for stick – the very images which the popular media call upon and name cool, stylish and sexy.

What we can see is the way in which lesbianism as a practice, lesbianism as a transgressive erotic charge and a signalling of the blurred edge between fashion and a sort of postmodern 'fuck you', *as well as* lesbianism representing the politics of feminism (increasingly attacked as politically correct, rigid, silencing and humourless) all appear much more openly in a variety of media representations. The way in which the lesbianism of the first categories is welcomed by some observers as validating sexual diversity and choice has to be pitted against the continuing, perhaps accelerating identification of the lesbian persona with the ridiculed and reviled radical politics of feminism and lesbian feminism. The two seemingly polarized images of the lesbian I have referred to do not necessarily form a coherent opposition to each other: the fashion shot redolent of lesbianism usually makes no reference to the stridently anti-fashion lesbian politico. The two images of lesbianism exist at the same time, one young and provocatively attractive and fashionable, the second older, dowdy, prescriptive and overtly political. Both images are fantastical; neither image corresponds any more to the multi-layered realities of lesbians' lives than other media caricatures of women do.

It's a difficult line to draw – or to walk. On the one hand there is much to critique in the feminisms and lesbian feminisms of the 1970s, but certainly not on mainstream media's terms! Within feminism and lesbian feminism many have expressed an interest in discussions of such things as ambivalence, desire, fantasy; about challenging overdetermined notions of female suffering and victimization as if there were never a space for negotiation or resistance; about exclusionary, racist and ethnocentric practices. The notion of shifting multiple identities giving texture and meaning to questions of race, class, sex and gender has appealed to many. But – and here is the rub – the way in which all this plays itself out in popular culture is quite different. Diversity, if it is devoid of any serious notion of resistance, is a bit like rainbow 'freedom rings' – pretty and possibly signifying friendliness but nothing much else. Why the hell shouldn't lesbians (or any women) be able to wear clothes which go against what girls are supposed to wear, clothes which are utilitarian and plain? What's wrong with making a political critique of the imperatives of femininity? Why shouldn't feminists strip away the froth in order to reveal the money-grabbing ugliness of the fashion and beauty business? But this sort of politics cannot be taken on whole by women's magazines – they can't digest it. However contradictory their contents have been for the past twenty years, these magazines are driven by huge industries, not only by cultural imperatives.

And yet … the disturbing but wonderful thing about news-stand women's magazines (and other forms of the media) is that I am continuously approaching them with critical ambivalence. I love the thing I am compelled to critique. In the present gallop to embrace popular culture, many lesbian feminists, in a reaction to an overly moralistic and proscriptive condemnation of all things popular (and overwhelmingly heterosexual) by earlier lesbian critics, seem to have lost their way. They wanted to escape the blanket denunciations of popular women's magazines which allowed no room for the possibility of personal pleasure when reading those magazines. But insisting that marginalized or disempowered people can 'read' dominant cultures with effect is one thing. Losing interest in attempts to create alternative challenges to dominant cultures is another. And a loss of interest in anything outside 'culture' is unforgivable.

There is no reason for lesbians to abandon even fierce criticisms, at the same time that they enjoy and consume popular culture. Popular culture as represented in women's magazines has never presented a monolithically smooth face – forget the models for now. At least since the 1970s these magazines have lost any unified frames for themes such as family, marriage, birth control, religion, abortion and, more and more, sexuality. Ironically, some of this was undoubtedly a response to the militancy and direct challenges with which feminism attacked the magazines. Turning the pages of many American, British and Australian magazines is like seeing a discourse stumble, destabilize itself and a page later straighten up and plunge on only to repeat the process.

However, delicious contradictions aside, women's magazines and women's features in newspapers are not the signal of a big new ground shift. To give them that power would be a mistake, even in a time of political uncertainty and the primacy given to representations and language as constitutive processes. There is no reason to give up partaking of women's magazines or some of the fashions they tout because of their weaknesses and conservatism, nor for their sad-assed attempts to co-opt a 'liberated' woman or chic lesbian into their pages. Most of us can come out unscathed after regular and continuing immersion in the glossy or not so glossy pages. And those passing pleasures can be separated from the necessary continuing critiques of the very object which brings pleasure. I refuse to abdicate my right or political need to criticize cultural artefacts which in my daily life I also enjoy. The pleasures I derive from reading and looking at women's magazine form a small part of my life as a lesbian still committed to resistance and change – and that's fun.

If I were magically given the choice between reading *Vanity Fair* and immediately achieving some of the radical goals of the sort of lesbian feminism I believe in, I'm not worried about which way I'd go. But the reality of the non-magical world is that change is not immediate, we live our everyday lives, work for and dream of change, all at the same time. Who knows, perhaps lesbians will create new subversive possibilities through *their* appropriation of popular culture's eager but limited fascination with yet another marginalized group's exotic possibilities.

Let's face it, style and fashion are pretty ephemeral wherever they occur – in the pages of women's magazines, hyped up for sales, or on the streets of urban cities, where succeding age and identity groups lay special claim to the importance and meanings of their look, their style. Lesbian appearance in magazines is often contradictory and deeply ambivalent. The fashion industry constantly searches out novelty (and capitalism new markets). The politics of a generation of women who identify with the naughty but exciting image of lesbians, which surfaces with more frequency in the fashion spreads of various news-stand magazines, will have to sharpen in order to maintain more than a superficial pose of rebellion. They can still wear lipstick and leather if they want. They may still discover that lipstick and leather look hopelessly old-fashioned in ten years' time.

A sharper politics would challenge the co-option of the sexy young kinky girl into fashion at the expense of any coherent politics. It might discover that style is only skin deep and that the questions which 1970s feminists posed deserve attention, possibly new answers, and definitely new tactics, from lesbians in the 1990s. It would not necessarily be a politics to warm the cockles of many older lesbian feminists' hearts. A recognition that the struggles of feminists in the 1970s and 1980s has brought us to a place where their sullen or sexy stares can grace the pages of the fashion mag.

My Queer Heaven – or A Dyke's Dilemma

– FIRST PRESENTED AT HARES AND HYENAS LESBIAN AND GAY BOOKSHOP, MELBOURNE, 1993

Searching frantically through my written work to find something to fit into today's festivities, something which could at least slide sideways into the queer paradigm, I found chapters and articles and notes on sex, HIV transmission, censorship, erotica, pornography, breast cancer, dreams and radical politics. Surely something would fit the bill? But ultimately it was clear that little of my work was unambiguously queer.

What the fuck was queer anyway? I saw contradictory evidence. It seemed to promise a thousand delights and hide a thousand sins. I was both attracted and repelled. It was what I wanted it to be when I liked it and what I was contemptuous of when I disliked it. It was squishy and malleable under its prickly surface. Once you found its soft underbelly you could suck it and poke it and roll around with it and find some pleasure in it, but you could also shoot it full of holes. For friends of young queer this might not be a huge problem but it creates an easy target for its enemies. Today queer politics only offends with jabby little prickles, offering no proof of its staying power or ability to effect more than illusory change.

I did some work in London at the beginning of 1992 on some of Channel 4's OUT programmes. In the process of researching one on 'gay genes' I talked to a number of young men who all defined themselves as queer. Gay was boring. Queer was exciting. What, pray tell was queer? In the USA the climate for queer was the dismissal of an assumed (and somehow strangely unified) lesbian and gay trend towards assimilation into the mainstream. But in Britain it was all about believing that everyone has deviant desires and queer was an in-your-face freeing-up and living-out of that. Queer was the popularization of the theoretical notion that sexual desire is constructed and not necessarily unchanging. Looking at sex through this lens problematizes heterosexuality as well as homosexuality, which can't be a bad thing.

These Brit boys said that queer in London was not like its American counterpart in that it was necessarily confrontational. Its political edge was in the literal living-out of desire – in clubs, in pubs, on the youth scene in general. They said they felt more at home with others who were open to their own desires and possible deviancy whether they were homosexual, bisexual, transgendered or heterosexual, than with the older, clone-dominated boring old farts in gay discos. Of course heterosexuals could be queer, look at Madonna.

The London activist group, OutRage! has been characterized as confrontational and queer. This group prides itself on its creative action-oriented style. But underneath all its 'shocking' up-front language, with its 'We're Here, Join the Queers' leaflets full of attitude, it is possible to discern a surprisingly old-fashioned political agenda all dressed up in new clothes, queer clothes.

One OutRage! flyer was colourful in its language, challenging queers to get off their arses: 'We are totally FUCKED off with the way the government, the media, the police and the public treat us like shit!' The final punchline from the 'queers with attitude' leaflet was to join a demonstration outside parliament for 'Equality Now'! Wow – now that's a really bold new political idea. Queer has a chameleon-like quality which gives spurious meaning to whatever it is attached to. Now we have queer film, queer literature, queer activism, queer bad girls, queer bad boys, queer sensibilities, queer nation, absolutely queer, and some might claim, queer overkill, and we still aren't certain what the point is – or if maybe that's the point.

A 1992 issue of the now defunct American publication, *OutLook*, ran a cover story called 'Greetings From a Queer Planet – from Moscow to Acapulco'. Every single report from all the countries covered was about lesbian and gay organizations, projects or people. Not one report mentioned the word queer. Queer was the buzz word on the cover created by California based *OutLook* but was totally absent from the reports from around the world outside.

Of course the part of all this which fucks off someone of my age, my experience and my outlook – besides the fact that most of the most insistent supporters of queer seem to find comfort primarily in the company of men (nothing wrong with that but why trumpet the primacy of sexual fluidity and inclusiveness) – is that it's such kids' stuff. Yes, it can be cute and sassy, but it's going to fade fast. As the writer Sarah Schulman said recently, 'Visibility is not what the lesbian and gay community needs as much as power.' The bloom of its youth, dancing on E, as pleasurable and real as it may be, will inevitably need to encompass the issues such as class, race, sex inequality and oppression. Yes, the thrill of confrontation can continue way into midlife and beyond but it is hardly enough to sustain life in opposition or to move from innovative tactics to strategies which have a chance of success. I have yet to see a queer in-your-face initiative around childcare, self-insemination or breast cancer – not very queer or exciting issues really.

Many of us are tired of the old *formulations* of difficulty, inequality and sometimes dislike between lesbians and gay men. But that doesn't mean all those nasty old problems have shrivelled up, even if some of us work successfully with some gay men. As the black gay American writer Samuel Delany says, 'The situation of the lesbian in America is vastly different from the situation of the gay male. A clear acknowledgement of this fact, especially by male homosexuals, is almost the first requirement for any sophisticated discussion of homosexual politics in this country.' I'll bet my bottom Australian dollar that the same holds true here.

Queer poses itself as the way out of the boredom with old ways of describing and naming. It insists that it is expressive of a new *inclusiveness*, it embraces diversity, it is willing to take on *difference* and *change*. But these are descriptive claims which indicate desire not practice. When pressed, the queer boys in London recognized the importance of sex and race in relation to privilege and power but said that in queer it didn't matter, those things would follow along. Queer was inclusive! Of course now that American queers have tripped up on the exclusiveness of the white queer clique, now that it is quite clear that queer is primarily a new, stylish boy's club, these statements are a bit pathetic.

Identity and diversity – the buzz words of queer – represent the conundrum, the tension within queer. Queer has taken up the inclination to knock traditional binary oppositions – for instance, male/female, masculine/feminine, homosexual/heterosexual. These stereotyped markers of identity have been under attack for quite a few years. In theory, queer arms have opened simultaneously to a proliferation of new 'transgressive' or marginalized identities scrambling for a place in the sun. Diversity is golden in the realm of rhetoric. But the wild underbelly of identity can still throw it out of whack. Who in queer gets to decide the parameters of inclusion? Queer black women and men get tired of queer racism. Trannys want recognition, not homogenizing inclusion. Women wonder at diversity devoid of the recognition of sexism. What's it all about without recognition of the social conditions and relations of exploitation and oppression? Identity is about sameness, diversity is about difference. Can the two tango in tension and not trip up? It can't happen in a queer playroom void, no matter how great the music is.

And yet queer rhetoric remains and is not without resonance. What was possibly the first fumblings of a naive but self-conscious postmodernist political moment revealed very quickly the weakness of that formulation, illustrated how fast some postmodernist approaches can wiggle up their own ass. Its strengths remain now in what were its political weaknesses – its reliance on culture and media. I am attracted to spicy bites of queer but cynical about its political nouce and above and beyond any of that the world moves on, the fucking wars, and rapes and mutilation of peoples and land continue, and even if it sounds boring, the rich get richer and the poor poorer, racism and AIDS devastate, so what the fuck does queer care about that? What we are left with is a wish, a desire for a coalition of deviants to come together unproblematically and celebrate/ confront. The celebration would be a confrontation; the confrontation would be a celebration.

I do not feel angry at queer even as I try to define its weaknesses, even as I think that, well maybe I'm not ideal queer fodder, even though I guess I won't be sucking fleshy cocks in my lifetime. Because I also love queer, love the looseness of it, the coltishness and irony, the reclaiming of an outsider's delicious position. The politics of desire, identity and practice is an enticing one and queer is eager to explore it. Our imaginations will not free us from oppression, but without imagination what would freedom be like?

I like the challenge queer can offer. Getting up people's noses is not a bad thing – it can make them think and it can be a hell of a lot of fun. Queer has also given to younger deviants a possible identity which lesbian and gay may no longer offer. It has given space to a significant number of younger lesbians to break open the increasingly rigid marriage of identity, gender and sex acts. I have heard claims that queer speaks (at least possibilities) to some racial and ethnic groups often invisible within a pasty mainstream movement more than what they call the rigid, baggage-ridden categories of lesbian and gay.

I will continue to play around with queer on the side, even as I maintain my place in lesbiana. I will continue to assert that the lesbian feminism I care about is not one which clings tenaciously to the past or is exclusive, open only to those who tow some rigid, fundamentalist line. But I will argue passionately with queers of any variety that feminism is not a dirty or boring word and that queers' adherence to inclusion might include taking note of and learning from the very radical history and politics of different tendencies within lesbian feminism and gay liberation.

In the end my cry is: Resist either/or formulations. Challenge everything, including yourself. Fuck it – I want it both ways; that's the solution for us ambivalent types. For me that means more than embracing both queerness and lesbianism. It means maintaining a critical stance in relation to both and taking pleasure in having my cake and eating it and demanding to know what happened to the pretzels.

Where Does Political Correctness Come From? Does it Drop from the Sky?

– FROM *CULTURAL STUDIES: PLURALISM AND THEORY*, 1994

The Speaker's Anxiety

I awoke in the middle of the night in high anxiety. Those people who can't stand anything that they say smacks of political correctness were attacking me for being politically correct. I turned, only to find that those who are labelled politically correct were attacking me for abandoning them and the principles I say I believe in. In the morning I remain, as ever, ambivalent. Which is not to say I cannot take a passionate stand on anything. I can and I do. However, at the heart of so many matters I find the worm of ambivalence and contradiction (and therefore of excitement and possibility).

I think of the words 'politically correct', or 'PC' as we fondly call them. Where do correct ideas come from, after all? Please correct your mistakes. She is a very correct young lady. The House of Correction. I shall have to administer a corrective – politically or otherwise.

The word in itself is not an evil one although, coupled with politics, it has a tendency to become whatever its definer defines. I see the word 'correct' being uttered (oh my god) by older, white, stern men, by headmistresses, by old Maoists and by dominatrixes. I see the word 'correct' being spoken by others – angry, marginalized, self-righteous, desperate, frustrated.

I also see the words defused, used as an internal joke. PC then becomes shorthand for joking about someone's uptightness or is part of a more gossipy descriptive process as in, 'Oh my god, she's far too PC for you, honey.'

Let the Seriousness Begin

I believe there are two major realms of discourse around political correctness, separated by vast seas of difference, yet existing now simultaneously and uncomfortably linked. What first springs to mind is what has gone on in different radical groupings for at least the past twelve years, primarily in the USA and Britain. I know I'm not the only person with a history of involvement in radical politics of some kind who has also been involved in long, sometimes very bitter divisions and splits, loaded with accusations of political incorrectness. Or, interestingly, perhaps I have experienced these differences as transgressions from some assumed politically correct position.

The second scenario is a more recent one, dating from around the mid 1980s, and, in a more general sense, only from the past couple of years. In it, politically correct attitudes and demands are seen as wrecking devices, bent on destroying (witlessly, at times) decent, liberal society as we all know and love it. In this situation, PC is used as a term of abuse, something to be thrown at anyone who challenges the norms of society, whatever the hell they are.

Radical Comes First

My experience in British radical politics during the past twenty-five years, particularly in its feminist and lesbian manifestations, tells me that the notion of PC that I described first began to operate in the late 1970s and the early 1980s in countries that had spawned vital and dramatic movements for social change – springing from hitherto dispossessed or disadvantaged groups in those societies. Guess who's coming to dinner? Uppity black people, uppity women, uppity lesbians and gays. Plus a whole other range of social identities formulated in the ferment of the politics of the late 1960s and 1970s. Class, in its traditional Marxist sense, in its social-democratic guise, and in its newer ranking in identity politics, had to struggle to hold up its end, even though, when things got tough, class often emerged as a subtext in other struggles around identity.

At the points where these spontaneous movements became large and popular and stretched out to their boundaries as distinct social movements, at these points they began to throw up internal dissension, differences and divisions which were not necessarily overcome or resolved. They began to fracture and splinter. The social conditions that gave rise to their existence still remained – changed, modified certainly, but not overcome. Racism, institutional, individual, conscious and unconscious, still exists and the same is true in relation to sexism and heterosexism. After all, we know that popular movements do not a revolution make.

By the 1980s the vitality and optimism of those social movements had diminished considerably. The politics that were combative, confrontational and moved thousands of people to change their lives – not because they were told they must, but because they wanted to – began a descent into rhetoric. What had been played out as the creative, difficult parts of a movement now attached itself increasingly to rules and regulations. Many men and women still committed to change, still believing in the politics of a range of progressive movements, were left with the words (often the increasingly politically correct words) that reflected a recognition of difference.

Something to Hang on to in Uncertain Times
Looking back, it is tempting to tidy things up (it's often tempting to approve of one's own tidying impulses) and explain it all by saying that political correctness in motion is what we ended up with when various movements got wrecked on the impossibility of sustaining a totalizing politics based on a simplistic and one-levelled notion of identity. For instance, the fracturing of the women's movement in Britain since the early 1980s took place at the same time as (not because of) a growing recognition that women were – surprise, surprise! – not all of the middle-class, white, heavily Anglo-American, English or Australian variety. This was and is an important recognition, which came at the insistence of those who were excluded. But it also fostered a moralistic notion of hierarchies of oppression which involved demands to 'give up power'. It seemed as if everyone was desperate to get it all – correct! All feminists should get the correct line on a lengthening list of issues: race, ethnicity, class, age, religious background, sexuality, disability, looks, weight … one could go on. However, the story of PC is but a small part of a much larger saga regarding the development and history of radical politics of the late twentieth century.

Today, the wind seems to have gone out of many a PC sail. Take, for example, what was perceived as PC within the lesbian community in

London in the early 1980s and until the latter part of that decade. There were lesbians who were telling other lesbians what constituted correct lesbian sex, correct lesbian desire, correct lesbian fantasy, as well as dress and demeanour. Lezzo etiquette schools, here we come! However, during the past five years or so, there has been a defusing, a refusal to take on a particular role on becoming a lesbian or else a throwing-off of previously obeyed rules, and an oppositional embracing of plurality and exploration. This stance may present its own political and ethical problems. Certainly, all is not roses in the lesbian secret garden, but we won't go into that now.

A (Much) Later Conservative Beat-Up

In my second scenario, situated in the mainstream, labelling someone politically correct is now assumed to be a shorthand way of discrediting them, making them appear ludicrous, while conferring on the name-caller a trendy contemptuousness of such destructive and boring behaviour. The person labelled politically correct now conjures up a heady mix of silliness (usually when associated with what is designated as superficial language changes such as, yawn, 'chairpersons') and partially submerged danger, often in regard to old and valuable academic heritages which form part of the very underpinnings of our culture. These 'silly', 'dangerous' people include women and black people who dare to challenge the dominance of the old masters in the academy.

About a year ago, in a series called 'Fin de Siècle' on Channel 4 in Britain, four venerable, white, male writers were gathered together in the USA to talk about the current state of Western culture. These men sat around and worked themselves up into quite a lather about all the ways in which black people, women and gay men were inappropriately and dangerously challenging the achievements of the culture they represented. Okay, okay – but this restrained hysteria got to the point where they seemed to be suggesting that the very fabric of society as we know it was being rent, ripped to pieces, destroyed by these attacks.

It was left to Gore Vidal and Toni Morrison, filmed outside of the discussion, to point out that the people these men were so heatedly discussing did not hold power in their hands – were still, disproportionately, among the poor, the disadvantaged, the despised. The challenge to the hegemony of what is now rather predictably called 'dead white European men' is not a challenge coming from equals. Please! And if it is so offensive to describe writers as men, or white, or European, why is it perfectly fine to call female writers 'women writers', or writers who happen to be black, 'black writers'? And if such people can destroy the fabric of the nation, how come they can't get health insurance for the sixty million Americans who, over any two-year period, don't have it?

(Wilkins 1992). How come wealth has been upwardly redistributed in the USA? (Wilkins 1992). How come schools that service the most disadvantaged in this country are closed down? How come rape increases, seemingly everywhere? How come the murder of gay men and lesbians continues in the USA, in Australia, in England? How come unemployment among American black men has never been under 10 per cent between 1979 and the present, averaging 12.9 per cent over that time? (Wilkins 1992). And on and on and on.

It's Still Not Simple

Of course, the question arises and bedevils: within the mainstream scene, who decides when a challenge to the dominant culture is more than juvenile carping? When is it more than, or different from, the product of a disturbed mind, or of an egomaniac, or of an exponent of a specific, rigid righteousness? A book about censorship recently published by the American civil-libertarian, Nat Hentoff, is called *Free Speech for Me – But Not for Thee* (Hentoff 1992). A mainly admiring review in a recent *Guardian Weekly* illustrates the problems of a mono-level civil-libertarian position. He says,

> The extremes to which this enforced conformity has been taken at times transcend the merely ludicrous. Take, for example, Stanford University, which in recent years has made a practice of outdoing itself in lunacy upon lunacy. Advocates of a speech code there argued 'that the white majority, as a whole, should not be protected from hateful speech as much as groups that have suffered discrimination'. (Yardley 1992)

– with the result, according to one law professor, that 'calling a white a "honky" is not the same as calling a black a "nigger"'. Now, I don't believe speech codes actually change racist or sexist beliefs and I think it is far more likely that they get driven under the carpet, ready to emerge dirty and loathsome at a later point. However, I would maintain that for a white person to be called a honky in racist America is significantly different from and less serious than calling a black person a nigger! How can I or anyone else ignore the tragic weight of history in regard to race relations in the USA and act as if we were somehow equal participants in nasty name calling?

Another example comes from a recent issue of *Vanity Fair* in an article about the murder of a Boston feminist law professor and the resultant upheavals at Harvard Law School. The passage I'll quote concerns a so-called parody written by two male law undergrads in a Harvard Law School spoof magazine, *Law Revue*, about the dead Mary Joe Frug's last written article. Two famous law professors are lined up on opposite sides in the vicious wrangling. Alan Dershowitz is defending the students' actions and is quoted as saying,

The overreaction to the parody is a reflection of the power of women and blacks to define the content of what is politically correct and incorrect on college and law school campuses... Women and blacks are entirely free to attack white men ... in the most offensive of terms. Radical feminists can accuse all men of being rapists, and radical African-Americans can accuse all whites of being racists, without fear of discipline or rebuke. But even an unintentionally offensive parody of women or blacks provides the occasion for demanding the resignation of deans, the disciplining of students and an atmosphere reminiscent of McCarthyism. (Collier, 1992)

Well, my, my! It appears that these days women and black people are free to attack and upset – whom? We don't really need to be told, because 'they' are still the assumed starting point for any discussion on the state of the world. Women and black people and, in other discussions, gay men and lesbians and anyone else who happens to get named as 'other', must be defined and named, because they are still coming in from the margins. 'They' are still men who happen still (by coincidence?) to be mainly white and middle class, but, of course, it is boring to say such things these days. These unnamed men are free to continue to run and control things. It doesn't really seem such a good deal. It's enough to make a woman of the nineties consider radical feminism all over again.

Obviously, I am dismissive of this sort of mystification, the squeals of those who cannot believe their 'natural' place at the centre is being challenged by people who don't even necessarily want a piece of their botched-up cake. But what really gets up my nose is the absurd notion that we are all arguing equally in one big, neutral landscape.

Is Sitting on the Fence a Sexual Position?

Yet, in the radical groupings, past and present, that I call myself part of, I am as often the transgressor as the other way round. I have been labelled a pornographer by other lesbian feminists as recently as 1990. Within the feminist discourse about pornography, erotica, violence and rape, this was not meant as an exciting revelation. In the early 1980s I was once denounced as a Zionist apologist in heated debates going on about whether or not we at *Spare Rib* magazine should publish any letters from Jewish feminists critical of our coverage of the struggle in the Lebanon. From 1979 to 1984, I experienced tense, continuous, sharp conflicts at *Spare Rib* over issues of feminism, race, sexuality and language. At times, I have had to admit to myself painfully that some criticisms were, well, correct. At other times, I have felt absolutely awful, but determined that my position was not what was being claimed and that I would not accept responsibility, out of some sort of misguided guilt, for what I didn't espouse. And at other times, particularly over the pornography and censorship fights I have been involved in much more recently, I have felt the criticisms were a bunch of old codswallop, and even if it hurt or was difficult to be the object of so much ire and hate, it simply had to be lived through. I have never denied that the issues associated with politically correct or incorrect behaviour were not important ones.

These sorts of situations have occurred in many different settings and to a variety of people. However, political correctness did not invent the urge to impose a correct line in the countries on which I have been focusing. Moral imperatives have been around for a long, long time. I remember well the American phrase 'Right On!' and how not being right-on was tantamount to our current definition of PC.

As well, the accusation that political correctness is the suppression of free speech and even the desire to control ideas, has some truth in it, and I feel quite comfortable with that admission. The situations I have described, which developed within and between radical groups themselves, brought up heated discussions about the role, value and limitations of free speech, censorship, privilege and power and, very importantly, about how one engages in a non-coercive politics that successfully challenges and changes both individual and institutional reactionary ideas and practices at more than superficial levels. These are important arguments in which we should all be involved. However, accusations of political correctness flung about as a short cut to dismissing, devaluing and showing contempt for oppositional views aren't anything to do with championing free speech. They're designed to condone the status quo or even to roll the clock back on changes that have given some recognition to black people, women, gay men and lesbians.

Political correctness probably originated in the USA, coming out of radical political groupings in their own struggles to understand and incorporate an often simplistic notion of difference. It made its way across the water to Britain and found resonance in British radical politics. However, in the past few years there has been a lot of jostling going on and PC had almost become a joke about the past. Unfortunately, it didn't die; its limp and almost lifeless body was scooped up by the media, by opponents of radical politics, by angry and fearful men in variety of academic positions. It has now been recreated – a creature of the desperation of those who would like to be obeyed because they want things to remain as they have been or, at least, as they decide they should change. A minor sub-group within the PC play-off includes those, like Camille Paglia, who condescendingly attack those in their own subcultures whom they consider uncool or boring. In the USA, the majority of media attention to PC has played itself out primarily through attacks on black people, women, lesbians and gay men, especially as they raise their heads to challenge or complain. In England, PC has replaced the wonderful old chestnut, 'the loony' – left, lesbian, individual or institution – which had in its own time overtaken the venerable bearded weirdie. In Australia, the resonance of the PC furore, whether historical or current, may be next to nothing. I wonder how immune to the ideas underneath it Australians really are, and will watch its use or disuse here with interest.

References

Collier, P. (1992) 'Blood on the Charles'. *Vanity Fair*, October, pp. 58-67.
Wilkins, R. (1992) 'White Out'. *Mother Jones*, November/December, pp. 45-48.
Yardley, J. (1992) 'Among True Believers'. *Guardian Weekly*, 6 December.

Gender Transformations and Transsexuality
– FIRST PRESENTED AT A GIRLS IN NEW ALLIANCE (GINA) FORUM, MELBOURNE, 1994

Why is there such fear expressed about a few male to female trannys (MTF) who identify as lesbian and want to find a place within lesbian feminism? This group is a minority within a minority, a virtual handful who are drawn to lesbianism and feminism, a minuscule number who ironically are the ones most likely to have critiqued mainstream definitions of womanhood and found them wanting.

My own history in relation to trannys, if not dominated by fear, was peppered with confusion. I remember my first encounter with trans-sexuality came in London in the 1970s when a left-wing academic man became a woman and simply shifted her revolutionary certainties to women's liberation. I had all the stereotypical responses, from calling her him, to fascination, to utter incomprehension. Many of the women present at meetings Carol attended confided to each other with a thrill of nasty guilt that she behaved in a very male-defined way: articulate, confident in presenting political ideas, talking a lot. As I remember it, many of us tended to stumble, small voices expressing our lack of confidence. Carol was not one of us and the resentment simmered.

Since then, transsexuality has cropped up as an issue from time to time, sometimes centered on a particular person, sometimes around questions of inclusion or exclusion from feminist or lesbian events. But even if I could not fully accept or understand transsexuality in the seventies and into the eighties, I was shocked by the hatred and vehemence which greeted the presence of one or two lone transsexuals at various feminist social events in London of those decades. The time and energy this took was ludicrous; what was the big deal? The more women wound themselves up in righteous anger, the more they claimed the presence of one or two transsexuals made them do it. But I stood on the sides, despising those who whipped up fear, loathing and copious tears all in the name of feminism and women's safety, while only a few courageous women stood up and bravely criticized such behaviour. To little avail.

Today when there are more visible numbers of transsexuals I wonder if such people are more welcome in groups organized around gender and/or sexual identity? Are gay men opening their arms to FTM gays, for instance? Some straight men and women, attuned to tolerance, may find it easier to accept a transsexual, adding that person on to their list of hip sexual oddballs, a little weirder but in the same category as other sexual deviants, like your garden-variety gay, lesbian or bisexual. And what is it about gay men who adore drag queens but can't take FTM gays? Evidently lesbian unease with transsexuality is not unique. Some- one who upsets even deviant gender and sex expectations is upsetting to many people. Including myself, especially in relation to FTMs. I'm drawn to butch women but would be immensely saddened if a butch I fancied decided she wanted to be a man. I want butch to be complete. But so fucking what? Transsexuals aren't me nor do they make their decisions with me in mind.

Why are transsexuals perceived to be such a threat to lesbians? Sure, they are upsetting certainties about gender and sex, but they are not the only ones posing difficult questions for an older lesbian feminist politics. Some 'women born women' dykes have been doing that all on their own for at least fifteen years. It is therefore bizarre to find transsexuals accused of destroying the implied unity and stability of lesbianism when ongoing schisms and divisions have beset lesbian feminism and lesbian sub- cultures for years.

What is specifically weird is that lesbians are not getting over their agitation, nor exploring the roots of their exclusionary impulses and it is this I would like to dig into a bit more. Because what I have found is that the alien aspect of transsexual people has lessened considerably as I become accustomed to their difference. As I am pushed to question what the meaning is of the differences between me and other lesbians and then turn to transsexual lesbians, much of my unease begins to transform itself. I no longer see transsexuality as a monolithic whole, but rather as a series of questions, possibilities, problems – and as part of a wider sexual politics.

Focusing on 'the things that divide us', on difference, has been instructive as I try to unravel personal and political responses to trans- sexuality. I begin to see a larger picture, not a male conspiracy to infiltrate lesbian feminism or women's space (as if these were located on an illegally obtained secret map) but one much, much closer to home.

Divisions and differences, denunciations and tears, bitterness and betrayal are all words which have surfaced in ongoing fights between women around such things as class, race, sexual practice, attitudes to prostitution, pornography and censorship. These have existed for years in lesbian communities.

It is interesting that with all these bitter differences between 'proper' women that the difference between 'women born women' lesbians and trannys becomes loaded with so much meaning. Suddenly all these differences are projected onto the machiavellian tranny who becomes *the* disruptive (male) force, ruining 'our' definition of who 'we' are, creating divisions between us. Please. We've been doing just fine at excluding other 'female born women' dykes from various aspects of lesbian 'belonging' without any help from a few lesbian-identified trannys.

In the face of such an 'outsider', a group of lesbians organizing, for instance, a conference or lesbian project present themselves as a unitary, unified group. What else? 'Women born women' lesbians, that's what. This group is then threatened with disruption by an 'outside' force imbued with double-trouble otherness. In her human form this force has a medically constructed female body but her male past and privilege betray her as less than a 'real' woman. Keep her out, she is disruptive, how typically male! As the Draft Outline Paper for the Autonomous Lesbian Movement in Sydney stated in 1994, 'It is not just a matter of individual (MTF) trannys identifying as lesbians, because in so doing they redefine all lesbians, and put at risk the right of female-born lesbians to define their own way.' (Included in a pack of position papers soliciting support for a tranny-free Lesbian Space Project in Sydney. Sent out by Backwoodswimmin in New South Wales, 3 November 1994.)

The politics of difference which I have been interested in for years is about how identity politics in an unravelled world of meanings can come to grief and confusion. Identity politics have given voice and substance to varied women since the late 1960s. But fast on the heels of those fabulous feelings of identity certainty – women together, black people together, gays and lesbians together – came the discordant calls of deviation or distinction, leading in its most fractured and absurd stages to hierarchies of oppression which soared higher and higher as newly delineated differences were claimed and named. These explorations of difference, often based in the stark realities of material divisions of exploitation and power which previously had been minimalized within feminism, were necessary. A problem arises when difference becomes the be-all and end-all, frozen into rigid identities, no longer located within social relationships and the possibility of change or alliances – let alone any understanding of layers of identity within groups of people or individuals. Nuance? What's that?

But nothing stays the same. Within the fragmentation the possibility of connecting is recreated. What seems fearful or confusing today is not necessarily so tomorrow. Is the so-called maleness of the tranny something innate or so deeply ingrained by society she cannot change it? If an individual transsexual lesbian is behaving in a way which is perceived as negatively 'male' why can't she be challenged and asked to change her ways? The accusation of behaving in a male way is often cheap and lazy. A way of dismissing another woman whose politics or pleasures or style differ.

The irony of so-called MTF tranny male privilege is that many of them didn't get the male thing right anyway. Isn't it just as possible that MTF trannys didn't want to be men and therefore they might be keen to work on any oppressive aspects of maleness they still carry within them? In the current arguments transsexuals are often presented as being unable to transcend their essential 'maleness' or their male social conditioning. Think about it – if a transsexual women, lesbian or straight, fits other women's expectations of what a women (or lesbian) looks like, if she sounds and acts so much like people expect a woman to that no one guesses her secret – what would the 'truth' be? Would hearing the news that she was a transsexual suddenly change everything? And what would it mean about 'women born women' who don't look, or sound, or act like what is expected?

We who were born biologically female and became lesbians go against the tide of assumed heterosexuality and reinvent our lives in line with our lesbian desires. Some lesbians claim they always knew they were lesbians. Others of us say that we became lesbians. Why can't a transsexual say the same things?

I wonder if some lesbians, possibly even more than heterosexual women, can't believe that a man would genuinely want to be a woman or a lesbian? Certainly I've heard it said many times that snipping off the bits and balls doesn't 'make' a man a woman. She hasn't experienced all the years of being a woman in a male dominated society. While there is some truth in this, the underside of it is a rather bleak and one dimensional view of what it means to be a woman. It's almost as if those women are saying, 'You haven't paid your female oppression dues! We're a miserable and down-trodden lot. We're just beginning to have a bit of confidence, a dash of fun. How dare you jump on the lesbian bandwagon after a life of privilege.' I think to myself, is life really chock-a-block full of privilege for men who grow up different, outsiders, not at home with their maleness? Is life for those of us born biologically women within systems of male power *only* trench warfare and dismal oppression? For myself, the answer is no.

What do exclusion and inclusion mean for feminists – lesbian, bisexual or heterosexual – when regarding transsexuality? My perspective on transsexuality is based on daily life and politics – not the presumed hidden male agenda of the MTF tranny. I lean towards inclusion in the larger framework while recognizing that the nature of many groups is often exclusive. We make principled and practical decisions all the time which excludes some people. We do it in women-only groups or spaces and I'm not opposed to those.

The nature of many groups may be exclusive. Who would allow an overt racist to be a member of an anti-racist group? Why would a radical feminist study group invite a socialist feminist to join? Or an anti-lesbian porn action group open its doors to lesbians in favour of the development of lesbian porn? Or women meeting together to share their experiences of being HIV positive want HIV-negative women to join in? However, presumably any one of the above groups could expect to make use of an inclusive lesbian or women's space or make fruitful connections with women who don't share their specific experiences.

We would also feel suspicious of and angry at a group of women who excluded others on the basis of superiority which mimicked the dominant society. Would a group which advertised itself as excluding black women, or said 'for rich women only', or 'no ugly women need come', or 'no disabled welcome' be allowed to use a women's space? Obviously what we need is a clear appreciation of what makes certain exclusivities okay, or even excellent, and others nasty or downright reactionary. This is not as simple as it might first appear. Think transsexuals, think sm, think queer, think bisexual. What one women or group thinks is obvious, others think is unclear. Disputed behaviours, identities, desires.

The problem arises when the woman-only event, or lesbian space is billed as inclusive, or is presented as a community or public space for a wide range of women, implying that a variety of different groups or individuals more or less 'inclusive' or 'exclusive' can make use of it, and it turns out that in fact there was a hidden agenda which says, well, all women are welcome but some women aren't. In some ways the notion of the lesbian space or the women's centre is a holdover from the days when all lesbians or all women were proclaimed as happily co-exsisting under the wide-spread umbrella of inclusion based on a marginalised identity. We may know better these days but now inclusion is claimed on the basis of the right line or something very much like liberal tolerance – uneasy bed mates which sometimes lead to conflict.

Trouble may also arise when the space is claimed a 'safe' space for a particular group. For instance, one wonders how long it would be before some of the dykes supporting the exclusion of lesbian-identified trannys from the Sydney Lesbian Space Project decided it was not only transsexuals who made it 'unsafe' for 'real' lesbians? Obviously people want to be 'safe' – on the streets, at home or where they work. However, the wish to extend safety to mean protection from what offends you is fraught with problems, especially when the 'danger' is purportedly coming from within self-proclaimed identity groupings. Yet again it seems as if bondings brought about by a claimed identity are most susceptible to these problems. Safe space and exclusion often run in tandem. Lesbian pornography (or erotica) and lesbian sadomasochism are two phenomena from which opposing lesbians have demanded 'safe space'.

Up till now I've tried to look critically at what I see as current feminist and lesbian feminist reactions to the phenomena of transsexuality outside of academia and queer theory, concentrating mostly on male to female transsexuality. I've tried to implicate myself in this criticism and to indicate how we might move from a sort of formless, emotional ambivalence to a clearer appreciation of some of the issues involved.

I have moved considerably on the issue of transsexuality. My unease has shifted. That doesn't mean I have no worries or that I have abandoned all criticisms. For instance, my deep distrust of the medical profession and way in which transsexuals are by default medicalized, remains. I have been a women's health activist for over twenty years. I am not going to let go of my critical feminist framework when it comes to shrinks, surgeons, drugs, and their relationship to transsexuality.

I wish to support and open up space for transsexual lesbians in the places where this is possible *and* hold onto my critical stance towards aspects of transsexuality which worry me. In other words, I'm not going to be boxed into one corner or the other over this issue. I want all the corners covered and then everything that's not in the corners.

As someone involved for many years in a politics of health, particularly focusing on women, lesbians and sexual health, I cannot feel easy about the medicalization of gender and bodies. The person who decides to change his or her biological sex is inevitably going to consume large quantities of drugs and hormones, some of them for the rest of their lives. They may undergo surgical interventions which end up causing health problems. For twenty-five years I have been angry at the medical profession and drug companies for pushing hormones down women's throats. I don't trust the medical profession when it comes to declarations of safety. Why should I drop this stance when it comes to transsexuals? People will take hormones and make their own choices out of need, desperation, ignorance or approval and I accept that. It doesn't mean I shut up.

Furthermore, I would like to see more discussion outside of American author Janice Raymond's perspective of disapproval on transsexuality, but one which still looks at the way in which some aspects of transsexuality are medically and technologically driven. How much does the medical model actually create, or at least feed into, the desire to change one's body through medical intervention? There are a lot of bucks changing hands as we line up to have our breasts, necks, cunts and penises squeezed, reduced, augmented, cut off and sewed back up and on. It's not only transsexuals who want body changes.

My second area of concern is around identity and gender. If being female or male is socially constructed, why can't a man be more like a woman and vice versa, without taking off or adding on 'bits and boobs'? My worry is compounded when some transsexuals embrace gender stereotypes without a flicker of embarrassment. I'll give you an example: a few years ago, I saw a film about Max, a female-to-male transsexual living in San Francisco. Previously she was a lesbian – now he desires women.

The thing that disturbed me about Max was how biologically he saw things, and how quickly he claimed certain behaviours were testosterone driven. He walks down the street and ogles women and he understands that this is just a 'normal' male thing and gets off on it. He doesn't cry much anymore. He has lots of energy. A dyke around my age in London, a self-defined butch lesbian, wrote to me that when this film was shown she found it strange and upsetting how many of the younger women thought Max was so cool. She was distressed and enraged when several femmy acquaintances asked if she was thinking of taking the tranny FTM route. Wasn't it the next logical (fashionable?) step for such a consummate butch?

I am sick to death of hearing about testosterone whether it's from feminists like Germine Greer or Camille Paglia or from men themselves. Whatever testosterone may predispose men to feel, it does not drive their actual behaviour. Achieving a patchy beard or a deeper voice are not the same as becoming a snorting bull. Nor are women made or driven by their raging hormones. What on earth have we been talking and working on for the past quarter of a century anyway?

So why can't a man be more like a woman without resorting to hormones and surgery? The fluidity of gender and sex may be a goal but living it out in real life, in the real world is much more problematic. Today, for a man to feel and behave and look more like a woman and vice versa is not a simple thing, nor is it always possible.

Gender dysphoria can hardly be totally solved by a 'sex change' at a point when gender and sex disruption and uncertainty are so common. But *exactly* because of this confusion, transsexuality becomes one option. For those people who are profoundly and daily unhappy with their gender and their sexed body, *playing* around with gender and sex, with masculinity and femininity may not be enough. Nor is pinning hopes on some future utopia. Then the individual solution of transsexuality may offer a way out of the dilemma. Perhaps the differences between growing up female and growing up male in our societies mean that *within* women's subordination it is still easier to be masculine than for men to be feminine within male supremacy. Women don't have to be drag queens or kings in order to wear trousers or work boots or tuxedos.

I am opposed to the notion of a 'true essence', a kernel of my real being which resides deep inside and which, if searched for can be liberated, the essential me set free. If I am opposed to this formulation, how then could I jump wholeheartedly on the particular transsexual bandwagon (there are a growing number, after all) which pleads that these are women, or men, who have the misfortune to be trapped in the wrong body? What does this mean? That we are born miniature women or men? That being a woman is ahistorical, transcultural? Bullshit.

It is a puzzle why fervid followers of all things postmodern, where fluidity and change are paramount, are the keenest supporters of transsexuality which is about taking one fixed position and changing it to another, even if it's only about getting rid of penises or getting breasts. Transsexuality appears almost trendy in certain circles; an extreme performance style. Subverting binaries is how some like to put it, especially those who combine traditional aspects of the male and female body – get rid of the breasts but forgo the less-than-perfect, medically-constructed penis; get some breasts but keep the dick. The 'new' tranny, perhaps best personified by American performing artist and writer Kate Bornstein, is pushing past these categories and rejects defensiveness about her past. 'I'm not a woman the way you're a woman. It's just a fact.' Yes, and that is what I'm trying to contend with. But at the same time I'm not a woman in the same way as other biological women. Stubborn as it may appear, I still can't quite grasp why surgery and hormones are necessary in order to be a different sort of woman.

Let me say again, if being male or female, or a man or a woman, or masculine or feminine are all socially constructed categories, then why can't a man be more like a woman and vice versa, without the extremes of surgery and drugs? And again, no, I don't believe we all have a tiny little crystal of truth which remains with us all our lives, telling us we were always lesbian, or always straight, or always a person trapped in the wrong body. Some heterosexual women and lesbians clearly believe that the so-called maleness of the MTF tranny is something innate or so deeply ingrained by society that she cannot change it. By this logic, lesbians and feminists can go against the grain and defy a range of socially-determined expectations, but if you are transsexual you're either a dupe, a fake or an infiltration.

Many lesbians, individually or in groups, still long for and want a community which is not fractured or uncertain. But I don't believe that what can make it possible for us to be in the same room or work together on chosen projects or dance together, is that we are all 'womyn born womyn' – lesbians or heterosexuals or bisexuals. Looking critically and clearly at the emotions and meanings behind identity and difference and figuring out where they come from is the way forward. Then the over-burdened figure of the transsexual might be able to negotiate her place in a range of differences between lesbians.

I think I've come to a place in which I can acknowledge my initial unease when I meet a transsexual person and then get on with it. I have come to a place in which I know unease can be replaced by ease attached to a recognition of difference. In the past I have had similar experiences with other groups of people I was different from, including for a brief spell, lesbians. I am freed finally to make judgements on actions and politics, not identities.

The fluidity of gender and sex may be a goal but living it out in real life is much more problematic. I intend to hold on to my politics *and* allow people, real live, breathing, feeling people, including myself, to negotiate solutions which in years to come may not be necessary. This is not liberal, a sell-out or patronizing. The current crisis in gender and sex, of which transsexuality is a part, creates the possibility to think critically and creatively about sexual politics. It does not mean an emphasis on the exclusion of individuals from spaces when we should be exploring why so few women of any variety are drawn to them in the first place.

All identities are, to use the dreaded words again, at least partially socially constructed and none come imbued with a 'natural' politics. I will never have the experience of groups of people different from myself, nor will I be oppressed in ways in which some groups are. But in the end, I will judge on the politics and actions of a person or group of people with any identity, be they white lesbians, black lesbians, working-class lesbians, older lesbians, transsexual lesbians. Beyond that I will continue to wonder what the hell identity means, even as I partially define myself through it. And outside of that framework, I will be drawn to some individuals more than others for emotional reasons I may never fully understand.

In the not so distant past, I experienced ambivalence and unease when faced with transsexual lesbians. It was only when I was pushed to explore the roots of my *own* uneasy exclusionary impulses that these feelings began to dissolve. What I'm talking about is a problem for those of us who are or have been frightened of or antagonistic to transsexuality. It isn't a question of 'being kind to trannys', it's a question of opening up the baggage of our assumed gender certainties.

Postscript
My disquiet about FTM transsexuals has not abated. To be blunt, I despise some of the rhetoric coming out of the newer FTM interviews and gossip I have heard since the GINA forum. Whereas I can accept an

MTF tranny wanting to be a lesbian feminist, I have great difficulty with the female-to-male former lesbians who utter sexist banalities and pontificate on what it means to be male in ridiculously stereotyped tones. The recent recorded voices of lesbians who have become men are not reassuring to me, with their self-satisfied tales of testosterone-driven blokish behaviour.

Last year Cherry Smyth wrote about the new transgendered lesbians in San Francisco ('What Makes a Man?' *Attitude*). Throughout the article Jordy, Stafford, Texas, Shadow, David and others tell us proudly of manipulating their bodies and emotions with testosterone. (The only thing they don't claim is that they've got smarter. Thank god.) Although Cherry Smyth draws out some of the contradictions from her subjects' assertions, she is a too generous presenter. Her interviewees are allowed to mouth the wearying downward spiral of a popularized postmodernism. From the high point of Judith Butler's gender as performance theoretical position, through Kate Bornstein's virtual performances, we finally end at the utterly threadbare where Texas drawls out that, 'We all perform gender everyday and my decision to go a step further was to stretch the limits of what is a dyke by doing this performance.' Oh really?

Some time later, I was leafing through one of my favourite Australian magazines (*HQ* July/Aug 1995) and guess what? There was an article ('Girl Meets Boy') about Stafford and Jordy, now joined by Frankie. In this article the interviewees say more overtly worrying things. Frankie: whose most exciting discovery is that men have '… got a lot more strength. They can run longer. I need about an hour less sleep now and have so much more basic energy. Colours are brighter, things are more three-dimensional. I feel more in the world than I used to.' Stafford: 'I used to cry when I read the newspaper over both sad or happy things. Now I *can't* cry … Now I'm driven by more physical urges than emotional ones.' The author goes on to say that 'Stafford is much more aggressive than she used to be and is quicker to anger'.

In a 1994 article in the lesbian and gay newspaper *The Melbourne Star Observer* ('Boys Will Be Boys Will Be …', Bridget Haire, 31 March 1994), Dale enthuses about energy: 'And energy! Now I only need to sleep for a few hours a night.' What is this about sleep? Come on, guys. Go tell it to the exhausted male toilers of the world. Tell it to the women who work long hours in the factory and come home to work half way through the night for their families – while they sleep.

What really gets my ire up though is the sexual nirvana these performers are all so surprised by and eager to explain testosteronally. Stafford went from 'wanting sex once a week to having to jerk off three or four times a day and I thought it was great'. And Jordy comes on a bit shy when she says, 'Although when I'm on my bicycle and I get a spontaneous hard-on in traffic it can be a bit distracting.' But in Cherry Smyth's article, Jordy explains that 'she/he/it' 'isn't trying to turn into a man'. The hard-on Jordy described is then a hormonally enlarged *clitoris*. Boys, where were you when you were girls?

Like Max earlier, Frankie goes the furthest of this new crop of 'gender performers': 'I'm a feminist, but I can really understand and empathize with teenage boys and the crazy things they do, like drive fast and rape girls.' Well, fuck that, Frankie. I suppose that there's a good possibility that at least half of what these particular transgendered FTM lads are saying is fantasy. What irritates and angers the most is the disingenuous way they are all so bloody unreflective; one is tempted to put it down to unusual thickness but that's the easy way out. I find myself unfashionably polarized – sympathetic to MTF lesbians who want a bit of acceptance in whatever lesbian and/or feminist community will open its doors to them and antagonistic to the publicized voices (I'm sure there are other FTMs around with alternative voices – where are they?) of the 'trendy' lesbians who take testosterone and 'perform' masculinity in an unimaginative and fairly unappealing way.

Whether or not this is simply an unreconstructed backward voice or maybe an indication that all tranny changes are not equal, I don't know. But there you are. Fence time again.

PART FOUR

The Sexually Explicit Bits

A lot of the work I do now involves talking about sex and sexual identities. I do training and workshops on health education and HIV/AIDS for a range of groups, including nurses, nursing students, undergraduate women's groups, lesbian groups, sexual health centres and groups within various lesbian sub-cultures. Sometimes I come in via HIV/AIDS and sometimes through focusing on sexuality. One of my aims is to break through professional walls of 'objectivity' around sexual practices. Another is to address people's ambivalences, silences, and embarrassments about sex. So much sex talk to so many people. But I continue to enjoy it. Sometimes more consistently than sex itself. I love it when initial tension or suspicion is defused by a bout of laughter, or when a young woman is given support and validation after getting up the nerve to ask an explicit question.

While working at *Spare Rib* a few of us tried to get a series of articles going which examined sex in long-term relationships. We put out a call in the magazine's pages and in poured women's writing. Almost all were from lesbians; we rifled through submissions to locate the heterosexuals. There were hardly any. We hadn't defined long-term in the notice. We were amused and startled by the number of lesbians who wrote telling us about their long-term liaisons – three months, six months, a year. It wasn't what we had in mind but maybe we weren't in touch with these real-life young dykes. The project foundered.

A few years after I arrived at Sheba Feminist Publishers, we decided to pull together our own anthology of lesbian erotic writing. We often talked about sex – personally and in relation to what we wanted to read and what we might publish – so we were all enthusiastic about the project and it very quickly became a collective baby.

That book was *Serious Pleasure: Lesbian Erotic Stories and Poetry*, published in 1989, and was followed the next year by *More Serious Pleasure*. In the first book we wrote a long introduction:

> Was the aim of a 'good' erotic story to explore a crucial dimension of lesbian identity in a revealing, yet sensitive way or was the aim to titillate, turn on, lead to masturbation or making love with someone? Our discussions were endless. We did not reach a conclusion, but decided that the two aims could co-exist. Curling up with a well-crafted, imaginative, innovative lesbian novel or short story which deals with sex can inform

our identity as lesbians, and bring us to a new place in our creative lives. At the same time, it can move us sexually. Getting into a story whose primary aim is to arouse us sexually is neither wrong, nor necessarily separate from any other aim of fiction.

We do not expect every lesbian to like, approve of, or be driven to having sex by every story in this book. Some are about rough sex, some about soft and gentle encounters, some entertain fantasies which we yearn for and others we fear may become a reality. Some of us like both these facets in our sexual lives, others like one or the other, some may not like either, but how are we to know if such stories do not exist?

We see the collection as representing the diversity not only of our experiences and histories but of our desires and sexual practices. We do not label this approach liberal; the differences within *Serious Pleasure* are framed by a feminist perspective which is informed by a radical approach to the politics of sex, race, class and culture. It is a perspective which celebrates the specificity of lesbian sexuality but does not see that sexuality as cut off from the rest of the world. We believe it is crucial for us to encompass all aspects of our sexual needs/desires, however contradictory they may seem to us, as well as all the other aspects of our lives which inform the very way in which we deal with the world and each other.

Perhaps the precise way in which we worded this introduction might change were we writing it today but I believe that many of the sentiments would be the same.

I have a story in *Serious Pleasure* – the first short erotic story I had ever written. I submitted it under a pseudonym because I didn't want my workmates to feel under any pressure to accept it because I was a colleague and friend. When it was shortlisted and then accepted I was relieved and nervous. Should I publish it under my real name? Would readers wonder if I got into the book because of working at Sheba? We decided to leave the *nom de plume* and escape the complications.

I have to admit I was relieved. What would readers or reviewers think? I wasn't afraid to take an open stand on political and theoretical debates about erotica, lesbian sexuality, or censorship, but fiction was a different story. It had been surprising to me what a turn-on it was to write about sex, but was this because it felt daring to create a story about sex? How could I judge the actual writing?

Serious Pleasure was a Sheba hit. The financial success of both the erotica books was greater than any other work of fiction we published and admired. This included books by Audre Lorde, bell hooks, Sarah Schulman, or any of our anthologies. It's a strange world and sex sells. Sheba's erotica was a first in Britain and compared with some of the American collections we had looked at the *Serious Pleasure* books were sophisticated and included some excellent writers. In the end it seemed that many lesbians wanted to read overtly sexual stories, were eager for writing which attempted to articulate what had been left up to male porn or the imagination for so long.

The first time I read explicitly sexual stories by lesbians I was turned on simply by the fact that they were there. Sadly this first cheap thrill soon lessened. After reading hundreds of erotic short stories, some in other anthologies, even more submitted to Sheba for our collections, I know in order to move me, an erotic story has to be more than permutations of limbs, lips, objects and orifices coming together. The imagery has to convince and progress beyond cliché. There is nothing wrong with the imagery of fruit, flowers, water, waves and shells but if they are crutches I am bored by them. I am much more interested in the *tension* between awkward limbs, recalcitrant desires and pounding waves or lush fruit.

Reading, writing and publishing lesbian erotica did not make it crystal clear what the division between erotica and porn was. It did lead me to read more selectively. I grew bored with erotica or porn with nothing else going for it except transgression. I certainly didn't feel motivated to produce harder core material or to read it either. But I wasn't bored with sex or writing about it. Although some lesbians maintain there is a discernible division between what celebrates the beauty of women's bodies or sex and what objectifies and arouses, I have never thought that the best erotic or pornographic writing abandoned either possibility.

Dorothy Allison, in her most recent book of essays, *Skin*, writes, 'We have so may clichés in the way, only a few of which have any shared sexual power.' She continues,

> Even those who want to do something original and important with our work on sexuality have to address the fact that most people think about sex in very, very traditional terms, in scenarios from old movies and bad novels, in the fetishized language of the most sexist pornography. That stuff is there to be used or reframed, but it cannot be ignored.

The debate about porn and erotica goes on and women glare angrily at each other across the chasms between them. The accusations that Sheba produced porn, which we dressed up and tried to make acceptable by the use of the word erotica, illustrates the certainty some lesbians have about what porn is. Some lesbian feminists have given up trying to distinguish between the two – they reason that it is often a subjective judgement which labels one representation porn and another erotica. A Canadian photographic show that included a range of pictures of women, together, separate, partly clothed, naked, in literal and abstract images, asked viewers, 'Where do *you* draw the line?' The responses were incredibly diverse. I continue to be interested in asking, Where do you draw the line? What is acceptable to you? Does it change according to time and circumstance?

I am keenly aware that there is a lesbian-feminist position which claims it knows what is porn and what isn't. While sex can be 'logically' situated in fiction or film, 'the pornographic materials are the ones whose whole purpose is to manipulate me into a state of arousal, not to tell me anything, but to make me feel or do something': so writes D. A. Clarke in 'Consuming Passions: Some Thoughts on History, Sex, and Free Enterprise' (*Unleashing Feminism*, I. Reti (ed.) HerBooks, 1995). In this view, objectification is a male domain and part of male domination; domination and subordination is the name of the game under 'hetero-patriarchy', and the eroticization of subordination is the conspiratorial way we women are kept enslaved and asking for more. It must be wiped out in fantasy, fiction and daily life.

There are other honourable lesbian-feminist positions on this subject which are quite different. Carole Vance wrote in the early 1980s in her book, *Pleasure and Danger*, 'If we want to study sexuality, we need more information about individual responses to symbol and image. We need to know what the viewer brings with her to make an interpretation: a cultural frame, resonances, connections, and personal experiences.' She warns us about the dangers of limiting the discussion on sex and sexuality. 'There is a very fine line between talking about sex and setting norms ...' and goes on to suggest that, 'Being a sex radical at this time, as at most, is less a matter of what you do, and more a matter of what you are willing to think, entertain, and question.'

We need to debate, clarify and sharpen our sexual politics. Easy answers which include glib assertions about free choice and consent aren't good enough. What do these mean in a society in which choice is too often a sick joke, in which structures of inequality and exploitation exist? What does consent mean when two or more people do not always come together as equals?

However, rather than throw the baby out with the bath water and declare that sex is impossible except in the confines of 'eroticized equality', I would prefer to enter the fray, try to protect and parade, fuck and fight, lust and laugh.

I have included two pieces in this chapter which arise from living in the time of AIDS. The first was included in a book that Kate Thomson and I edited called *Positively Women – Living with AIDS*. I wanted to set safer sex within a much broader framework than the grid of high risk, low risk, no risk sexual practices. I hoped to engage women emotionally, not only with information.

The second is from a short book Pratibha Parmar and I wrote. *Lesbians Talk (Safer) Sex* was meant to gather together the bits and pieces of information about lesbians and HIV which were scattered all over the place and try to make sense of them. But we also wanted to make lesbian sexuality and sexual practices the underpinning for the discussion of the specifics of HIV. Therefore we included opening and inclusive sections on sex which we hoped would be a million miles away from any medicalizing or sex manual approach. I have included several sex sections from the book.

Pratibha and I wrote about lesbians and HIV in 1992. Controversy raged in certain circles about the riskiness of sex between women in regard to transmission. If vaguely worried, the majority of lesbians were untouched by the sound and fury of these debates. This situation continues today. Together Pratibha and I declared ourselves agnostics, doubtful that *sexual* transmission of HIV between lesbians was likely, at the same time we emphasized that lesbians were at risk through injecting drug use or from sleeping with infected men. Today, I find the agnostic position useful – after all, in a situation in which uncertainty is the byword it's not easy to write rules in stone – but I am now more provocative when I argue about the incredibly low to non-existent risk of women-to-women sex. Today it's as if there's a puzzle I can't quite figure out: why are the campaigners for lesbian safe sex (low risk doesn't mean no risk, they would say) so wedded to a crusade to assert lesbian sexual risk? Why isn't the agnostic's position attractive to more lesbian AIDS activists.

Finally I have chosen an unpublished piece on anal sex for this section. Two of my friends and I had the idea of a sex book for women which would weave safer sex discussions and information into the text. We wanted it to be sex positive and accessible. Oriented to a spectrum of sexual identities and practices and therefore inclusive. Non-judgmental but willing to take on belief systems. Admitting of the pleasures *and* pains of sex and relationships of all sorts. It was one of those halfway sensible and halfway unrealistic projects which finally settled into dusty files. The anal sex piece is from one of those files and I've dusted it off a bit. But I'm not sure. The tone is perilously close to the jollying, condescending sex manual style we hoped to avoid. In the past four or five years, anal sex has lost some of its hidden nature. Sometimes it seems like it's become the newest lesbian hot sex indicator in books and articles. Perhaps it would be more useful to produce something on anal health?

We need to have the courage to let a 100 flowers bloom in order to be able to have the kinds of arguments and discussions which would inform a future politics of sexuality, including the writing of erotica or porn by lesbians for lesbians. We need to unlock our guilt and fear and ambivalences over our desires, our fantasies and our actual sexual practices and set them in the light of the kinds of lives we lead everyday. In this way we can most effectively understand AIDS. Most, if not all of us, are attempting to be good and strong people. Most, if not all of us, try to treat our lovers with respect and equality. While our sexual desires and practices are certainly not separate from the rest of our lives or exempt from political demands, they are different from other areas of our lives. Rather than fear exploring our sex lives because of what we might find – sex lives easily kept secret from the rest of the world or even lied about – why don't we explode the silence? Is it really so dangerous, what we are dreaming about? Don't we deserve pleasure?

Ambivalence: A Short Story

– FIRST PUBLISHED IN *SERIOUS PLEASURE*, 1989, UNDER THE
NON-DE-PLUME, TINA BAYS

I was faced with having to make a choice. I didn't want to. I wanted, well, who knows what. That ambivalent desire to have no choice but to be overcome, not in control. A state I might yearn for in imagination but rebel against in practice. If, of course, I got the chance. Anyway it gripped me; I was head over heels in desire. Nothing was spoken. I read my fantasies onto her. She looked like my desires.

We met at social occasions from time to time and the peripheries of our political lives as lesbians intersected provocatively. Between times, I built my treasure house of fantasies. I didn't know her.

During that summer, away from cool days and colder nights of England, I slept by myself in a hot corner room in a house by the sea. Late at night, lying in bed, I would luxuriate in the heat, in my aloneness, in the muffled sound of the fog horn. I loved being there with the sea smells and sounds insinuating themselves into the hot, slightly claustrophobic room. No breeze those nights to stir the faded curtains or disturb the rising smoke from my cigarettes.

I would find myself thinking of her. An image, a feeling, merging into a fantasy. I was never aware until too late of what was happening. She made me do things; the confidence and certainty in her look, her voice, her actions allowed no compromises. And oh, how she wanted me! Any uncertainties about my desirability (and believe me, I had them) were reduced to trivia in the face of that desire. How my wetness was witness to the power of my fantasies.

It bemused me. I wasn't obsessed. I interacted as usual with friends and family, read, enjoyed food, went swimming and generally relaxed. But slowly in the summer evenings, alone, I filled my treasure house.

Grey, green London – home, away forever from home. Country girl in love with the city. I settle back into the familiar, back in the life. By contrived chance our lives begin to intersect again and much to my delight and terror there seems to be a different note of recognition in her eyes. Is something going on? I'm nervous of imagining that she really might have feelings for me. What if I'm wrong? What do I do about this? What might happen in a transfer from fantasy to reality?

Weeks later, walking together after a birthday meal for a mutual friend, it feels like a never-ending ritual dance. I feel attuned to her essence – me who sneers at any notion of essences. I brush aside a voice of warning. Too late; I slide in and out of physical encounters even though we never touch. The space divides and yet connects me to her. I'm almost breathless with sexual longing and tension. Surely it takes two to generate this much feeling. I want it this way forever. I want to make love without touching. I'm dying to touch. I want to back off, forget it, forget it. I want to stop her in her tracks, reach out, slowly draw her head to mine and stand there, forever, breathing her in. The ambivalence delights and frustrates me. In fact I'm already set on breaking it down. I may regret my impatience.

What patterns are being enacted here? What predictable patterns played out? I want to understand *and* to be out of control – irreconcilable. My gut heaves, my cunt is alive. I'm soaking wet, I'm dazed. I want my breasts touched, my nipples teased, then hard, harder, please harder, bite me, bite me. I want to kiss, brush her lips, trace her face, dive my fingers into her hair, run them from the crown back, then pull slowly out through thick, dark tangled curls.

I hear her voice talking as we walk: I nod, hmmm, but I'm off and away, out of control and nobody knows. I want to push her into a deep doorway, kiss her throat as I hold her head against the solid wood, slowly and with pressure run my fingers between her breasts, in turn stroke up and brush each nipple tracing circles, pulling out, then greedy cup hard, and still hold her pinned to the dark door as cars and people pass us by. I want to put her against that door, sink to my knees in front of her, magically manoeuvre her smart butch trousers down, eat her through her knickers, then hold onto her hips and pull the cloth down until she's naked from the waist to where her clothing entangles and holds her ankles. I want to tongue the soft skin of her thighs, deliberately run a line with my fingers right down her middle from belly to the top of springy, soft pubic hair, on to tease her clit and continue to the radiating heat and wetness of her cunt.

I want to force her legs apart, knowing she can't move far, open her lips, pull her towards my mouth. I want to hear her moaning for it, before I taste her, hungry with my tongue, tease round her cunt, run my fingers in circles around it, until finally, pulling her towards me with one hand holding her lovely arse, I enter her slowly as she cries out,

'Yes, more!'

Then me on my knees fucking her, licking and sucking her with passion and skill, my own cunt opening and burning, until she buckles with orgasm, stifling her cries for fear we'll be seen.

All this and we're still walking. How am I walking? In real life, late at night on a seedy street in London, I'm on the verge of coming. The object of my desire, whose fantasy fuck has left me wet and longing, stops to make a point. This real and flawed object has caught me miles away. Should I take her hand? I'm blushing; does she feel it? Jesus, does she guess? Now there's silence and I feel as if all sorts of sexual words and sounds are going to force their way into articulation. God, this must be so obvious to her. How could I feel such a current if it's not reciprocated? Do I really want reciprocation?

My lips are sealed. We walk on, refer to the burdens of work, say our goodbyes, and part at the tube to head off in different directions. Is this a courtship? Her separateness excites me. It's what attracts me and I embroider impossible desires onto her. I'm waiting for her to make a move. I don't know her.

Sex in Difficult Times

– FROM *POSITIVELY WOMEN*, 1992

'It isn't what you do, it's the way that you do it.'

'If sex is so simple, how come we worry about it all the time?'

'Safer sex, huh! I had problems getting my boyfriend to take birth control seriously, and his attitude about HIV doesn't seem very different.'

This is a chapter about women and sex. It isn't only about safer sex. How can we deal with safer sex when there is so much confusion, fear of rejection and lack of confidence about sex in general? All this without even taking the virus into account; and when we do take the virus into account, phew! There's stigma and secrecy and fear of death. We have to begin to open up and to contemplate the many layers of influences which affect how we feel sexually, how we see ourselves in the world sexually (wherever we happen to be in it), how we do and don't manage to acknowledge and negotiate the kinds of sexual relationships we want, and how we can begin to sort out our positions as women in a world which is still largely male-dominated.

Listen, we fall in love, we have sexual desires, we want sexual satisfaction, and we want to please our lovers. Many of us want to be with men, some of us want women, and others fancy both sexes. Many of us have discovered the delights of pleasuring ourselves through masturbation. But in different ways, within different contexts, most of us at some point in our lives are caught up in sexual attractions or pressures and the reality of having sex with someone else. If someone is ill or feeling sick, sex may be the last thing on their mind, but they may regret the loss of that possibility, even if it is only temporary. There are times as well, when we may have no desire for sex of any kind. Many women have discovered that in celibacy they found peace and relief at being out of the domain of sexual tension and expectation. Their lives have been as rich and varied as anyone else's.

It's only if sex is regarded as a variety of sexual acts that we can approach the subject in a relatively straightforward way. Even if that were possible, difficulties remain. After all, what is sex? What is 'real' sex? When sex between a man and a woman is being described, as in 'they had sex', whose sexual pleasure is being described? Is it the man's orgasm, achieved through intercourse, which defines having sex? What about kissing and stroking? Clitoral stimulation? Penetration with fingers? Oral sex? Is it 'real' sex if the woman doesn't have an orgasm? Is it 'real' sex if the woman or the man has an orgasm through any other means except penetration? Do orgasms matter? Does penetration matter to all women? Do two women making love have 'real' sex? It's time that women finally changed the definitions of sex altogether – 'real' sex is what brings mutual pleasure, full stop.

Some of us may know what we like, or wish we could try out or discover in practice. If we are heterosexual, penetration may not be our main aim. Even then, we may still believe that fucking is the only 'real' sex. For so long everything else has been described as foreplay that even if we're the lucky recipients of it and know that it can be, or is, the most pleasurable aspect of sex (and perhaps the only way we can get orgasms), somehow we feel it isn't as good as penetration. Of course, none of this means that many women don't love penetration, love fucking. Of course they do, but that doesn't invalidate the equally large number of women who don't, or the even larger numbers who value a whole variety of sexual acts equally, or who like one thing one time, and another the next time. Lots of women know this is a ridiculous state of affairs but because heterosexual women's desires are obviously intertwined with men, and because so many men are trapped in a mind-and-body set which only really values fucking, we go along with it.

Why do women go along with it? At the risk of sounding like an old record, a lot of it is because men still call the tune. Women may have come a long way in discarding feelings of inadequacy and second-rate status in relation to men, but many still feel vulnerable and lack confidence in sexual matters. This pattern of thought isn't only an attitude, it accurately reflects the power and prestige men still hold relative to women in our society.

But we don't have to be defined as victims of forces outside ourselves. Even if it's difficult, even if we have mixed feelings, women can make changes in their lives, including their sexual lives. Let's set the record straight. Sex, between anybody, may include penetration, whether it's with a penis, fingers, a dildo, or a nice fresh (and washed) cucumber. Penetration itself has many different moods, from sweaty lust, to deliberate, skilled thrusts. But sex is also touching, soft with gentle fingers, firm and holding, hard and pushing, squeezing. It's kissing, sweet, long, probing, feathery, wet, demanding and hungry. It's using lips and tongue on the body, tracing paths on backs, inside thighs, across an instep, on nipples. It's blowing breath on genitals, brushing clits, sucking and stroking with mouth and tongue, pushing fingers into cunts, holding pricks in mouths, tickling balls with fingernails. Sex is teasing around arseholes, it's sucking nipples and pressing and kissing and lying on top, and rolling around, and using sex toys like vibrators.

Sex is getting turned on – before, during, again. It may include having orgasms – sometimes, often, rarely. It's hundreds of variations, or only a few. It's passionate and intense, hilarious, boring, disastrous, satisfying, clumsy, expert, wanted, ordinary. It's simple, tried and true, or complicated and brand new. It's experimental, it's comfortable, it's scary, it's with a new partner, or an old love. It happens when you're young, middle-aged, old. It happens between men and women, women and women, men and men, and let's not forget, on your own. It has different boundaries and rules attached to it in different cultures and different historical times. It is not separate from the rest of our lives or concerns. We see it around us constantly, we read about it, we talk about it. And yet it remains, for the most part, an act between two people, carried out in private.

Yes, we talk about sex: with our closest friends, maybe to our doctor. But not very often with our partner. When we're girls and the talking could really help exploration, or the use of birth control, or the drawing of boundaries, or the use of safer sex, it's difficult. Boys still seem to think that the girl who talks about sex before it happens, expects it to happen. Therefore she's a slut. They think, if she's prepared and carrying a condom, then she must plan to have sex – with me! Clearly we need to change a lot more than helping girls feel more confident about negotiating safer sex!

What this illustrates is that even if we're grown-up women, sex doesn't happen in a vacuum. We are people who live in the world, who have histories, aspirations and dreams, and who experience contradictions in our lives. And so do our partners. Our desires do not spring, ready made, from our genitals. They are complicated things, not reducible to so-called 'natural' drives.

Which brings us to safer sex. We all know about the 'rules' of safer sex. They are on one level very simple. No exchange of bodily fluids or blood in which the HIV virus may be present. In sexual terms this is most important when considering semen. The ground rule of safer sex is no semen in the vagina or anus. Everything else is more or less open to interpretation or individual decisions. Of course the virus is present in other bodily fluids, including vaginal fluids, but the highest concentration is in semen and blood. But wait a minute: what about everything we've been talking about – the difficulties of reducing sex to straightforward physical acts, the problems of teasing sex out from other layers of influence and constraint? The complexity of relationships, especially with men? Is it true that everyone, HIV positive or not, should be practising safer sex? If sex is more than fucking, if 'real' sex is a variety of sexual activities, what about those activities? And what about the possibility of transmission of the virus from vaginal fluids?

All of us, to a greater or lesser degree, have problems about safer sex, and that includes positive women. Those women who are not positive, or do not know their status, may think of safer sex in terms of remaining free of the virus, but in our sexual relationships we are all subject to fears of rejection, fears of labelling or stigmatizing, and desires for intimacy and pleasure. If heterosexual, we have to negotiate our sexual relationships through sexism, and assumptions about women, whether we are positive or not, and this isn't always easy. It's important to realize too, that even if a man is the most tender, understanding person in the world, and sees his female partner as equal, the pervasiveness of sexual inequality is such that the woman may still fear rejection or difficulty if she insists on safer sex.

I've been concentrating on the complexity of sex so much because it's been far too simplified in so much safer sex material. When it turns out not to be such a simple task, we may feel that we've failed. We may give up, or give up sex, or feel guilty and bad if we haven't managed it 100 per cent of the time. What is needed is some understanding and acceptance of the complexity of the different situations we find ourselves in, and the knowledge that if we fail from time to time, we are not bad, and we can help ourselves to make safer choices the next time. This is true, no matter what our HIV status is.

Of course it is particularly important that positive women explore their own situations, perhaps with other positive women and with their partners. Positive women do not turn into saints the minute they know they are positive. Why should anyone expect that? But positive women are living with HIV, and therefore, by that very fact, living with the reality in all aspects of their lives. Positive women may have heightened fears of rejection by their partners, and their partners may be ambiguous about not wanting to reject their positive lover. That may become symbolized by a refusal to wear a condom. They may even have a romantic urge to share the risks with her. Positive women also have to take on board the knowledge that to become re-infected with the HIV virus could worsen their health. The question of pregnancy is also important to some positive women. A climate which assumes positive women should not have a baby, even though the risk of passing the virus to the baby is lower than originally thought, means that those women who desperately want one have few recourses other than unprotected sex with a man.

Too often the assumption made by heterosexuals who are not positive, or do not know their status, is that all will be fine if they avoid having sex with positive people. This is off beam in a number of ways. In the first place, there are positive people who do not know their status. Positive people are ordinary people; it's ridiculous to think that you can tell that someone is positive by looking at them. In the second place, what does this say about positive people? That they are unworthy of being fancied? Or loved? Of course they are worthy of both. Also HIV is a weak virus. It is a dangerous virus when it finds a home, but it can be quite easily shut out by, yes, practising safer sex, and not sharing injecting equipment when using drugs intravenously. By practising the ground rules of safer sex, no semen in the vagina or anus, which obviously means that the man should use an approved variety of condom every time he penetrates a woman vaginally or anally, the risks of transmission of the virus from a man to a woman or a woman to a man, will be hugely reduced.

As far as deciding whether or not you need to use safer sex, it is absolutely important to be 100 per cent certain that you can and do communicate honestly and clearly with your lover, and that it is reciprocated. Can you talk honestly and openly about your sexual and drug-related histories covering the past ten years or more? Do you believe your partner can? These are difficult questions to weigh up and it seems reasonable to at least take on safer sex as an important necessity in any new relationship. How often do people know each other inside out before they have sex together? How often do established relationships harbour sexual secrets, or hidden pasts? Taking on these complexities is an essential part of making decisions about safer sex, whoever you are.

There are disagreements about what constitutes the practice of safer sex and all the other sexual activities which people can and do explore. Information is contradictory, opinions range far and wide, new knowledge brings new guidelines and advice. And emotions are not always in tune with knowledge – sometimes a positive person may be scared of kissing, even though she knows it is not a risky activity, because she's frightened of passing the virus on, and thinks, 'What if …' The lover, who is not positive, may harbour fears of kissing, with similar knowledge of its lack of danger, because of a persistent voice saying, 'What if they're wrong and it can happen this way?' These feelings are understandable but they can change. Our feelings don't remain static and if they're not shoved under the carpet, ease can replace unease.

What are the current guidelines on safer sex and non-penetrative sexual activities? Again, we have to understand that nothing is fully understood and different 'experts' give different advice. We may desperately want total answers but they don't always exist. Learning to live with an element of uncertainty about HIV transmission is part of living in the time of AIDS, but uncertainty is not a new phenomenon. We live with uncertainty about other aspects of our lives. For up-to-date guidelines we have to get current advice and remember that because HIV and AIDS are not understood in any complete way, we have to look to new information as it is available and then try to build our own frame-work in which to fit the advice. This is the difficult part. No one can tell us for sure exactly what is and isn't safe apart from unprotected fucking in the vagina or anus.

Oral sex is a case in point. Lots of women adore getting oral sex. Is it risky? Advice directed at heterosexual women sometimes doesn't even mention it, and when it does, rarely in detail. Some advice indicates that it is a very low risk sexual practice. However, some lesbians and heterosexual women feel strongly that oral sex is a real and present risk, although not as risky as unprotected penile penetration, and that it is possible to transmit the virus through licking and sucking a woman's clitoris and vaginal area. Other women believe oral sex is so close to being totally safe that no one should be frightened of it. Most suggest that you should abstain from oral sex if the woman being licked has her period. One of the problems in evaluating women's risks from HIV is that the research, classifications, and surveys done to present have not concentrated on transmission from women to men or to women. There is anecdotal evidence that a few people have been infected from practising oral sex alone, usually when the woman has had her period. Wider anecdotal evidence suggests that it is not a risky activity. In other words very few people are reported to have acquired the virus through oral sex. In the decade or more that we have been aware of the virus, thousands of positive people have engaged in oral sex with partners who are not positive and who have not become infected.

But that doesn't mean you might not be worried about it, or that anyone can say that no one at all has, or won't, become infected through oral sex. Right now the way to deal with that worry or uncertainty is either to stop doing oral sex, or to work through the worry and decide that in your evaluation of the risk, it's okay to go ahead, or to use a barrier and lick through it. It also seems sensible to advise everyone to play it safer and avoid going down on a woman while she has her period, or to always use a barrier then. Dental dams were invented for use in dental surgery but have been co-opted by oral safer sex fans. These are latex squares which are held over the vaginal area by either partner. This isn't always easy to get the hang of, so some people have invented crotchless knickers with latex sewn in so the licking partner has his or her hands free. Dental dams aren't easy to come by; an alternative is to cut the tip off a condom and then cut it lengthwise – the advice is to use a water-based lubricant on the clit and vagina and then hold the latex over it. Licking lube off of latex isn't very tasty. The use of clingfilm as a barrier to HIV is doubtful, but it might be the material you use the first time in order to get the 'feel' of doing it.

As far as sucking off a man goes, the advice is again contradictory. In Britain the emphasis is on safer sex for fucking; currently the Terrence Higgins Trust does not advise men that blow jobs are risky. But others disagree. Similar anecdotal evidence exists about men being infected by having oral sex with other men as exists about cunnilingus (licking and sucking a woman's clitoris and vagina). However, if there is any worry or unease, the man can wear a condom. Some women love sucking their partner's prick, but others are put off, perhaps by the idea of semen in their mouth. In this case a condom might be attractive to a woman and give her partner a pleasure he hadn't had with her before.

Latex gloves are the accompaniment for other forms of sex in which one or both of the partners are worried that the activity may be risky. Again there is little or no evidence that anyone has become positive through putting their fingers in a vagina , or even an arsehole, let alone in a mouth. We have all heard about the cuts and sores allowing the virus in, or transmitting the virus to the body it is in. But remember, those cuts and sores would have to be open and bleeding in order for even theoretical transmission to take place. Latex gloves enable a worried man or woman to finger fuck. They can also be used when you want to stimulate the anus. Lube can be used for vaginal finger fucking with gloves, but you must always use it if you are going to penetrate the anus. Always check safer sex guidelines to see which kinds of lubes to use with latex. Latex gloves can be found in certain chemists and from some sex shops, particularly gay ones.

Sex toys are safer sex friendly. These include things like vibrators and dildos as well as silk scarves, lotions, body oils and sexy stories, among hundreds of other things. Fucking with a dildo is safe. The only proviso is that you wash it carefully with soap and water between shares. You can use a condom on sex toys like vibrators and dildos but remember, change it before you share the toy. A dildo is not a penis. The whole point is that you can have penetration if you want, finish, wash it up and toss it in your drawer. Not the same as a penis at all.

Remember that nothing that is being described here is necessary for you to do. For instance, some women may be shocked and horrified by the idea of a dildo, or of oral sex. There is no reason to disguise that. Sit down and think about it for a while. Where does the shock or disgust come from? Maybe it's only because it's something unknown. Maybe it's because it goes against everything you were ever taught or believed. Perhaps you have a history of sexual abuse. Whatever your answer, knowing about something doesn't mean you have to try it out or even if you do try it, like it, or ever do it again. One thing which HIV and AIDS has taught us is that we have to admit to the realms of possibility everything sexual which is consensual and practised by human beings. How else can we talk about sex and stopping the transmission of HIV and include everyone in the discussion?

Safer sex is primarily about HIV transmission. But it also has relevance for wider health concerns. Positive women will want to conserve their health; common sexually transmitted diseases (STDs) may have more serious negative effects on an HIV-positive woman. No one wants to get hepatitis, gonorrhoea, thrush or herpes, but for a positive woman it is even more important to avoid these, and safer sex can protect from a lot more than HIV. There is also evidence which suggests that the presence of an STD heightens the possibility of HIV transmission. When considering STDs, the use of latex squares for oral sex can be important.

Sex is a complicated business. It's not everything in life, but it can be puzzling and compelling. Let's take it seriously but not be too hard on ourselves or others. Success or failure isn't the best way to look at anything which is in process. Learning how to negotiate sex is difficult and ongoing, and includes trying and failing, trying and getting part way there, and trying successfully. For positive women the pressure may be intensified and the desire to get to grips with it greater. One of the biggest blocks we all have around sex is that we believe we're the only ones who have ambivalences or problems in sexual matters and so we stumble on feeling as if we're at fault. But we all have them, whether we're positive or not, and they definitely don't go away with a positive diagnosis. Opening up and talking about sex with a partner, a friend, within a group of friends, often dispels this myth. Sharing our ambivalences, our contra-dictory feelings and our desires to be a responsible person about HIV and AIDS helps us to demystify the process and make it more possible to play an active, confident part in our sexual relationships, whoever we are.

Talking Sex: Talking Serious, Talking Dirty

– WRITTEN WITH PRATIBHA PARMAR AND FIRST PUBLISHED IN
LESBIANS TALK (SAFER) SEX , 1992

As Beth Zemsky and others involved in HIV and AIDS work have pointed out, it's simply not possible to discuss the relation of HIV to lesbians without talking more openly among ourselves about sex. So we have included here our own, exploratory naming of words and of practices which lesbians might or might not do, or know nothing about. It's a start-out, a warm-up, and definitely to be added to.
Lesbian sex is:

- *looking* at women, at breasts, at eyes, at legs, at mouths, at hair, at clothes, at attitude, at dancing, at working, at play

- *flirting* at clubs, with girlfriends, with strangers

- *holding hands* on a bus, hidden in coat pockets on the street, watching television, at a party, meeting parents, going shopping

- *planning a seduction*

- *hoping to be seduced*

- *undressing* yourself, another woman, tearing off clothes, taking them off slowly, leaving some on, ripping off a slip, a T-shirt, coming naked into the room, removing underwear under the bedclothes

- *gazing and longing* for a long time, for a second or two, not at all

- *getting down* in bed, on the floor, in the kitchen, outside, in a dark street, a toilet, your mother's house, over a chair, on your knees, on all fours, on your back, side by side, one on top, head to feet, sitting up, across a table, on your own with a fantasy, together, with others watching, others touching, three or more together, on the beach, in a field, hidden but with people around, at the end of the world, in the water, in a bath, in a car, at a party, a club, a bar, a friend's, your own place, hers, a hotel, a conference

- *sucking* nipples, clits, toes, ears, necks, fingers

- *kissing* lips, with tongues, open mouths, ears, eyes, all over the body, cunts, arseholes, bellies, bums

- *hugging* hard, bearhugs, light ones, group hugs, love hugs

- *licking* vulvas, clits, marathon licking, teasing tongue darts, orgasm strokes, skin, arseholes, ears, tongue probing earholes, probing cunts, probing arseholes, licking feet, toes, necks, all over, thighs, fingers

- *pinching* nipples, bums, cheeks, with nipple clamps, with fingers, nipping with teeth

- *stroking* all over, backs, breasts, thighs, hair, faces, eyelids, eyebrows

- *slapping* bums, faces, cunts

- *fucking* finger-fucking the cunt, the arse, the mouth, putting the whole hand in the cunt, in the arsehole, fisting, finding the G-spot and stroke-fucking it, turning fingers in the cunt while fucking, one hand fucking the cunt while the other does the arse, tying her up and teasing her with the fuck to come, fucking with objects

- *dildos* in the cunt, up the arse, held in hands, worn in harnesses, under clothing, for show, used by a partner, on yourself, looking like penises, looking like cylindrical shapes, black, white, pink, shaped like dolphins, corncobs, made out of latex, plastic, wood, rubber, cucumbers, imaginations

- *butt plugs* small, medium, long, slim, large, inserted during masturbation, used as a small dildo, left in the arse while making love, fucking the arse with it

- *lubricants* for the cunt, for dryness, to make a cunt slippier, for fisting, non oil-based for using with latex gloves, dental dams, flavoured lubes, plain lubes, always lubes for anal entry, lubes for using on clits for vibrator pleasure

- *vibrators* for your own pleasure, for orgasms, for multiple orgasms, for using with a lover, for quickies, for taking on holidays, for using in semi-public places, for pushing against cunts and bums, for fucking with, for easing aching muscles

- *ejaculation* some find it cums easily, some don't find the spot, stimulating G-spot with fingers or dildo, bringing yourself or your lover to an ejaculation, in her face, wet the bed

- *food* avocadoes, honey, whipped cream, chocolate, grapes, champagne, brandy, salt, lemon juice, mangoes, ice-cream, ice cubes

- *fingers dancing* on clits, beside clits, on arseholes, across nipples, on lips, on palms, across backs

- *fingers moving* on clits, on tits, in cunts, on bodies

- *piss* artists, at orgasm, on someone, golden showers

- *orgasms* fast, taking forever, lasting forever, over in seconds, like a sneeze, like an earthquake, one of a number in a row, not worth it, the best thing ever, delicious, exquisite, ordinary, shaking, rolling around, out of control, off into space, rolling along like waves, cute, scary, makes you cry, makes you laugh, makes you growl, howl, shout, scream, moan, cry out her name, his name, the right name, the wrong name, makes you say the L word, makes you want more, makes you tired, helps period pains, puts you to sleep

- *do-me queens* she always gets it and is then too tired

- *making love* good sex, bad sex, routine sex, no sex, changing sex, new sex, old sex, moving in together sex

- *rubbing* cunts and clits together, cunts against thighs, against breasts, rubbing breasts against cunts, cunts against bums, tits against faces, hair over faces, over backs, over bellies, over cunts, hands against cunts, against arseholes

- *talking*
  talking sweet
  talking low
  talking dirty
  talking funny
  talking histories, futures
  talking fantasy
  talking rough
  talking love
  talking fears
  talking desire
  and much, much, more

Some sex language, some names, add your own:

- *cunt* vagina, pussy, slit, beaver, fanny

- *clit* clitoris, pearl, button, love spot

- *arsehole* anus, shit hole

- *secretions* wet, juices, cream, cum

- *breasts* boobs, tits

- *rimming* ass-licking

- *fisting* hand-fucking

- *cunnilingus* going down on, eating out, eating pussy, muff diver, pearl diver

- *fucking* screwing, making love, intercourse, bonking, rooting

- *female ejaculation* stimulating the G-spot makes some women spurt out a liquid – definitely not urine

It's not just because we live in the age of AIDS that we suggest that it's a positive and important thing for lesbians to talk about sex. We live in a world in which sex is continuously present, implied, conveyed – and repressed, misunderstood, judged – and desired. In most countries and cultures, lesbianism has been both unimaginable (invisible and/or disgusting) and titillating, a part of public and private fantasies. We have tended to have few public places in which to develop distinctly lesbian sub-cultures and have too often been invisible to each other. Recognizing the titillation value of lesbianism in the straight world has made us fearful of developing an explicit and popular lesbian language of lust and sex. Who might listen to our words and stories besides ourselves?

That lesbianism has become a sexual possibility for many more women in a number of countries during the past twenty years or so has helped create different lesbian sub-cultures, particularly in urban areas. But the fear of speaking publicly about what happens sexually between women has remained a continuing force. We talk around the subject: we talk about sexuality; we talk about love; we talk about who we fancy, who turns us on. But the majority of us don't talk about what we do, what we want to do, or what we fantasize about doing with another woman. Why?

First, many lesbians seem to believe that there is already a recognized and acceptable recipe for lesbian sex. But when questioned more closely, it often becomes clear that no one really knows what this recipe is, or who decided it was good and nutritious in the first place. It seems to go something like this: kissing, stroking, stimulating the clit with fingers or tongue, perhaps a finger or two inserted into the cunt. This can be romantic, swooning stuff, or sweaty, rolling-in-the-hay hard stuff. It can be mutually accomplished or not, although ideally each lover should have her needs met. All this is fine, but what do we really know? Do most lesbians go down on each other? How many use rubbing? Do fewer practise penetration? How do we know? Maybe some don't who are really dying for it? And what about everything else that girls might like to get up to with each other? What about heavy fucking with fingers, a hand or a dildo? How many get that, give that, want that? What about dressing up, playing roles, arse fucking, sitting on your lover's face, slurping into 69, tying her up, getting yourself blindfolded, and on and on and on? And what if you don't get sex? Don't want sex?

We're scared of talking. Scared we're going to be *wrong*, scared we're going to be judged.

> Part of the trouble is that lesbians have had a problem talking openly in our community about sex, both between women and whether or not we partner with men. This means that it's very controversial for a lesbian to talk about whether or not she uses sex toys, she fucks men, or whether or not she rims or is rimmed by her girlfriend. When we start to talk about safer sex, what sex acts are we worried about – oral sex, blood? – Amber Hollibaugh

We live in a society which maintains that it celebrates individual choice and development. Yet really we seem to want all the individuals who make up society to behave according to certain rules. Within the lesbian communities in Britain and in the US, divisive, bitter, accusatory sexual politics ruled the roost during the eighties. Certain kinds of sexual practice were considered bad, not really lesbian, dangerous to women. Generally these were thought to be SM practices, whatever that means, but they also often included butch/femme behaviour. The legacy of those days is still with us. Lesbians' historical reticence and nervousness about talking about sex has been exacerbated by the bitter debates within lesbian sexual politics. Who wanted to risk being denounced, ex-communicated from the lesbian club, labelled a terrible person because she talked openly or listened generously to a range of lesbian experiences?

But it isn't always about being judged for doing the supposedly 'wild' things. We're also scared of being judged by SM or pro-sex dykes who say or imply that if you aren't (at least) getting yourself strapped up and fucked with a dildo, then you're boring, caught up in your own fears and repressions. Where does the fear of being judged, caught out, embarrassed, thought silly, come from?

> The strange thing in the community I'm part of is that, on the one hand we talk a lot about sex, but on the other, there are so many prescriptive notions around which are the result of years of politics about what sex is acceptable and what isn't. Anything we do, like or desire that doesn't fit in with the supposed norms of whatever lesbian community you come from, is censored in any debate. And then there's still the business of being a woman and being worried you're doing something unacceptable. In order to explore issues which may be taboo and difficult, we have to stop being judgemental and start to be honest. – Da Choong

The ease with which we can talk about sex is informed by our personal histories and can be culturally specific, too.

> For a lot of Asian women, sex is a taboo subject in our families and culture and we never talk about it. I have found it difficult to talk about sex; then to talk about safer sex is another issue altogether. – Madhu

Perhaps some of our fear comes from the difficulty of being truthful about something so often private and elusive, and so hard to convey in words. Sex is physical and present, but it is also bound up with desire, which is cerebral, perverse, subconscious and unpredictable. Does acknowledging that you really want to be fucked up the arse, held and rocked like a baby, or talk dirty to your partner(s) convey to others where desires come from, or what place they hold in your emotions? What feels intensely sexual in the dim light can sound ridiculous and banal in a non-sexual talk about sex. We have to make it clear that we won't judge ourselves or others, that no matter how ridiculous it feels, it isn't going to hurt to say it, that someone else has felt it too.

What HIV and AIDS have made clear for lesbians (and for all sexual human beings) is that we can't afford to allow the *shoulds* and *shouldn'ts* of sexual correctness, or received wisdom, to stunt our discussions. We don't have the leisure, the time, the space, to wait, to put off until tomorrow: we have to break through whatever it is that keeps us prisoners of our own fear. Once permission is given, once the floodgates are open, we can begin to perceive the beginnings of a collective exploration of lesbian cultures of sexuality. It is only then that we will be an active part of the ferment which is taking place, in large part due to the AIDS crisis, around sexuality.

We want to be able to celebrate the diversity of lesbian sex with more knowledge of what that diversity means in practice. In itself this isn't enough, but it is essential in order to resist any fundamentalist attempts to restrict sexual acts to what a person, group or society thinks is correct or incorrect.

Safer Sex: To Suck or Not to Suck

> I used to practise safer sex but I stopped because of all the conflicting information and because I hate dental dams which I find really uncomfortable. But that doesn't mean I don't talk about it with whoever I'm with. It's being able to talk and negotiate your fears around it that's important. – Madhu

We believe that safer sex is something lesbians should know about, and should know how to practise if appropriate, for the following reasons:

• Safer sex techniques are possible ways of protecting lesbian sexual health from STDs in general, including herpes, chlamydia, warts, crabs, hepatitis, gardenerella and other vaginal infections. The possibility of using safer sex techniques selectively in relation to your own or a lover's STD is a health-and-sex-positive move. Lesbians having one-off sexual encounters, even if not worried about HIV, might think about other, more easily picked-up or passed-on, STDs. Repeated bouts of vaginal infections are not insignificant annoyances, and herpes is for life.

Lesbians do not take their sexual health seriously enough. Lesbians often believe that they 'don't pass on nasty things to each other'. Sorry girls, if you're lucky, fine, but lots of lesbians pass things on and back and forth. Others are nervous of going to a doctor or clinic because they fear anti-lesbianism, or a lack of understanding about lesbian sex. *My doctor told me I didn't need a cervical smear because lesbians didn't get cervical cancer. Even though that's a myth, I had to tell her that quite a few of us were heterosexual before.*

The success of the recently founded Sandra Bernhard Clinic for lesbian health in London shows the need for facilities lesbians can use, and medical staff who understand their needs.

> We set up the Sandra Bernhard Clinic in April 1992 because we felt that there was very little information about lesbians and sexually transmitted diseases. We were concerned that lesbians were not being given access to services they needed. Many lesbians have questions about their sexual practices and concerns about whether they could transmit certain sexual diseases to their partners. We wanted to create a safe environment for lesbians to be open, in which the onus isn't on them to come out to potentially hostile doctors. We also wanted to offer HIV testing and a safe space to discuss safer sex and give women the latest research and information. The clinic is fully booked for months in advance and is very popular. – Sandy Nelson

• For the lesbian who is already positive, safer sex can be a protection from STDs which might have more serious consequences in a positive body, particularly hepatitis B and C, thrush and herpes. Taking this into account is responsible and smart. Women who assume they are not positive could think about the possibility of having a sexual relationship or encounter with a positive woman not only in terms of the possibilities (or fears) of lesbian transmission, but also in terms of *what danger could I be to this wonderful woman I fancy and how can I be safer for her?*

> There are lots of STDs that are easy to pass on through lesbian sex and are much more likely to be transmitted through the kind of sex lesbians have than HIV is. But most lesbians don't know anything about them. There is also evidence emerging that STDs have quite a lot to do with transmission – as possible co-factors. And more lesbians have STDs than is popularly believed. It would be useful if the debate about HIV/AIDS

was a platform for lesbians to start taking their sexual health more seriously. I think that's important. – Da Choong

• Safer sex is a skill we can all know about and then choose to use or not as the situation demands. Identities can be multiple and changing. The woman who fucks only women today may be the one who falls for a man tomorrow. Safer sex in these circumstances takes on a very different meaning and priority. Having a lesbian identity does not protect you from HIV in other circumstances. Lesbianism in itself is not a condom!

• Safer sex can be a way of exploring different sexual practices. Latex gloves, with a coat of non-oil-based lubricant on the fingers, might enable some shit-scared lesbians to try a bit of anal stimulation (remembering that you never force fingers or objects into an unrelaxed anus). Using dental dams to cover up the arsehole and then licking (rimming) it could drive your sweetie wild, take away either partner's nervousness of shit, and protect from hepatitis (which is much more easily transmitted than HIV). Put a bit of non-oil-based lubricant on the arsehole before covering it with the latex – it makes it more pleasurable for the licked one. Doing the same with a dam for licking cunts and clits could free up women who are scared off by vaginal juices and smells, including menstrual ones.

• Playing with safer sex bits and bobs could be the first truly hysterically funny sexual encounter you have with a partner. The slurp and slush of a too-big latex glove while fucking your girlfriend's cunt is quite an experience. (Properly fitting latex gloves are the most easily eroticized safer sex accessory – some lesbians say that just hearing the snap of the glove going on gets them hot.)

• Talking about the ways you might want to use safer sex techniques can turn into a session of sexual openness and fantasy. And don't forget that sex toys are the easiest safer sex fun around. A dildo or vibrator only needs a change of condom between shares in order to protect from thrush, herpes and warts. If condoms aren't around, be sure to wash it well in hot water and soap, and rinse off.

• Uncertainty is part of life, particularly as millions of us live it today. Many old certainties have gone or transmuted, new ones are still around the corner. Perhaps for one woman it's more important to use clean needles when shooting up than to worry about the less likely possibility of becoming positive through lesbian sex. Perhaps someone else will decide that if there is a one-in-a-million chance of transmission, that's enough to cause worry, and so will want to practise safer sex and be able to stop worrying. If you believe (or fear) there is a minute possibility of transmission, then you might decide to evaluate it as you do other risky activities: driving in cars, walking alone at night, smoking.

• Finally, safer sex is part of a big and varied sexual conversation of the eighties and nineties, sometimes troubled and horrifying, sometimes new and exciting. That doesn't mean that all lesbians must practise it in order to be part of a new lesbian political correctness. But it does mean that everyone should know the rudiments of safer sex in order to be informed and to be able to make more than theoretical choices.

It is always instructive to ask yourself if you would go down on a woman (or man) who told you they were positive, especially if you assume you're negative. It might make you stop and think, no matter what your beliefs about woman-to-woman transmission. Even if your initial response is no, that doesn't mean you would continue to feel that way. Thinking, talking, getting information, can change feelings of fear. And if you are positive yourself, you may not want anyone to go down on you without using latex, for fear of picking up a secondary infection.

Who knows when a woman you want to make love with will ask you to use safer sex techniques? Or when knowledge and information about them would make it easier for you to start a seduction? Who knows when or where you might be called upon to educate someone: a friend's teenager, your own kids, their friends, your brother or sister, your friends, your mother, a colleague? We may not choose to deliver safer sex speeches at every opportunity, but we may find ourselves in situations where we are the only ones who will, or can, and we should be able to do it.

Safer Sex: The Basics

Where HIV is present

HIV is transmitted primarily through blood and semen. In theory, HIV can be found in all bodily fluids; however, its concentration in different bodily fluids varies hugely. The lower the concentration, the lower the likelihood of transmission of the virus.

Blood and semen have the highest concentrations; vaginal juices and pre-cum (what leaks from the penis before ejaculation) lower concentrations. The presence of a vaginal infection seems to increase the concentration of HIV in a positive woman's vagina. The concentration in tears, saliva and probably piss is so low as to present no chance of transmission at all. The bodily fluid in shit probably has a very low level of HIV, so shit in itself is probably not a dangerous route of HIV transmission (although it can carry other infectious amoebas and viruses). If shit contains infected blood, obviously that blood will contain higher levels of HIV. However, the small amount of blood in shit, unless a person is haemorrhaging, is very small, and by the time it is ready to come out, it may be old, dried blood in which the HIV is no longer active.

Routes of transmission

HIV is passed on when blood, semen or less often vaginal fluids or pre-cum from a positive person directly enters another person's bloodstream, either through actively open wounds or mucous membranes (the mucus-secreting linings of various cavities in the body such as the nose, anus and vagina). The mucous membrane of the anus is more delicate than that of the vagina, so anal fucking is more likely to create open cuts in the anus through which the virus can enter the bloodstream.

The main routes of HIV transmission are through unsafe sex with a positive person; through sharing unclean needles to inject drugs; through the use of unclean needles for injections in hospitals and clinics in countries where there is not enough money for disposable needles (inject-ing drugs with clean needles is safe in relation to HIV); through infected blood, blood products and donated organs that contain HIV (since 1985 all these have been tested for HIV before use in the UK and US); possibly through transfer from mother to baby during pregnancy. None of these activities is guaranteed to pass the virus on. As one positive woman said:

> You never know if it's going to be the third time, the thirty-ninth time, or the first time you have unsafe sex with a positive person that transmission of the virus happens. It's always a Russian roulette.

Sexual transmission most often occurs through infected semen being ejaculated into the vagina or anus. That's why the major safer sex message continues to be aimed at preventing men from depositing infected semen into vaginas and anuses. Condoms are the main way of keeping semen out of these places. Gay men who have used these for anal sex have been successful in stopping transmission.

A positive woman can transmit HIV to men through vaginal fucking, although it appears less likely to happen this way round than from man to woman. Again, condoms protect. Positive people of either sex will want to protect themselves from getting new infections of HIV which could compromise their health further.

Self-insemination

Lesbians have been concerned about whether or not there is a risk of HIV transmission to either themselves or their foetus if they are using donated sperm from a positive man for self-insemination. This is another grey area in which the risks are still unknown. Anyone wishing to use donated sperm for self-insemination will want to use healthy sperm and therefore to avoid HIV-positive sperm. Guidelines include having the donor – gay, straight or bisexual – test for HIV antibodies twice, six months apart, and for him to agree to practise only safer sex between tests and for the duration of the donation. The only information about transmission from donated sperm relates to an Australian case in 1985, in which four heterosexual women attending an infertility clinic sero-converted after being inseminated with the semen of a donor later found to be positive. We have never seen any other cases discussed or reported.

Inseminating with 'fresh' semen is more likely to result in pregnancy than the frozen stuff which has been tested twice for HIV that all clinics now use. And many lesbians fear rejection or judgement at fertility clinics, and therefore prefer self-insemination. Most gay donors will expect to be asked for HIV test results; straight men may well not have given an HIV test a thought. In the end, you have to trust your donor and feel confident he will tell you the truth about his status and sexual practice.

> Ultimately it comes down to trust. However many tests he does it means nothing if you don't trust he's always going to practise safer sex in between. – Da Choong

Are we positive?

Not everyone who is HIV positive knows, or even suspects it. Unfortunately, there are men (and women) who do suspect or know their positive status and who continue to have unsafe sex. It therefore makes sense for heterosexuals, bisexuals and gay men to know about and practise safer sex if there is any reason at all to doubt their own or their partner's status, whether in a long-term relationship or not.

Even committed couples find it difficult to be 100 per cent truthful about their sexual histories, past and present. How many times have we heard women say, 'It came as a complete and utter shock to me. I honestly believed we were faithful to each other and there were no signs that he/she was sleeping with anyone else.' On the other hand, blanket rules about *everyone* needing to practise safer sex don't help the credibility of safer sex education. For some couples, it is fair enough to make the decision that they truly are monogamous and have been for long enough or are sure enough of their status not to worry about sexual transmission of the virus. Of course they have to trust that if the situation changes, they will tell one another and so can change the rules.

Assessing the Risks

These are the basics of safer sex. Everything else has to be evaluated by individuals or communities in the light of new information, acceptability of risk, or even, in the absence of clear guidelines, a 'better safe than sorry' outlook.

No one contests that HIV exists in vaginal secretions at lower levels of concentration than in blood or semen. But does it exist in high enough concentrations to be transmitted during oral sex? Very little safer sex advice for heterosexuals contains negative information about mouth-vagina oral sex. There is evidence which suggests that saliva has a neutralizing effect on the virus, rendering it harmless, especially when it is present in a low concentration, as in vaginal juices. In addition, it is known that HIV is destroyed by stomach juices, so even gay men are now being advised by many gay HIV health workers and health activists that oral sex is not dangerous.

HIV can be transmitted from women to men during vaginal fucking, probably through cuts in the tender skin of the unprotected penis. Transmission from the vagina would be much less likely to happen through finger-fucking, even if there were tiny sores on the fingers. And it would be even more difficult for a positive person's fingers, even chewed ones, to transmit HIV to a partner's cunt. *RELAX!* It's good to remember that in order to get in, the virus has to come into contact with actively open cuts and sores. It has to go right into the bloodstream. In most circumstances this is a very weak virus – it doesn't survive well outside certain conditions in the human body. As has been said a million times, you don't get it from toilet seats, from drinking glasses, from coughs or sneezes, or from kissing. And it seems clearer and clearer that all sex is not equally risky.

> Things have changed a lot in the last year or two. When I first joined Terrence Higgins Trust the talk was all about dental dams. Providing dental dams was a way of discussing the issue with lesbians and a way for them to start thinking about it seriously. Dental dams have never been tested as an HIV barrier, aren't easily available and are not easy to use. But we were providing condoms for men, so we had to provide something for lesbians to use. That was the thinking at the time, although there are still lots of women who believe it. But it is inconsistent. Dental dams have never been pushed for heterosexuals: they are always for lesbians. So I do think that it was a way of introducing the subject to the lesbian community. – Da Choong

Lists of high-, middle- and low-risk sexual behaviours can become obsessive, frightening and confusing. In the past, we wondered why fisting (insertion of the whole hand in the arse or vagina) was listed as high risk in many safer sex do's and don'ts. Was the risk to the fisting person or to the fisted person? If the fisting person was wearing a latex glove, was that safe? Given that semen was the major problem and hands don't (call us naïve) produce it directly, why were fisting hands up in the list along with fucking with unprotected penises? If the fisted person was in danger, what from? Blood from the fister? Surely it was very unlikely either that someone would put a profusely bleeding hand into a cunt or an arsehole or that vaginal juices or anal matter would pose much risk to a hand?

It seems that the logic of the advice (largely unstated) was that fisting anally or vaginally could cause cuts or abrasions – especially in the arse. If the fisted (and injured) person was then fucked with an unprotected penis, there was a higher chance of transmission of HIV. Why wasn't this stated clearly? Along with commentators like Pat Califia, we can only surmise that safer sex guidelines, especially older ones, incorporated the writers' prejudices and fears about sex. Fisting is not considered proper or acceptable gay sexual behaviour by some gay men and lesbians. The same story could be told about SM sexual practices, which often found their way into the riskiest lists when in fact most should have been included in the safest list, whatever the list-makers thought of SM.

All this illustrates how important it is to separate off acknowledgment and acceptance of consensual sexual practices from personal endorsement of what's exciting and not exciting in sex. *Whatever anyone thinks of a particular sexual activity should not have anything to do with how it is analysed in relation to safer sex.*

As we open up discussions of lesbian sex, less known, more 'daring' sexual acts may appear as better, more exciting, and the women who do them may present themselves or be seen by others as being freer and more open. We've said it before and we'll say it again. Just because someone fists a woman, wearing leather, upside down, with nipple clamps on, does not mean she is any more exciting, interesting, witty, funny, sexually skilled or successful than anyone else. Someone who promotes vanilla sex is not necessarily a better lesbian feminist. 'Daring' sex can be kissing. Skilled, successful, hot sex can be cunnilingus. Exciting people can prefer vanilla. Interesting people can like SM. Witty women can adore massage. Funny dykes can desire a dildo. Just as being a lesbian doesn't automatically mean a woman is politically progressive or radical, so certain forms of lesbian sex do not automatically imply anything else about the women who practise them.

Demystifying our sex lives by talking about what we do, and seeing that communication as part of safer sex in its widest sense, can only help create a collective idea of the meaning of HIV in lesbian lives.

The Agnostic Position

We know that HIV and AIDS have not struck different lesbian communities with the same ferocity as they have gay mens'. We know that there have not been large numbers of women infected through lesbian sex before that route was considered a possible route of transmission. Thankfully, we are not in the position of gay men, who have to make safer sex part of their sexual lives.

But this does not mean that we don't worry about the breadth of our choices. Even if we don't believe that woman-to-woman transmission is a risk worth all of us practising safer sex for, we may still end up dreaming dreadful dreams of vaginal juices, saliva, shit, tears and menstrual blood teaming with HIV. Or we may believe that there are cases of lesbian sexual transmission, and that unless we are sure of our own and our partner's status, safer sex is an essential safeguard. Or that while, as lesbians or in our own particular relationship(s) we don't need actively to engage in safer sex, we do see it as important to put our energies into HIV/AIDS work and activism, into pushing for more research on women and HIV, as well as for more resources for gay men and other affected communities.

For us, the agnostic position feels the safest. It leaves the way open for those lesbians who are worried, and can't resolve that worry, to use safer sex. But it also indicates how pressing it is for us to build a framework in which to place our worries, our information, our politics, our uncertainties and our knowledge. Not all decisions are rational or make total sense, especially those around sex! Deciding to practise safer sex with another women in specific circumstances may not always be rational, but may make that sexual encounter a freer, more exciting, more caring experience. Conversely, deciding not to practise safer sex with another woman in specific circumstances may be a rational risk assessment of the danger of HIV transmission, but leaves herpes or hepatitis out of the equation. Deciding that making love with your sweetie with no reference to safer sex is not a risk in relation to HIV seems a possible responsible choice for lesbians as well. In celebration of our perversity, we should be revelling in the wealth and breadth of the sexual choices we can make in the time of AIDS and joining with others to end the epidemic, to continue to care for those affected by it and to be a strong, radical force in sexual politics.

Make no mistake. We need to be open and accepting of our sexual lives and desires in all their diversity and mystery in order to be strong in our sexual politics. Even if lesbians are not in danger of transmitting HIV through woman-to-woman sex, it does not mean that we are mere onlookers in the AIDS crisis, involving ourselves as 'ladies with lamps'.

Worldwide sexual politics is in flux. HIV and AIDS have become the vehicle for wider struggles over sexual freedom, homosexuality, women's liberation, family values and sexual pleasure, diversity and difference. We are a part of this and without doubt the outcomes of these various debates and struggles will have perfound and far-reaching effects on our lives.

Lesbians and a Politics of HIV
We want to talk about what HIV and AIDS means for us as lesbians and queers in a hostile world.

• We want to begin to build a flexible framework of ideas that will help lesbians (and others) to make sense of their uncertainty and confusion in relation to HIV and AIDS.

• We want to talk openly about lesbian sexual practices, because until that happens, collectively and individually, we can't be confident about where we fit into any AIDS discourse. We are pro-sex, but non-judgementally critical women, and we believe that lesbians need to open up, to stop being so fearful of being wrong – about what they do in bed, what they want to do there, or even what they don't want to do in bed or anywhere else.

• We want to point out where we think logic breaks down in sexual health messages to lesbians, particularly those to do with safer sex.

• But we are not interested in either/or messages – either we're at risk from unsafe lesbian sex or we're not, full stop. We believe that the AIDS crisis affects everyone, but with different intensities. A vital and radical challenge to AIDS would weave together these differences, while fully acknowledging and validating the pain, anger and needs of gay men in the face of homophobia and indifference, and the undeniable continuing impact AIDS has on them.

• This challenge would consider the devastation of people in Asia and Africa, and the impact of the virus on poor and/or black people in the US, both situations undeniably bound up with an ongoing history of racism and exploitation.

• It would recognize the different ways the epidemic is affecting a range of groups and would consign to the rubbish heap the notion that different groups asserting their need of AIDS resources takes away from other groups. The idea that *gay men* are competing with *women*, are competing with *drug users*, are competing with *Africans*, are competing with *Asians* for resources fits very nicely into a divide-and-rule-perspective.

• We can only meet the needs of specific groups if we admit *everyone* affected by HIV and AIDS to the arena. Supporting the differing needs of groups and communities need not take away from the groups most in need, or most disowned by society. It need not ignore or downplay the serious health crises women face besides HIV and AIDS – such as breast cancer. Rather, a united response could be a more effective means of exerting enough pressure on governments and agencies and people with money, power and resources to meet the needs of everyone affected by HIV.

• Our challenge would *develop* the different levels of response to HIV and AIDS that lesbians could have and would understand that most people do not live in hermetically sealed communities. The recognition that positive lesbians exist challenges old fixed notions of lesbian identity. These are lesbians who have mostly become positive through IV drug use or having sex with men. They should be supported and accepted in our lesbian cultures, our homes and our hearts.

Anal Matters
– UNPUBLISHED

For many women anal sex is still a taboo subject. We've had books on reproduction, been encouraged to get familiar with our sexual organs, to lose our inhibitions about masturbation, you name it. But very few talk or write openly about anal pleasure or desire – or the lack of it.

The crazy thing though, is that research indicates that about 40 per cent of American heterosexual couples indulge in anal penetrative sex at one time or another. This is the hidden reality of a practice which is popularly considered gay men's territory. Straight men's paranoia about the sanctity of their butts and the fear of gay men is complex. Desire and fear all mixed up.

Too often anal sex is understood as full penetration and many women either imagine (or have had) an unpleasant or painful experience of this. Maybe a man has shoved his penis or an object up your ass when it was tense and unreceptive or, even worse, when it was not wanted at all.

Still it is worth being clear why you might be adamantly opposed to any anal stimulation. Perhaps it brings back horrible memories of painful times, perhaps you were anally raped or abused as a child or woman. These are totally understandable reasons for wanting to avoid anal penetration. But some taboos women hold on to are based on less traumatic reasons. After some thought or discussion with a partner or friend you might decide you want to explore the possibility of anal sex. You might not want to. No one should be under any obligation to like anal sex in order to be sexually fulfilled, adventurous, uninhibited or happy. Force, bullying or spurious notions of 'liberated' sexual attitudes have no place in sexual exploration.

The anus is exquisitely sensitive and pleasurably so for some people. But there are many exquisitely and pleasurably sensitive areas of the body and ultimately, it's up to each woman to explore, or decide what gives them enjoyment.

If you are interested but a bit nervous, here are some guidelines and explanations. First of all, start on your own and try stroking your anus while you're in the bath – whatever you do or don't do sexually with a lover, it's a good thing to be aware of your own body, its different sensations, tensions and feelings. After the bath, take a look at your anus in a mirror. It won't hurt. Again, even if this is the extent of your exploration, it's a positive step. Far too many people are so cut off from their bums that any day-to-day awareness or sensation 'down there' has been repressed. It's good health practice to be aware of your whole body. Anal stimulation doesn't necessarily have anything to do with penetration. Many women enjoy having their anus gently brushed or circled by their partner's fingers while he or she is going down on them, licking their cunt and clitoris. Others like to begin with a back massage and start getting turned on as their partner reaches their bottom; this becomes more intensified when a hand slips between cheeks and runs suggestive fingers over and around the anus. Still others have been delighted by feathers or silky material being drawn across their anus. All this is anal sex.

These are also sexual activities which can lead to further anal pleasures if you want them to. The major thing to remember for any form of anal penetration is relaxation. If your sphincter muscles are not relaxed then penetration will be painful. Pushing in harder is not the solution. You do not need to 'stretch' the anus or 'get used to it'. There should be no penetration if you aren't relaxed enough.

Sometimes people spontaneously relax those muscles, allowing a finger to slip in easily, or even a penis or dildo. But for others it takes some learning and experimenting. Some people maintain that visualizing their muscles relaxing or imagining being warm and open down there helps. Others find that a finger can be inserted and then held still for a minute while the muscles relax further around it. Some women find that after the slow, gentle insertion of fingers or a penis, they build up to wanting more and more inside, and they lead the way to stronger and harder fucking. For them, face buried in a pillow, arse up and open, it is sweaty sex at its best. Positions for anal penetration are varied – on your back, your stomach, on all fours – it depends on your body and your partner's on what excites and works for you, and what's going up your arse.

If you are keen on anal penetration and want to try it out, think lubricants. KY jelly is fine or you might try to find one of the fancier lubes. Always use a water-based one if you are using a condom because oil-based lubes can destroy the latex. Some lubes contain nonoxynol 9 which can irritate the anal skin. Check this out by putting some on your wrist. The anal canal doesn't lubricate during sexual arousal and is naturally less moist than the vagina. Penetration without a lube can be painful even if you are relaxed and can result in tears in the anal canal. The two main guidelines are relaxation and lubricants, whether penetration is with fingers, penis or an object.

Speaking of penises, the other major issue to consider when thinking about anal penetration is HIV/AIDS. It is this more than anything else which has changed considerations about penile penetrative anal sex. It is no longer an unproblematic choice to fuck anally with an uncovered penis. The base line for safer sex is no semen in the vagina or rectum. If you are HIV positive it would be risky for your negative partner. It also appears that the receptive partner is more likely to be infected by someone who is positive than the other way round.

Semen seems to be a factor in helping the virus along its way in both the anal canal and in the vagina. The reality of HIV will be a necessary consideration which influences you about anal penetrative sex involving a penis. Condoms make safer anal sex possible but there is a slight possibility a condom might tear or be incorrectly used. Most mishaps happen because the wrong sort of condom is used or it isn't put on properly, so following proper instruction is important. Condoms for anal sex are tougher than those designed for vaginal fucking. If you wouldn't have unprotected vaginal penetration because of HIV, then that should hold doubly true for the anal variety. However, stroking the anus, licking it, or using fingers or a dildo for penetration are all safe activities in relation to HIV transmission.

If you already know you like full anal penetration with something more than one or two fingers, you might consider a dildo. This universal object has the advantage of being useful to heterosexuals, lesbians, gay men and bisexuals. For maximum sexual health, it should be washed carefully between uses or covered with a one-time-only condom. Lubricant is a necessity. The same guidelines apply as for any other anal penetration – relaxation, cleanliness and the desire to do it. It is possible to use a dildo anally on yourself and be in complete control of what goes on. It's possible to buy dildos which resemble anatomical penises or much more abstract shapes.

Some sex shops, particularly those catering for gay men, sell butt plugs which are tapered shapes in various sizes with a wide flat base. These can be inserted and left in place before, during or after sex. They also can be used as mini dildos. It's important to remember that if you insert anything into your anus it should have a base which prevents the whole thing slipping into your rectum. Unlike the vagina, the rectum goes on for a long way. Things can get lost. Sad but true, doctors have extracted amazing objects from people's bottoms – including salt shakers and candles.

Some women have been experimenting recently with dental dams for safer vaginal oral sex. There is no reason why dental dams shouldn't be used for rimming. Rimming is when someone stimulates your anus by licking and probing it with their tongue. If you like it, you probably love it, although it is one of those activities which seems to have more 'do me' devotees than doers. The shit factor bothers some people. A bath or shower before you start messing around helps allay fears, but to avoid taking in any amoebas, which although not life threatening can be serious (the most severe of these is hepatitis B which can seriously damage your health and sometimes lead to death) you could give dental dams a try. These are squares or rectangles of latex which are placed over the area to be licked. Then you simply go to work through the smooth, thin barrier. It is equally true that latex gloves can be used by a lover who plans to play with your arse. Lube up the latexed fingers first. Buy them in sex shops or get them from a sexual health clinic.

Speaking of shit, and there's no shying away from the subject when thinking anally, many of us associate the anus with dirtiness and shame. Learning to control one's sphincter as a toddler is often a messy and emotional process. The shitting we once were so proud and unashamed of is transformed through adult insistence into a more or less controlled function done in private.

There are health care practitioners around who maintain that large numbers of grown up people manifest their bodily tensions primarily in the anal area. There is also evidence that many of us are so alienated from our bums that we can't properly comprehend when our body is telling us to shit. It's a complex part of the body, fulfilling a natural but culturally sensitive function and it's no wonder many people are ambivalent about their arseholes.

The funny thing about shit is that as mothers, women become incredibly casual about cleaning it up. They wipe off the baby's bum, wash the nappies, and give their own hands a proper scrub after handling the stuff. But most seem content that they're not in danger of contamination or germs if they wash up. So why such disgust and nervousness about possible contact in sexual encounters?

If you are nervous about shit, your own or others, here are a few suggestions and some information. For the first three or four inches the anal canal is often completely free of faecal matter. In the best of all worlds, that's the way all anal canals would be. But because so many of us eat unhealthy diets and are out of touch with the natural rhythms of elimination, this is not always the case. In fact, there may be bits of it in those first inches. (By the way, shit gathers further up the tract and is guarded by another set of muscles which when functioning correctly, relax when the section above them is full, giving plenty of physical warning that you need to shit. If this happens, the muscles of the canal actually push the shit out in waves, making the red-faced, grunting agony many experience while sitting on the toilet unnecessary.)

The possibility of getting a bit of shit on fingers or dildos can be dealt with by a good wash with soap and water afterwards, or use latex gloves or condoms, whip these off when finished and dispose of them. Of course, it is a bit of a drag because those digits or objects shouldn't go into a vagina or mouth after indulging in anal fun until they have been washed or the latex removed. If you are licking a naked anus, there is the possibility that you will smell a vaguely shitty smell (which some people like) or more seriously that you will take in microscopic bits of faecal matter which may contain germs. The riskiest of these is hepatitis B.

Increased anal awareness within a context of sexual health and pleasure would be progress for many women. There are anal problems or health concerns which could be positively affected by greater awareness. Piles and anal fissures create pain and ongoing medicalization of the bum. STDs such as warts or gonorrhoea can and do infect the anal area and canal. More familiarity and less stress around the anus could mean more effective avoidance of anal STDs, possibly more awareness of the importance of diet and anal health. Learning to relax tension in the anus and to be more in tune with what your bowl is telling you could reduce the incidence of anal fissures. There's nothing to lose but your piles.

Beyond health, describing the attractions of anal sex is as difficult as describing any other sexual pleasure. The outside of the anus is filled with nerves and is as sensitive to stimulation as the lips or labia. What makes anal penetration pleasurable to some women is harder to explain. Unlike men there is no prostate gland to be stimulated by penetration. However, for some women the sensation of being filled up anally and the sensation of something pulling in and out of the arse is very exciting.

And who knows what role the forbidden nature of anal sex of any sort plays in sexual excitement and desire? Some women find that their orgasm, especially when someone is going down on them, is heightened or even brought on by the gentle insertion of a finger into the arse.

What we do know is that men and women, in variations of sexual couplings, have partaken of anal sex of some sort for thousands of years and in many different cultures. So if it turns you on, in fantasy or reality, enjoy. If it doesn't don't worry. Good sex is not about amassing the longest list of sexual practices, it's about discovering what is exciting and desirous and being open to the possibility of experiencing them.

PART FIVE

Taking Sides

This is the hardest to write – things that seem vitally important to me, events and debates that have occupied me for years, people whose behaviour and politics have angered me. The danger is that in taking a loud and definite side, I simply exacerbate and freeze divisions more firmly. The danger with forever sitting on a fence, no matter how good the views are on all sides, is that you don't engage fully with the people and politics you oppose. The danger is being too timid to say what you really think in a public forum.

Striking out for the brief pleasure of hitting your target doesn't justify the strike. It doesn't mean I never do it. With the exception of the last piece on Camille which revels in its own nastiness and which I maintain Paglia deserves for writing a book which ruined my life for the two weeks I worked on this review, the other writings in this section pertain to arguments within feminism and mostly within lesbian feminism.

My life has spun itself out in a British context for over thirty years and most recently in Australia: the politics and people I deal with on a day-to-day basis in Britain and Australia therefore reverberate most strongly for me. If I were living in the United States my critical eye might be fastened on Andrea Dworkin or Catherine MacKinnon and the particular turmoils their positions throw up. But, as much as feminism internationally absorbs me, I like digging around in my back yard best.

Taking sides, naming names, being explicit in relation to the particular politics and personalities represented in this final section came about when I realized I could no longer be nice about what was going on in specific, discrete situations. By the time Susan Ardill and I wrote 'Upsetting an Applecart: Difference, Desire and Lesbian Sadomasochism' (published in 1986) we had, as far as the brand of feminism we were critiquing was concerned, burnt our bridges. Nothing less than a full 'conversion' would make things friendly again.

Yet in 'Upsetting an Applecart' Susan and I also rejected binary oppositions. We were itching to develop a critique of a strand of lesbian feminism and to unravel the place of a certain sort of identity politics within that strand. That persistent itch was brought on by the practical politics we were involved in. What motivated the women we opposed? Where did their righteousness come from? How could we dissect their positions the better to understand and stand up to them? But in opposing, let's say, Lesbians Against Sadomasochism (LASM), we also stood back from the 'other side', London's precursors to queer, the Sexual Fringe whose utterances and writings we also found problematic even if we were more sympathetic to them.

Never mind. No one from the Sexual Fringe identified us as the enemy, even if some were pissed off at us for our criticisms. But many from Lesbians Against Sadomasochism were livid. Women I had known and worked with for years stopped talking to me. I didn't really care, but nor did I really understand how deep the animosity went or how many repercussions it would have.

Taking sides is hard to do – that's my experience. Yet to enter, however innocently, political arenas and seriously contemplate what you find there may at some point present this necessity. 'Upsetting an Applecart' came out of an intensely fraught time. I am fascinated by how difficult it is today to convey an episode filled with so much tension, which drove so many women to extremes. Not exactly ancient history, especially as the issues are still bubbling and festering away, not resolved at all, and yet it feels a million years ago. Perhaps I have changed although I don't want to repudiate what Susan and I wrote. I'm sure whether it makes me glad or sad that I would not have as much patience today with the arguments of our opponents about whether or not SM groups or individuals could use a lesbian and gay centre. (The centre we wrote about soared up, bright and beautiful, coasted and then crashed, brought to its end by bad management and indifference after seven years of existence.)

Susan and I had worked together since our *Spare Rib* days. We had remained there through another, earlier time of mind boggling intensity and struggle when the emotional and political fires of race and racism, anti-Semitism, and sexual identity had seared everyone on the collective. We had all floundered, some had dropped by the wayside and others staggered on. I took uneasy sides, but often I stubbornly refused, trying to voice other choices. In practice, we didn't know how to plot the dividing lines between a hierarchy of righteousness based on *identity*, and the real racism in the magazine and on the collective.

Today we might maintain that if *Spare Rib* were to happen all over again we would play out our roles with more political confidence because of what we ultimately learned there. Not as much cowering in fear of being labelled racists if we disagreed with a line being put forth by a Black woman. More understanding of the desperation which led Black and third-world women to present a unified front to the white women on the collective. More clarity about the real role personality conflicts play in organizations. More incisiveness about the way white women wallowed in guilt and then dropped out 'exhausted' by it all. Less patience with the primacy of an ongoing, unresolved drama which took on a life of its own. At the same time, I know we would both agree that the reality and importance of racism on the *Spare Rib* collective was painfully real and its resolution, in more than rhetoric, a speck on the horizon.

By the time the sexuality applecart tipped over, Susan and I were on slightly more certain ground. First of all, as much as we were writing against unitary politics of a particular kind, we were also on the ground of our own lesbian identity. This ground might be as treacherous as any other but we believed we belonged there as much as any other lesbian. Secondly, we were more seasoned to the familiar acrimonious divisions between feminists. And thirdly, we realized the fights we were having were far-reaching and were not going to be resolved by time or goodwill. Lastly, we believed we could make a difference in this situation.

It's not a coincidence that our comparative clarity about the political divisions between lesbians was based more firmly on differences in ideological approach and the meanings of various subdivisions of *lesbian* identity. In our 'sex war' skirmish all the cries of pain and oppression and patriarchal outlook from our opponents were like water off a duck's back. Almost. Ironically, our own lesbian *identities* bolstered our sense of belonging in this fracas. As we set about deconstructing a notion of a privileging lesbian identity, at the same time that was made possible by our own lesbian identities – even if we problematized them.

The rest flowed from that. It flowed on and on. It was exacerbated by the professional and personal friendships I made with American lesbian feminists who were already placed and labelled as anti-feminist within the British/North American/Australian lopsided sex war lines, women like Joan Nestle, Sarah Schulman, Cindy Patton and later Gayle Rubin and Carole Vance.

Susan and I continued writing shorter articles which are included here and in Part Two. 'Sex in the Summer of '88' was published in *Feminist Review* in 1989 and in it we rather disingenuously signal the lessening of the power of groups like LASM and the moralistic grip this kind of lesbianism appeared to have on lesbian intellectual, social and political life in London. In it we note a new spirit of openness although we are less sure about what this signifies.

My own involvement in the summer's activities centred on Sheba's publication of Joan Nestle's *A Restricted Country* and her two-week visit to Britain to help launch it. All four of us on the Sheba collective loved the book and were thrilled about Joan's visit. We brainstormed madly. What Sheba events could we organize to focus attention on the book and also draw out the implications for Britain? Araba Mercer and Michelle McKenzie were keen that we include gay men in our large public meeting, 'Putting the Sex Back into Sexual Politics'. Both were involved in attempts to set up a Black lesbian and gay centre in London, both were strong and confident feminists, both wanted Black gay men to be present.

Rae Ann Robertson and I agreed that Sheba was ready to organize a public meeting for women and men. Later on we would joke that event was a prefiguration of queer in London.

Susan and I analysed the events of the summer of '88, including the Sheba forum. I mention it here to make clear that all of us on Sheba took an active part in publishing decisions. The dynamics of our collaboration were based on mutual respect and support. We came from very different places and ages. We were Black and white. We felt, no matter how briefly, as if we were top of the world, publishing exciting books, poor as dormice, connected to a growing community of diverse women.

By the time I went to the International Feminist Book Fair in Barcelona in 1990, representing Sheba, I was a member of Feminists Against Censorship. I didn't feel easy with a straightforward civil libertarian position on pornography but felt I could grapple with my ambivalence there better than sitting around and doing nothing, as other feminists drew the lines of what was to be relegated to the dust heap of patriarchy when it came to porn. I was facing up to my own contradictory position on erotica/porn which for a while absolved lesbian and gay erotic writing from the supposedly inherent sexism of heterosexual porn/erotica. Porn of any variety, which was racist, sexist and violent should be resisted and fought against through means outside the legal or institutionalized channels of the bourgeois state. But not all porn was inherently destructive.

When I returned from Barcelona and reflected on the way I had been turfed off the fair's major lesbian platform at the insistence of women who declared I was a 'known pornographer' I concluded that I wasn't going to sit passively on my butt and take it. No more nice girl, always trying to see the larger picture, worried about individualizing things too much. If a few fundamentalists were going to play dirty then I was going to play hard, name names and lay some blame.

I'm a stubborn sort. I can't stand people telling me, 'There's nothing you can do. Ignore it. It's not important. Who cares anyway?' I have no illusions about being able to solve things, single-handedly change them or anything like that. But I won't go out of this life without trying, or without registering opposition. With these sentiments in mind, I have chosen to include a long letter I wrote to an American feminist publication, the *Lesbian Review of Books*. I sent it after a particular debate I felt strongly about had run its course in the paper, so I never expected it to be printed. It wasn't, although the editor sent me an interesting reply.

The last piece in this section is my Paglia rant. I can't stand her writing or her 'persona'. So what's new? I wanted to go beyond her cheap denunciations of feminists and feminism and get to grips with some of the underpinnings in her book. I combed her essays and so tedious and boring were they that they almost drove me mad. I decided to write using her sort of venom and see if I could apply it and still forage my way through the endless layers of bluster and verbiage she foists upon the reader. Paglia does not represent an aspect of feminism; she is a parasite with no interest in feminism other than denigrating and helping to destroy it wherever she can. I had no compunction about tossing 'nice' out of the window and getting dirty with Camille.

As I write, the Beijing Women's Conference is happening, the pope has made his appeal to women, gay bashings are increasing in the USA, Australia and Britain, and a vicious backlash is underway against anything which can be tagged with the 'politically correct' label. Victims are out. Long live victims. And yet ... the visibility and actuality of lesbians has never been higher. Finally, taking sides is something you do out of necessity.

Upsetting an Applecart:
Difference, Desire and Lesbian Sadomasochism
– WRITTEN WITH SUSAN ARDILL AND FIRST PUBLISHED IN
FEMINIST REVIEW 23, SUMMER 1986, 'SPECIAL ISSUE:
SOCIALIST-FEMINISM: OUT OF THE BLUE'

This article is about an ideological and politcal set-to over defining, discussing and organizing around sexuality as lesbians in the mid eighties in Britian.

We were both involved in the battle at the London Lesbian and Gay Centre (LLGC) over whether SM (sadomasochism) groups should be able to meet there. This battle went on for almost six months in 1985 – explosively, at times viciously. It was not just confined to the centre. Battlelines were drawn in many lesbian groups, women's centres, even bars and discos. The consequences linger today.

We want to talk about the different feminist politics which informed the groups engaged in the tactics and open fights which went on over the months. We want critically to examine SM and its lesbian feminist manifestations. We want to discuss politics which arise out of and around our sexual pratices.

Although this was ostensibly a political struggle over a sexual practice, sex remained the silent item on the agenda.

It seems to us that in the London Women's Liberation Movement (WLM) there is often a chasm between discussions about the 'politics of sexuality' and discussions about what our actual different sexual practices are. Over and over, workshops at conferences, even whole conferences, bill themselves as being about sexuality, only to turn into talk shops about the things which *determine* sexuality, or how frightening it is actually to talk about sex. Evocative words are thrown around, like 'pleasure', 'danger', 'lust', 'romance', but as often as not, on the day, it's other words which apply, like distance, analysis, evasion – and above all, frustration, confusion and boredom.

Sexuality is for both of us a political and personal concept and fact. Intriguing, jagged, hurting, sunlight and shadows, movement and moment. Recalled alone and recalling together. But the divide remains as we attempt to bridge it. That's the skirmish which we, two socialist-feminist lesbian friends, are having to go through to get this article out.

We approach our sexuality to capture it. But is it ever steady enough to capture? To haul into the political arena? Can we break through the reactions of our feminists sisters, lovers and friends? Their disapproval or feigned boredom makes us falter, blush and backtrack. Is talking about sex political? Can politics encompass sex? Is feminism a dour tendency? Do feminists do peculiar things in secret? Do we tend to come unstuck in sex? Do we get stuck up about sex? Is secret sexy? Does any of it matter in cold, cruel light?

Here *we* are, with daring words to start yet knowing another page will be quite ordinary. But that's it: how to talk about sex – boring, passionate, regular, surprising, absent – and how it intersects with different women's daily lives as Black or white women, as workers, as people in relationships, with or without children, as feminists meeting all the oppressions and hierachies of this society. Because it *does* matter – though it matters differently in different historical moments, in different geographical areas. The literature of oppressed people so often contains the dreams which sexuality seems to offer, intertwined with the struggles to do with class, with race and imperialism, and with other gender roles.

The movements for gay, lesbian and women's liberation have offered a way to understand, change or enhance those dreams. Or, rather, they have increasingly offered many *different ways*.

Shattering Reality
This article is being written at a time of depression and lack of confidence in feminist and left-wing politics. The reality of fragmentation and the development of politics around the autonomy of 'new' political constituencies – women, Black people, gay men, lesbians, old, disabled – has thrown up its own theoretical discussion around 'difference'.

From the beginning of the women's liberation movement in the West, when differences were sheltered (and hidden) under the benign umbrella of sisterhood, we moved to the situation of the early 1980s when 'differences' pulled down the umbrella and claimed sisterhood as an autonomous state for their own group. A multitude of identities defined lives, loyalties and political correctness, as the totalizing world view feminism offered to some, mainly white, women cracked open. Conflict became the keynote.

This article is about one such conflict – one which was crucially concerned with differences *between* lesbians. It struck both of us that while recognition for the oppression of different 'other' groups of people constantly came up during this struggle, in fact our political opponents had a basic difficulty in acknowledging that within our own shared identity of lesbianism, other women could drastically differ from them in attitude or practice. We wanted to take apart this apparent contradiction, wondering if it could offer us any insights into the roots of the bitterness of the conflict, or give us any help in creating the alliances or coalitions we must make to affect radical change.

Hello. What's Your Name?
What we felt happened with the increasing dominance of 'identity' as the organizing factor of so many feminist activities and discussions is that 'naming' and 'claiming' came to be invested with a peculiar moral authority. Just to *name* yourself as part of a given group is to *claim* a moral backing for your words and actions.

Where does this sort of 'naming' get its power? Why have certain words become icons? In the LLGC battle, for example, speeches by women who were opposing SM often began with a declaration of identity: for example, 'I am a lesbian mother and I think ...' In this context the words 'lesbian mother' are meant to convey a specific moral weight, not just that of personal experience. What was being invoked was a particular feminist ideology. We cannot *name* this ideology. It's not a simple political tendency, but an amalgam of various strands of feminist politics. As we see it, there are two key ingredients: an analysis of the world as made up of a fixed hierarchy of oppressions (or a select collection of oppressions) around gender, sexuality, race and ethnicity, age and ability; and notions of the 'authenticity' of subjective experience – experience which can be understood only with reference to the hierarchy. So, to say, 'I am a lesbian mother' within this mode of politics during the LLGC struggle was to allude to a whole set of oppressions as a way of validating the speaker's current political position. (A number of other things were going on too, but here we want to get to the root of the tone of self-righteousness we often heard.) Within these politics, there's little room for distinguishing between politics and those who speak them, little space for such things as evaluation of strategies or criticism, or making mistakes.

Somehow, the radical power of uncovering by describing, creating language for experiences that have previously gone unarticulated, just becomes labelling, slotting things neatly into place. In this value system 'naming' and 'experience' are privileged – but there is little room for movement once the words are out. To speak experiences, to claim identities, is to be tied into positions, and everything is assumed to follow on from them. A lesbian mother, then, will automatically have certain positions on men, women, money … sex.

The inherent problem with taking subjective experience as the main key to political action is that people have differing experiences. Not only that, they may also interpret the same experience in differing ways. The solution of some feminists, be they revolutionary feminists, cultural feminists or socialist feminists, is to fall back on their own particular hierarchy model; those more towards the bottom bear more of the weight so our/their experiences must speak more 'truthfully' of oppression. In this context, any clash, whether between groups or individuals, becomes a matter of rank determining righteousness. While this hierarchy model has developed partly as a response to difference and conflict, it doesn't do particularly well with diversity or contradiction. It too easily lends itself to a politics of 'truth'. Taken to extremes, if there are divisions within the same 'rank' or group, suppression becomes necessary, so as to protect the 'official' version's claim to define and describe the oppression.

These basic premises, with their reliance on the truth of the hierarchy or the sacrosanct nature of a collection of oppressions, and the claiming of identities, have increasingly become an implicit part of much feminist politics. They act as the framework, the supports, for political positions around the different issues.

Feminists' ideas about lesbianism have formed and changed over time. In the last few years one ideology of lesbian feminism became dominant and claimed feminism for itself. This ideology operates within the framework we have just outlined. 'Anger', 'identitiy', 'experience' have become the hallowed passwords among large numbers of lesbian feminists.

Imagine their consternation, then, if another group of lesbians pops up – who are *angry* and who want to *identify* around a different *experience* and *interpretation* of it. But this interpretation, in the realm of sexuality (that most subjectively experienced area), upsets the whole previous applecart of lesbian-feminist assumptions about who lesbians are. It is this fundamental clash which forms the basis of the entanglements over SM, and because it's a struggle over definitions and the power to define, now at the crux of some political positions, emotions ran high. Unravelling the tangles at the roots of the bitterness that fuelled the LLGC SM debate has been emotionally fraught for us as participants, and difficult to do. But ultimately that unravelling exposes many of the underpinnings of the various politics involved. It presents possibilities for stating differences and divisions while working to change and challenge exploiting power. And, in the course of the struggle at the LLGC, it's just possible there started a fracture which could impede the ascendancy of a brand of lesbian feminist politics which has been prevalent in this country for long enough.

The Premise of the Premises

The London Lesbian and Gay Centre is the result of certain possibilites meeting certain perceived needs. It would not exist in the form it does today without the politics which the radical Labour GLC embraced and propagated. It wouldn't exist as it does now if a particular cross-section of gay men and lesbians hadn't come together with an understanding of all this and with a vision of a centre.

The centre, an old four-storey building, almost across from London's Farringdon tube, opened unofficially and unfinished in late December 1984. The plans were for stylish and well-appointed premises that would meet the needs of a wide variety of London's gay and lesbian population. Included were the inevitable disco/bar/theatre space, a café and kitchen, another bar, a bookshop run by Gay's the Word, a crêche, a large lounge and meeting room for lesbians, a media resource floor, various centre offices and a number of spaces for rent to gay and lesbian projects and enterprises.

By the time of the 'official' opening in March 1985 the centre was being booked for meeting space by a number of different groups. The co-opted management committee (MC) had already discussed the issues that would soon break out into bitter fighting between users or potential users of the centre. Wendy Clark, one of the co-opted MC members, told us, 'We knew from the women's movement what some of the issues would be and that sometimes clashed with some of the views that the men held.'[1]

Bisexuality, paedophilia, sadomasochism, transsexuality, dress codes – all came up in the MC discussions about who could or should be welcomed into the centre. At the same time the MC, an all-white group of men and women, discussed making the centre accessible to more Black and working-class gay men and lesbians.

Wendy Clark maintains that the majority of the women on the MC were antagonistic to the SM groups who wanted to hold meetings in the centre, and in particular they were not keen about the men. Yet the centre's ideological underpinning was a liberal tolerance which incorporated the 'wide diversity of the gay community'. This contradiction was not fully faced, until it hit them in the face.

Zoning in on the Centre

It was in this context that the first stirrrings of more public debate about SM and the centre occurred. Different eddies and currents, already swirling elswhere in the WLM, settled on the centre with histories already in the process of gelling, with scuffles recorded and bad guys and good guys named. A coalition of lesbian feminists saw that the centre was (unenthusiastically) giving a place for SM groups to meet. Already they had managed to trounce the possibility of any of this ugly business happening at A Women's Place (the central London women's centre) or of SM being discussed in the central London women's newsletter. Letters arrived at the centre from these women demanding that SM groups be forthwith excluded. They declared with their usual confidence that they represented *the* lesbian feminist position on the subject.

By the time the centre opened officially, the 'debate' was underway, particularly within the weekly meetings of lesbians who were trying to co-ordinate events in the lesbian-only lounge and work out the relationship that space had to the rest of the centre.

It was not a new debate – only the instance and place made a difference. Political positions over the SM issue by no means followed a clear-cut path. But certain trends could be discerned.

Sexuality and Feminism

In the mid seventies lesbianism and/or separatism were first presented within the women's liberation movement as possibilities for all women to take up as part of their political struggle. For many feminists the printing of the CLIT statement from the USA in issue after issue of the London Women's Liberation Workshop newsletter was shocking, frightening and led to the first significant withdrawal of women from under the umbrella of sisterhood. (We're aware that many, particularly Black and working-class women never got under it in the first place.) In the CLIT statement all heterosexual women were named as untrustworthy dupes at best, or, at worst, as active collaborators with the enemy. Given that, the only feminist choice was withdrawal from men and bonding with women.

In London there was no sustained political rebuttal of CLIT – only the outraged cries of wounded and angry heterosexual feminists. In this instance, heterosexuality was attacked on moral/political grounds and the response was moral/personal outrage. No one spoke directly about sex; there was no ongoing discussion about desire or sexuality. But, after this, the earlier possibilities for heterosexual feminists to explore their relations with men didn't exist in the same way. Being a heterosexual feminist, even an angry-with-men one, was not enough any more.

However, from then until the emergence of revolutionary feminism, and in particular the Leeds revolutionary feminist writing on political lesbianism in 1979, heterosexuality was still the assumed sexual identity of most, if not all, women in most feminist circles. Lesbians had certainly made their presence known inside the WLM, but often they still had to assert their presence in order to avoid being incorporated back into the assumed heterosexuality of all women. This was true even on *Spare Rib*, a magazine of women's liberation. Continued sorties against that assumption were made by lesbians and/or separatists. Often the basis of the criticism was confused. In some cases it veered towards biological determination, as in the then-infamous 'boy children' debate in London, where the presence of the boys of feminists at women's centres created a furore. In other instances the argument tended to be couched in terms of lesbianism's 'natural' subversive and revolutionary character in relation to the patriarchy.

Revolutionary feminism, as distinct from radical feminism or socialist feminism, is the forerunner of a particular English feminist politics which six years later ended up fighting SM at the LLGC in the garb of Lesbians Against Sadomasochism (LASM). LASM had links, through particular women and, more importantly, through its political opposition to SM, with the early political lesbianism of the Leeds revolutionary feminists, and with the anti-porn politics of Women Against Violence Against Women (WAVAW): 'Porn's the Theory, Rape's the Practice'. But other lesbian feminist political positions were also present in the anti-SM grouping.

Radical feminists, even if in relationships with men, tended to say that they rejected male sexuality as it is now, totally. But on *Spare Rib* magazine, the early years produced confident articles on sexuality; articles which were going to teach women how to have orgasms, how to demand what they wanted from men. By the late seventies that confidence had gone.

Spare Rib spent much of 1980 tearing itself apart over the issue of sexuality. The collective was split over whether a submitted article claiming that lesbians had silenced heterosexuals in the women's movement was anti-lesbian and, secondly, whether *Spare Rib* should print it. The lesbians and heterosexuals on *Spare Rib* (all white women at that time) differed over the article and the lesbians differed among themselves. However, the 'naming' and 'claiming' tone was set by those lesbians on the collective who felt that the article was anti-lesbian and that they suffered as a result of it. Because they suffered, their position had to hold sway. The other lesbians, who either did not think the article was anti-lesbian or who felt that the best way to deal with anti-lesbianism among feminists was to bring it out in the open, air it, confront it and struggle with it, did not count. They didn't display the requisite pain. The *expression* of anti-lesbiansim in whatever form, from whoever, became the *oppression* of lesbians, full stop. The article was not printed and the collective went on in a confused, moralistic and contradictory way to confront and be confronted by racism, Zionism and anti-Semitism.

What's That You're Grappling With?

The rise of revolutionary feminism in the late 1970s claimed a certain place for sexuality on the feminist agenda – firmly in the centre. Men's sexuality was the key problem, but in a different way from the view of many radical feminists. In revolutionary feminism, male sexuality was, for the foreseeable future, irredeemable. Feminists' struggle was against male sexuality, not *with* it; they mobilized against it in WAVAW and anti-pornography groups. Women's sexuality was the key to both her oppression and liberation.

Suddenly everyone was grappling with compulsory heterosexuality and political lesbianism, separatism, non-monogamy, lesbian lifestyle, lesbianism as the pratice of feminism. Where was socialist feminism in all this? Despite the brief existence of Lesbian Left, the terrain around lesbianism seems to have been left wide open for revolutionary and radical feminism to claim as their own. In the late seventies and early eighties heterosexual socialist feminists, confronted with the growing divisions in the autonomous women's movement, not the least of which were accusations of consorting with the enemy, dropped out in droves. And they made a beeline for the mixed organizations of the left – trade unions, the Labour Party, campaigning groups – leaving those socialist-feminist lesbians who remained socially and/or politically active in the grassroots of the WLM not a little isolated in the face of the now dominant assumptions about lesbianism and feminism.

It is ironic that while many of the best-known socialist-feminist intel-lectuals are lesbians, over the years socialist feminism has come to be associated with heterosexuality. It has concentrated on analysing desire in the abstract and has virtually nothing to say about lesbianism. It has made no significant political intervention in the ongoing messy debates about sexuality, heterosexuality and lesbianism. This is a schematic view, of course, but one which we think accurately describes the relative power (or lack thereof) of socialist feminism *vis-à-vis* radical/revolutionary feminism in speaking to lesbians about the experience and politics of sexuality.

Tipping the Cart

So, 'women-identified' ruled ok. Then *Sex Heresies* came along, published in the spring of 1981. This issue of an American feminist periodical was an attempt to combat the latent feminist assumptions about how we, hets or dykes, 'should' express sexuality. With a paucity of feminist writing around sex, and after a few years of *The Joy of Lesbian Sex* and others of that ilk, it was definitely exciting. And shocking to some – with articles on butch-femme relationships, sadomasochism, masturbation and celibacy, prostitution, fag hags and feminist erotica. Whatever else, *Sex Heresies* signalled a move to put the erotic back into sex. Whereas the British revolutionary feminists appeared to see sex as a pleasant possibility between women who had withdrawn from men, *Sex Heresies* underlined the deep and confusing currents of desire between women.

In the USA *Sex Heresies* seems to have been the first salvo in a battle over sexuality which has been intense, overt and wide-ranging. A loose coalition of sexual radicals (who include lesbians, heterosexual feminists and gay men) has sprung up, stringing together the unrespectable issues, like paedophilia, SM, promiscuity, willing to dissect, bring into the open and mostly defend all the variations of sexual pleasure and desire. All of these overlapping issues have had specific ramifications among lesbians – but, in the lesbian-feminist sub-culture, SM has become the peg from which all the others have been hung. And it was the SM debate that turned up among lesbians in Britain.

SM's Shifty Meanings

Why do we keep naming it 'the SM debate'? One of the most difficult aspects of this ideological struggle around sexuality has been sifting through a quagmire of shifting definitions. A simple description of SM might be the sexual dramatization or acting-out of power relations, with its own history of codes and meaning, of ritual and paraphernalia. But is SM a clearly delineated physical practice which only a certain percentage of lesbians will ever be into? Is it therefore of limited relevance to most lesbians? Or is SM the crystallization of the most vital components of *all* erotic tension: teasing, titillation, compulsion and denial, control and struggle, pleasure and pain. Alternatively it could just be that, in the vacuum of lesbians speaking and writing about sex, the language of sexual excitement used in, for example, *Coming to Power: Writings and Graphics on Lesbian SM*, resonates with a great many women who are not, technically speaking, into SM (SAMOIS, 1981).

Debates specifically around lesbian SM *have* taken place in the context of a general challenge to feminist sexual orthodoxy. SMers indeed have aligned themselves with other self-defined 'sexual outlaws' – prostitutes, butch and femme lesbians, bisexuals. Several things seem to have been happening at once, and at times it's hard to keep a grasp on exactly what it is at any given moment.

SM lesbians have been engaged in a struggle to 'come out SM', to be open and proud of their sexual practices. Because of the negative connotations of sadism and masochism (linked to actual torture, cruelty and emotional suffering), and the hegemony of political lesbianism, they have been come down on – hard – by large sections of lesbian feminists. Other lesbians, including many socialist lesbians like ourselves, have acted in defence of SM dykes around issues of censorship and exclusion. This defence has necessarily broadened into an intense struggle over definitions of feminsim and lesbianism, the rights and wrongs of lesbian sexual pratice, desires and fantasies in general.

In participating in these struggles, we've become aware of the absence of language that can deal with different lesbian sexualities. To some extent, SMers have captured the market of sexual description. But it's plainly no use dividing all lesbians (as some SMers do) into SM and vanilla dykes. During the last year we've been dismissed as liberals (from both sides) because we've appeared to be just tolerantly defending the rights of others. However, we don't disavow our own interest or involvement in some aspects of SM. We do think, though, that a socialist-feminist critique of SM as a political theory and pleasure as a supposedly neutral playground is needed.

In Britain, the struggle around lesbian sexuality has been muted and spasmodic, though accompanied by often violently intense reactions. This struggle to retrieve eroticism in the face of, among other things, the political desexualization of lesbianism, has been characterized here by an almost complete absence of talking or writing about sex. A magazine like the explicit Californian *On Our Backs* seems unthinkable in London. Even the sexual liberationists, in discussions about 'Pleasure and Danger' in the avant-garde *Square Peg* (No. 10, 1985), resort to allusions to 'tops' and 'bottoms' and various interpersonal dynamics. Having bought their under-the-counter (yes – from Sisterwrite in London) copies of *Coming to Power*, lesbians might make either covert references to their 'favourite article', or disdainful jokes. The possibility of having, for example, a frank and public discusion on the lesbian gang 'rape' fantasy ('Girl Gang' by Crystal Bailey) seems out of the question in London – and yet one of us has been in on a discussion on that, and many others like it, in Australia. We're forced to fall back on the suspicion that sex itself *is* relatively more hidden in British society, and that goes for the women's movement too.

Reactions

The reaction against *Sex Heresies* and all it stood for was well under way by late 1981. Articles in the internally published *Revolutionary and Radical Feminist Newsletter* posed a dichotomy between sexual liberation and women's liberation reminiscent of the early 1970s – only this time it was some forms of lesbianism, not just heterosexuality, that were under attack. Revolutionary feminists and some radical feminists sought to set the terms of the discussion: political lesbianism (lesbianism as a political strategy for fighting male power) was such a central tenet of their politics that any challenge to the orthodoxy of lesbian sex was a challenge to the entirety of their feminism. Anyone mounting such a challenge was not a 'true' feminist.

But the sexual pleasure brigade continued to make inroads, in books, conferences, discussions. By late 1982 articles in the *Revolutionary and Radical Feminist Newsletter* had to take some of the issues on board, though still with a completely hardline rejection of SM. They were obviously worried that talk of sexual fantasy, masochistic feelings and erotic pleasure was ringing a few bells among lesbians. They felt the 'SM lobby' was capitalizing on the silence of its opponents, so their strategy became one of talking about sexuality. They wanted to demonstrate that most lesbian feminists had perfectly reasonable non-oppressive sex lives (and thus didn't need SM). They acknowledged that many women had masochistic (even sadistic) fantasies. However, if feminists were 'afflicted' with the 'internalization of the male (hetero) sexual model', change was possible and necessary for feminism.

With this strategy in mind, revolutionary feminists organized the Lesbian Sex Conference in London in April 1983. However, although they planned it and wrote all the pre-distributed papers, the conference ended up having a non-specific atmosphere. Attended by hundreds of women, with workshop titles from 'Lesbians and Fashion' to 'Monogamy' to 'Heterosexism', there was a general air of waiting to see what would happen. With organized speakers in workshops, and no plenary session, complete pot luck determined any individual's experience of the weekend (see Egerton, 1983). There was the odd rumour of disagreement from the SM workshops, and there were conflicts involving the felt exclusion of some working-class women and the physical exclusion of women with disabilities. But in general nothing much seemed to happen. If there were few open discussions about sex, neither was revolutionary feminism much in evidence. It was a diffuse and defused occasion.

In the following two years, questions of sex and sexuality went slightly out of focus, as struggles and eruptions, especially around racism and anti-socialism, took centre stage in the WLM. The 'sex' debate had been, in Britain, primarily conducted between two (or more) camps of white women, with individual contributions by some Black lesbian feminists (Bellos, 1984). This, we think, is unlike in the USA where the concerns and theories around sex of Black women and women of colour had a strong voice among the pro-pleasure groupings, though not without hard criticism of the racist elements of much white theory. Here, the increasingly organized and powerful presence of Black lesbians has had a gradual impact on the terms of reference of the SM debate. Some Black lesbians have made it clear they don't want anti-racist rhetoric used in an opportunistic way to bolster up *either* side of the debate, particularly as it has remained a white-dominated discussion. Racism in sexuality remains largely unacknowledged on the white lesbian political agenda.

It's Getting Closer

On to the next round of skirmishes. During the winter of 1983-84, the *London Women's Liberation Newsletter* refused to carry a notice about a meeting called by SM Dykes to discuss sadomasochism. The few individuals (including members of a lesbian sexuality discussion group we were in) who raised voices in protest at the censorship were shot down in a barrage of abuse and condemnation.

At the 1984 Lesbian Strength March the storm in a teacup blew up again when SM Dykes appeared with a provocative banner (lesbian symbol intertwined in chains). *Newsletter* writers raged at the shame and horror of it all. SM Dykes, having been silenced, kept silent in feminist circles.

Less than a year later, the LLGC opened its doors and the anti-SM lesbians were busily writing letters to the MC protesting about any SM presence there. A few of these women started to attend the weekly meetings of the Lesbian Co-ordinating Committee, set up as an open voluntary group to plan and organize the lesbian-only space. Instead the meetings (in which we took part) spent a lot of time skirmishing, fighting, going over and over the subjects of SM, lesbian identity, political acceptability and the role of the centre. No one talked about SM *sex* or whether anyone should do it. We were talking about the presence of small groups of women and men who might use the centre for meetings on the same basis as many other lesbian or gay groups. No one defended the 'right' of any fascist or racist group to meet at the centre, no matter how 'well' they might behave. In fact the centre's constitution clearly excluded any such groups from meeting in it. The argument remained one about definitions of SM, and the supposed behaviour of SMers.

Because no one really believed SMers were going to do 'it' in the centre, the focus was on their presence – how they looked became all-important. The practice of lesbian SM was, on both sides of the debate, described with dualistic pairings of words: power and submission; pleasure and pain; dominance and subordination; passive and active; top and bottom. Alongside these went the apparel and (optional!) accessories: whips, chains, dog collars, caps, leather, studs, handcuffs. The 'look' (often indistinguishable from punk) became overloaded with meaning, and as threatening as the acts themselves. The question of women who might take part in SM sex without dressing the part was never dealt with. An extreme image was set up to be knocked down.

SM acts were, in the eyes of LASM women, irredeemably connected to heterosexuality. As most heterosexuality was considered violence to women, the added ritualization in SM sex made it more horrific and dangerous. In lesbian SM the fact that the oppressor (man) wasn't actually doing it made it even more reprehensible.

The Leeds Revolutionary Feminist Group had written their paper 'Political Lesbianism: The Case Against Heterosexuality' in 1979. In it they said '... it is specifically through sexuality that the fundamental oppression, that of men over women, is maintained' (Leeds Revolutionary Feminist Group, 1981). The Leeds group stated it very directly. In 1979 they wrote as if class, race and disability didn't exist, even if they were heavily criticized for this at the time. Now the same revolutionary-feminist analysis came shored up with the opportunistic use of race, class, anti-Semitism and disability. In a sense these became the stage props of the central drama which, for them, is still the determining division between men and women. But this is our interpretation and lies beneath the surface of the politics we are describing. The debate over lesbian SM was carried out by using their hierarchies of oppression, their collections of 'most oppressed', and attaching them to the practice of SM sex – thereby 'proving' how dangerous, disgusting and politically incorrect SM is. SM Dykes became the walking repositories of racism, fascism and male violence.

Mixing It Up
It seems in retrospect, no coincidence that this long-running drama in lesbian feminist circles finally came to a head in a mixed centre, though at first glance it might seem strange that women whose political position tends towards separatism even bothered to care about what would go on there. After years of separation, the LLGC marked an auspicious attempt for lesbians and gays to bridge the gap. A whole generation of lesbian feminists had gained their political experience in women-only centres and groups. It may have been a shock, even an affront to some that an attractive, well equipped centre was opening outside of their assumed sole claim to lesbian politics.

Lesbian SM, and SM Dykes themselves, had been fairly easily squeezed out of the increasingly prescriptive feminist channels of organization and communication. (Long gone are the days when a feminist cabaret act could call itself the Sadista Sisters and get away with it!) But owing to the different historical development of gay liberation politics, a mixed gay centre potentially offered them a home. Confirmation to its oppenents, perhaps, that SM *is* an essentially 'male' practice, and that the struggle against it is part and parcel of the larger feminist struggle.

At times during this struggle, LASM's main argument was against the contamination of lesbianism *and* the centre with a violent 'male' ideology. At other times it seemed that some anti-SM women were in complete opposition to any alliances or solidarity with (gay) men at all, and that was really the basis for their involvement at the LLGC. It was when this fundamentally destruction-minded position seemed to be gaining the upper hand that some of the group of women we were working with gave ourselves the somewhat dull title of Lesbian Feminists for the Centre.

Not that our support for the centre, or for working with men, was unproblematic, but then, we had entered into it anticipating that. When the SM debate came along, the primary aspect for us two was the struggle over ideologies of sexuality and lesbianism. The playing out of antagonisms between lesbians in front of men obviously posed difficulties. We had to be very wary of colluding with the view of feminists as spoilsport puritans perpetuated by some gay men (and women). One of us was disturbed by the anti-feminist tone of some statements at the first meeting of the Sexual Fringe (a coalition of women and men who defined themselves as sexual radicals). On the other hand, we would have liked to know how to protest openly at some lesbian behaviour towards men at the mass meetings, without swelling male egos. Too often we found ourselves silent, loyalties and politics pulling us all ways at once. Our main concern was to focus on the other lesbians involved, and to mobilize more lesbians to get involved. So, throughout the struggle we organized in an autonomous group of women. We wanted to keep distinct from the centre, and from men, in order to engage fully with LASM women within a feminist framework. But at no time did we consider the presence of men as incidental, or something we'd rather have done without. When it become apparent that we'd struck, and were up against, a deep anti-coalition vein within feminism, our commitment to this mixed centre clarified. It become, then, partly also a struggle to maintain the right to political optimism; to retain a sense of the possibilities for new things which the centre stood for.

Putting the Extraordinary into EGM

In April 1985, the first extraordinary general meeting (EGM) was held at the newly opened LLGC. Most women and men came thinking that they were there to discuss and resolve the issue of SM at the centre. The management committee, after its initial acceptance of SM groups meeting at the centre, had reserved that decision. After receiving letters and protests from LASM women and their supporters, they changed their minds. Wendy Clark says, 'So we took an interim decision that as a group they couldn't meet until there had been an open meeting or the first general meeting of the centre members and ask them to decide.' In fact SM groups took legal advice, consulted the constitution and called the first EGM.

It was a packed, tense meeting. Nothing was resolved. For constitutional reasons we were unable to take a vote on the proposed ban. For us the tension arose from our own silence and inability to support SM groups meeting in the centre in the face of the emotive presence of LASM women and their supporters, some of whom had never set foot in the centre before. Immediately after some angry scenes, *lesbians* were invited upstairs to a meeting in the lesbian meeting room. When some of us went our presence was challenged because we were 'pro-SM'. By this point feminism and lesbianism were claimed as LASM's own.

LASM's reports of the meeting were outraged. In newsletters and on the grapevine came news of a meeting packed out by SM men and women dressed in fascist gear who, by displaying continuous misogyny and hatred of children, oppressed the LASM women. The act of opposing their demand for exclusion of SM groups was, they claimed, an SM act in itself. (As far as dress goes, some strange outfits were worn, some leather and a few studded collars and leather caps. We saw no fascist gear.) The North London Lesbian Mothers Group, supporters of LASM, produced a leaflet for the EGM which illustrates some of their politics. 'For those of you who claim to oppose censorship of any kind, ask yourselves if you would allow a group calling itself "Gay Fascists" to organize in the Centre. There have to be *limits* in order to *prevent oppression* of all kinds' (our emphasis).

Here is the usual equation of SM with fascism. But we are interested in other aspects of the quote. So – oppression of all kinds can be prevented by imposing limits! Well, unfortunately oppression is not the product of 'no limits'. It comes, in however devious a route, from particular social systems and from particular sets of relationships that are part and parcel of those social, economic and cultural systems. To propose setting 'limits' as if that could take care of oppression and exploitation in our society is a travesty of the sort of changes we need to go through in order to transform anything. Our criticsim of the lesbian mothers' leaflet is on this basis, not about whether or not 'limits' are sometimes necessary or a good thing.

The static moralism of this political position is ripe for reformism too. It's been noted often enough how many socialist feminists have been drawn into municipal socialism and the Labour Party. What has not been noticed at all is the number of revolutionary feminists and those influenced by them now working in the same institutions, usually around women's issues. It would be interesting to trace out the reception their politics are getting in the Labour Party, and the influence they are having.

An Extraordinary Repeat
After the April EGM many centre users became more organized. Spurred on by LASM's tactics at the first EGM and ashamed of our

inertia around that event, Lesbians for the Centre began to meet independently to formulate a proposal for the next EGM (on 9 June at Conway Hall) and to discuss how we should go about trying to engage with LASM in order to defeat it. Our politics were diverse; we were not a group of SMers, nor were we all socialist feminists. We lacked a common theoretical base, but shared general agreement in pratice about the centre. We knew that LASM would propose an outright ban on SM groups, and that the Sexual Fringe wanted a completely 'anything goes' situation. We wanted to defend strongly the rights of the SM groups, while raising questions about what *could* be problems in such a centre in terms of dress and behaviour.

Stuck in Dilemmas

This led us into hours of debate over a dress code. Our proposal reflected the compromises we all made. Tagged on to the end is the one dress ban we all agreed on (the swastika, in the West a symbol of fascism past *and* present) and the one we compromised on: that no one should be led around the centre on a leash or chain. (Yes, we know it sounds ridiculous.)

No one in our group questioned that certain clothing or equipment evoked images of reaction and oppression. What we divided over was whether some styles or equipment – handcuffs, for instance – were in themselves symbols of oppression and therefore in themselves racist, fascist or anti-Semitic. The two of us agreed that meanings of objects are socially and culturally constructed. That did not mean that certain dress or behaviour could not be contested or even banned, but it should be on the basis of political discussion about the relationships between people in the centre and between the centre and the outside. Our motion said:

> The LLGC is a centre for a wide variety of lesbians and gay men who have different political perspectives. We are committed to an outreach programme to actively encourage the participation of Black and ethnic minority lesbians and gay men, disabled lesbians and gay men, and younger gay people. In order to ensure participation, the centre holds a firm policy of anti-fascism, anti-racism, anti-sexism, and an opposition to anti-Semitism and aggressive behaviour. The centre is closed to any group that advocates fascism, racism, anti-Semitism or sexism as any part of their stated aims or philosophy.
>
> Lesbians and gay men have a diverse range of 'sexualities'. We advocate no one sexuality for lesbians and gay men, understanding that sexuality is very complex, but we do recognize that the centre should be a place for constructive discussion around all aspects of our sexuality.
>
> Certain symbols and actions will not be permitted in the centre, namely the wearing and displaying of swastikas, and the leading around of individuals by means of chains or leads.

Of course this was seen as the very life blood of liberalism by LASM. Our aim neither to identify with a simplistic pro-SM stance which absolved anyone of critically looking at that sexual practice nor to dismiss the fears of LASM was not particularly appreciated by anyone.

In any case, the second EGM was beset by similar constitutional problems as the first, and the few motions or proposals discussed could be voted on only in order to ascertain the sense of the meeting. A large group of LASM women and their supporters demanded and got separate votes for men and women, obviously in order to *prove* the connection between 'male values' and pro-SM politics. Finally, about one third of the women present and three-fifths of the men voted to allow SM groups to meet in the centre.

The meeting was as acrimonious as the first, at times disintegrating into shouting matches. When a small group of women (about twelve of us) who sat together on one side of the hall raised out hands to oppose a ban, women on the other side of the room, LASM supporters, stood up to stare at us. The divide by the aisle was as literal as the divide between our politics.

Gathering Forces

All during the spring other groups had been meeting and politicking around the centre. The Sexual Fringe included SM lesbians and men as well as bisexuals, transsexuals and celibates. They saw themselves romantically as sexual outlaws, wherein the very fact of 'difference' put them in the same political position. They produced several leaflets which took on what they called prescriptive feminism.

When LASM put out a leaflet headed 'What Is This Big Fuss About Sado-Masochism?' it sparked off a number of responses. The LASM leaflet itself is interesting. Its pompous question-and-answer format compares very closely with the Leeds Revolutionary Feminist paper of 1979 on political lesbianism. There, the same irritating, moralist question-and-answer format places the authors in the superior, vanguardist position of explaining it all to backward children: For instance:

Q: But we don't do penetration, my boyfriend and me.

A: If you engage in any form of sexual activity with a man you are reinforcing his class power.

Q: But I like fucking.

A: Giving up fucking for a feminist is about taking your politics seriously.

Q: Are all lesbian feminists political lesbians?

A: No. Some women who are lesbians and feminists work closely with men in the male left (either in their groups or in women's caucuses within them) or provide mouthpieces within the women's liberation movement for men's ideas even when non-aligned.

The 1986 LASM leaflet, 'What Is This Big Fuss ...' includes 'answers' too:

S/Ms often wear clothes expressing real power, pain and humiliation, e.g. Nazi-style caps, dog collars, chains. This is racist, anti-Semitic and offensive to all oppressed people.

A pathetic questioner goes on to ask:

Q: But isn't Lesbian and Gay Liberation about freedom, not more limitations?

A: Total freedom is the freedom of the powerful to oppress – do you condone racism, anti-Semitism, heterosexism?

Q: But I like wearing long spiked belts and dog collars – and I'm not into SM.

A: So what. If you don't care that others see them as racist, anti-Semitic, etc. then you are being racist, anti-Semitic, fascist.

In that leaflet and in another called 'Sado-Masochism – the Reality', which was produced after the second EGM in June, SM takes on vast meaning: 'Remember that SM was a significant part of the "decadent" social scene in 1930s Berlin – part of the political climate of the day. People acclimatized to SM brutality would have failed to notice the threat of the "real Nazis" approaching.' Not only is SM equated with racism, fascism and anti-Semitism, but it also appears now to have allowed the rise of fascism in Germany! A view of 'decadent homosexuality' which is uncomfortably similar to the Moral Right's. The leaflet goes on to say: 'Similarly, we are all brought up to have racist feelings, otherwise the institution of racism could not survive.' These are the sentiments which fuel much of the racism – and heterosexism – awareness training industry: it is feelings that allow the institutions to survive.

The Sexual Fringe members responded to these lectures with some wit and precision, though their libertarian outlook sometimes weakened their insights. However, one of their leaflets which appeared before the second EGM was more sophisticated and responded to LASM's equation of SM and fascism. In 'Who Are the Real Fascists?' they say:

To label SM fascist is to trivialize the real fight against fascism. To throw the word fascism about with no reference to what it means is to make the real fight more difficult. To use people's sexual revulsion as a scare tactic against sexual freedom is a real insult to fascism's victims.

In an unpublished letter to *Feminist Review* last summer, four women members of the Sexual Fringe wrote:

> We feel that the women's movement has become more concerned with constructing and policing its own categories of sexual identity than with attempting to understand the complex and often contradictory construction of women's sexuality in a male-dominated, capitalist society.

All of these positions and arguments circulated in the weeks leading up to the second EGM and afterwards before the Lesbian Strength March and the July AGM. The LASM women were furious and disgusted when they lost. The fallout was heavy. Various lesbian groups had to decide what to do after the defeat. Some decided not to hold any meetings at the centre – fair enough. But at least two or three groups wrote letters to the GLC claiming that the centre was racist, fascist and excluded lesbians. They wanted the GLC to chop its financial support. A few LASM supporters inside the GLC even attempted to represent LASM's position on SM and the centre as the one and only true feminist one. It's quite a turn-up when lesbian feminists, some of whom advocate withdrawal from men on an individual sexual basis as a political stance, run to a male-dominated bureaucracy to denounce other lesbians and gay men. All that was quite shocking and indicative of the bankruptcy of their politics.

In the weeks leading up to the Lesbian Strength and Gay Pride March in June and before the AGM at the end of July, leaflets attacking the centre were distributed at women's venues, clubs and discos. Immediately before the Lesbian Strength March, when the centre served as a meeting point and the evening celebrations were in the lesbian lounge, a warning was handed out to women in London: 'Warning. Do not go to the London Lesbian and Gay Centre unless you are prepared to be in an environment that is rife with fascists, racists, misogynists and sadomasochists.' It offered an alternative social event after the march at Tindlemanor, a women's centre. Hundreds of women ignored this, and a fantastic evening followed. The centre was claimed as a place for many of London's lesbians.

Opening Up the Space to Explore

So what were the consequences of all this fighting? The centre doesn't appear to have been overrun with whips and chains – at times it's a positively tame place to be. A large number of lesbian feminists undoubtedly stay away. But many others do come. Most significantly, for us, a politics founded on an apocalyptic vision of what would happen if SM groups merely met at the LLGC has been publicly defeated and proven wrong. We definitely get a sense that LASM's ideology has suffered quite a big dent, and that some space has opened up for more discussion about lesbian sexuality. For, if anything, this debate showed that we are hardly at the beginning of being able to talk about it.

SM literature has said much about sexual daring, openness and excitement. It has said a lot to verify our own experiences, to incite us to further fantasies and possibilities. It has brought into the open naked desires. But it hasn't said much about situations where desire is absent or fantasies won't come; much less about, for example, the mundanities of a fetish-less long-term relationship.

We don't want to fall into the trap of posing these as opposites of each other (cruising *v* monogamy!). We're not saying that SM Dykes are responsible for articulating all sexual possibilities. The struggle around the rights of SMers has made space for more writing about sex – some great, some awful – though there's still far too little of the good stuff about. However, we do think that the Sexual Fringe (not an SM group, but from within the same political stream), during the LLGC struggle, *failed to acknowledge* that 'vanilla' sex can be exciting or that sexuality can be problematic (and not just because of 'repression'). By default, their position seemed to amount to one of 'uninhibited pursuit of the sexual high' – which leaves a lot to be desired!

Ultimately the Sexual Fringe's libertarianism ended up glorifying a kind of individualism. They romanticized categories of 'deviant' sexual practice – if you can't claim one of their identities, well, frankly, you're boring.

Boring equals vanilla sex, which is what? For lesbian SMers and for us, the ritual of the sexual interchange is very important. But for us an SM interchange can be as much about finding pleasure in the unplanned holding down of one lover by the other. 'The way we think about sex fashions the way we live it' (Weeks, 1985). Our own political position on SM is that we are all on a continuum. (We refuse the label liberal over this – stuff it.) Is the thrill of deliberate touch on muscle, a pressure on shoulders, done with a sense of dominance, accepted with a sense of submission, any less exciting than tying someone up? We suspect most of our sex lives and sexual histories are very uneven: cuddly sex, bondage, kisses and affection, one-night stands, dressing-up – any of these can be what we crave or pursue at any given time.

We should make it clear that, issue by issue, we would line up with the Sexual Fringe in defence and support of a radical sexual politics and practice. The question of desire is crucial to our understanding of sexuality. Where we disagree is over the context for those politics.

The centre's 'Fringe' and the SM groups saw their rebellion against society's 'norms' and, further, against the 'norms' of what constitutes 'acceptable' sexual practice according to certain groups of lesbians, as a radical act with political significance. In denying that playing out society's power roles in bed had any causal connection to the continuance or development of such relationships in the big wide world, they tended to exclude any discussion about the ways in which sexual relations *are* related to the rest of our lives. For instance, around housing, work, family – as well as state institutions. Lesbian SM literature suggests that organizing around oppositional sexual difference constitutes not just a political practice but a whole political perspective. It's here that SMers come unstuck. By failing to situate themselves as within particular sub-cultures, linked to certain life-style requirements, they inflate their sexual politics with a universality it almost certainly does not have.

The most absurd extension of the SM political position is the implication that if we all played out our SM fantasies in bed, the world would be a better place. The connecting line between this mode of thinking and the LASM one is striking, even if they draw the opposite conclusions.

LASM women claim they they have no real interest in the acts of SM sex except as they represent and become all of the pain, horror and degradation of women, Black people, Jewish people, mothers, disabled people, and so on. Unlike the SMers who deny any harmful reality of sexism, fascism and racism in SM sex roles or rituals, LASM goes to the opposite extreme and claims that things like tying up, spanking, whipping and wearing collars or belts with studs are in themselves violence against all the oppressed people of the world. LASM say they 'do not consent to being terrorized in the presence of the symbols of brutality, which are *just* as threatening as the presence of the real thing' (our emphasis). They deny any possibility of consensual agreement or equality in SM sex, just as the political lesbians do to women in 'ordinary' heterosexual sex. In an unquestioning SM view, we can choose our stage and role. In LASM's view we are acted *upon*; we are permanent victims (or bearers of oppression) except when we refuse the acts, deny the feelings that make us victims. We are implicated in our own victim status if we refuse to do that. This is where morality makes its entrance. (It's a remarkably religious scenario.)

Neither of these views sees the world in movement, in tension, dialectically. Still, is any of this SM debate/struggle really important enough to go on about? Why do we care so much?

Taking a Stand
Sexuality in Britain in the 1980s sits uneasily in the political domain, with other matters such as class despair, racist attacks and economic

depression demanding feminist attention. They demand our attention too, but we don't want to loosen our claim to the sexual as political and as important to our everyday lives. The thoroughgoing heterosexism of this society makes the struggle around sexuality an especially crucial one for us as lesbians.

Both of us live out our lives at least partially within the lesbian sub-cultures – socially and politically. We have no intention of quitting that world, and every intention of standing our ground there as lesbian feminists. As lesbians we have chosen to criticize the words and actions of other lesbians, we hope in a way consistent with our politics. A LASM leaflet said about *us*:

> SM Dykes have in fact never spoken up at any of these meetings, leaving the shouting to SM Gays and a group of 'liberal' women – none of whom are interested in defending any 'minority groups' other than the so-called 'sexual fringe' groups. The 'rights' of SMs, paedophiles and transsexuals are given priority over the rights of women who are Black/ Jewish/Irish/of Colour/disabled – and all other women who are threatened by male violence and are therefore excluded from the centre.

That leaflet exemplifies the sort of intimidatory tactic which has fuelled our anger during this struggle. We think this sort of tactic has serious implications for lesbians and for feminism. We know of many individual lesbians who have taken up the LASM position on the centre because it was presented so heavily as the 'correct line'. This represents a wider trend. Doubts, ambiguities, confusions are shoved under the carpet under this sort of pressure. The mere expression of dissenting ideas has become synonymous with endorsing oppression. There is no room in the LASM view for struggle, for admitting that we all can harbour reactionary ideas at the same time that we hold on to progressive ones.

Exploring complexities within the framework of the need for socialist-feminist change is a way of understanding where we are now – alone, together, in different groups. As lesbians, we do not want to be restrictively told what we are, or should be. As women, we do not want to be presented with a feminism predicated on a false portrayal of ourselves. That will not take us anywhere.

To Sum Up, Then
The fight between feminists about SM groups meeting at the LLGC represented a lot more than that. It was the location, for a brief and tumultuous time, of a battle around particular feminist politics. It was ostensibly about sexuality and yet sexuality was hardly mentioned in detail. For us it was largely a political struggle between different groups of lesbians. We don't believe for a moment that many of the LASM women

gave two hoots about the centre. In that way it was a symbolic occasion for the anti-SM women and, even though we were very involved in the centre, for us too.

History, in the short and long term, while open to analysis, has a messy daily life. It's a sad if not unsurprising irony that a socialist understanding, one which could help explain at least some of the reasons behind the exploiting divisions between particular groups of people, has not 'fitted' in a lasting way with the development of the women's liberation movement here. All through the 1970s the voices of excluded, ignored or patronized women sang angrily, accusingly about class, about race, about sexuality. Yet the practice of the white-dominated women's movement, with a large and vital socialist-feminist presence in it, was unable to answer those voices.

Whether this says more about British socialist history, contesting Marxist analysis of the 1970s, or about women's attempts to merge socialism and feminism, is open to debate. In any case, by the late seventies and early eighties those different voices finally resonated in many of the organizations, structures and publications of feminism. 'Difference', so long acknowledged but not dealt with, came home to roost, at the same time that socialist confidence in affecting social change was waning. It was then that the whole reality of unequal power relations between feminists and in the world was taken on board by an increasingly dispersed WLM. In some instances, the resulting lessons and achievements offer exciting possibilities for really radical change. But, for some, 'difference' became *in itself* an explanation, an organizing method, a static and moralistic world view. The anxieties about differences between women provided fertile ground for the rise of a simplistic politics within lesbian feminism which grasped for the seemingly easy answer of 'authentic experience'.

The possibility socialist feminism had of pushing forward a historical and dialectical analysis of difference between feminists and women in general which could produce a politics that could move, embrace, challenge yet forgive, had been overtaken by a rigid feminist politics which elevated some differences to the basic underpinning of political organization. What any one individual 'makes' of what she undeniably feels is open to many possibilities. The 'truthfulness' of the experience of the individual is not what we would question. Nor the reality of conditions which gave rise to the experience. But the fact that there is no one unifying response to sexism, to racism, to class exploitation, to heterosexism, forces us to examine the *place* that individual experience should hold in the development of theory and practice.

The contradictory responses of people to their particular oppression and/or situations alerts us to the often contradictory and complicated intertwining of the forces that course through the body politic. Far from making us throw up our hands in despair, we believe feminists can use that reality to develop an analysis and practice which takes into account the messiness of real life, the hopes, fears, angers and acquiescences.

The 'things that divide us' are as hard to discern as a sliver of glass and as huge as a boulder. The individual experience, however subjective, is an engagement with a force with a half life of its own and another half owned by other social forces. Racism exists. Sexism exists. Class exploitation exists. Imperialism exists. But each tangles with the other, feeds from or subtracts, adds to or bloats up another.

The way we 'feel' or experience any of these forces, either directly or indirectly, either one or the other or all, cannot be claimed as the only authentic one. In the first place that totally individualizes the effects of social forces. The social construction of an individual neither means 'free will' nor victim status. And secondly it removes individual constructions of feeling or experience from the impact of historical, economic and cultural forces. Thirdly, it proposes that there is a straight, short line from experience, to consciousness, to understanding and, finally, to political action.

What we feel as women from a thousand different realities, as oppressed and oppressor, actor and object, is a vital *part* of what goes into our political analysis as feminists. Often it is the key to our political awareness, or our awakening. But we don't base our understanding of women's continuing oppression and exploitation on it. No white person can claim to define a Black person's experience, nor a man a women's nor a heterosexual a homosexual's. Any of us must be able to develop politics which make us sensitive and open to learning from the experience of others *and* provide us with the tools and a framework for critically assessing theoretical analyses and daily political life.

It is the absence of discerning, exciting and accessible feminist and left political theory and practice at this particular point that makes it so difficult to stand up against the politics of experience or 'identity' politics. It's one of the elements that has swept through so many of the bitter eruptions in British feminist politics during the past five years in particular. It's what we falteringly and finally tried to come to grips with at the London Lesbian and Gay Centre.

Notes

Thanks to *Feminist Review* members for helpful notes and reactions. We would both like to thank the women with whom we worked politically during this debate. As well, Susan would like to thank Penny, Gerri, Anne and Paula for comments on the article, and Norie and Kim for thought-provoking discussions about sexual politics while writing it. Sue would like to thank Ruthie, Jill and Diane for long discussions on sexual politics over the years.

1. From a very helpful interview we did with Wendy Clark in September 1985.

References

Ardill, Susan and Neumark, Norie (1982) 'Putting Sex Back into Lesbianism'. *Gay Information* No. 11.
Bellos, Linda (1984) 'For Lesbian Sex, Against Sado-Masochism' in Kanter *et al.* (1984).
Echols, Alice (1984) 'The Taming of the Id: Feminist Sexual Politics 1968-83' in Vance (1984).
Egerton, Jayne (1983) in *Trouble and Strife* No. 1 (Winter).
France, Marie (1984) 'Sadomasochism and Feminism'. *Feminist Review* No. 16.
Heresies (1981) (a feminist publication of art and politics). *Sex Heresies* Issue 12, Vol 3, No. 4.
Kanter, Hannah, Lefanu, Sarah, Shah, Shaila and Spedding, Carole (1984) (eds) *Sweeping Statements: Writings form the Women's Liberation Movement, 1981-83* London: The Women's Press.
Leeds Revolutionary Feminist Group (1981) *Love Your Enemy? The Debate Between Heterosexual Feminism and Political Lesbianism*. London: Onlywomen Press.
Samois (a lesbian/feminist/SM organization) (1981) editors *Coming to Power: Writings and Graphics on Lesbian S/M*. Alyson Publications.
Snitow, Ann, Stansell, Christine and Thompson, Sharon (1984*) Desire: The Politics of Sexuality.* London: Virago Press.
Vance, Carole (1984) (ed.) *Pleasure and Danger: Exploring Female Sexuality.* London: Routledge & Kegan Paul.
Weeks, Jeffrey (1985) *Sexuality and its Discontents: Meanings, Myths and Modern Sexuality.* London: Routledge & Kegan Paul.

Sex in the Summer of '88

– WRITTEN WITH SUSAN ARDILL AND FIRST PUBLISHED IN *FEMINIST REVIEW* 31, SPRING 1989. SPECIAL ISSUE 'THE PAST BEFORE US: TWENTY YEARS OF FEMINISM'

After a couple of years of quietude, events took place in London during the summer of 1988 which indicate new shifts in struggles around lesbian sexuality. In this short article we will give a résumé of those events and speculate on the new map of sexual politics which seems to be emerging.

Although many lesbians had been active, some for the first time, in the campaign against Section 28 in the half year prior to this summer, these campaigns were primarily pragmatic and did not necessarily engage with theoretical issues. (Section 28 of the 1988 Local Government Act prohibits local authorities from the 'intentional promotion of homosexuality' and forbids the teaching of the 'acceptability of homosexuality as a pretended family relationship'.) Yet in defending ourselves against what has so far remained largely an intimidating ideological attack, lesbians and gay men did have to negotiate some fundamental theoretical questions, such as whether or not we are born or made this way. (A surprising level of acceptance of essentialist notions, as in 'we've always been here and we don't harm you, so why not leave us alone', was manifest throughout the wave of activism.) Also, having our sexual identities become the focus of such attack inevitably meant that collective underlying anxieties and unresolved political conflicts were stirred up. And Section 28 gave rise to a new urgency propelling us towards each other – the search for emotional and political solidarity had an edge that was not present before. (Were we correct in sensing a grudging element to this solidarity, as though we were forced together out of need rather than desire – was this characteristic of Thatcherite Britain?)

We feel that all of this contributed to the particular atmosphere of the events that summer: there was a groundswell of enthusiasm for discussing ambiguities and confusions: a desire to reappraise the old questions in the light of new conditions; and at the same time a sense of unease caused perhaps by the fact that realignments and new alignments had occurred (including coalitions between differing lesbian politics and with gay men) which had not yet been synthesized.

She Must Be Seeing Things

Events often arbitrarily signal beginnings or ends, and we are not suggesting that the Lesbian Summer School which took place in London in July 1988 was the start of something new – but we will start there with the notorious *She Must Be Seeing Things* scandal. Accounts were often contradictory, but it is clear that this American lesbian film and what it was reported to contain (brutal scenes of lesbian sadomasochism, heterosexual rape, mindless role-playing: in fact one article said 'the entire film consists of violence against women') became the focus of an angry and emotional clash. The handful of women who saw it as a pornographic film physically attempted to prevent long extracts from it being screened in an open evening session about lesbian representation in film. They also condemned outright the session organisers and members of the Lesbian Archive who defended their right to show the film.

It seems clear that a small minority of women at the Summer School wanted an outright ban of the film; it seems equally clear that some women who stayed to watch were upset by what they saw and walked out.

What did they see, and were they seeing things? Many of the issues around lesbian sexuality which have been simmering and occasionally boiling over for a few years previous to 1988 – butch/femme; domination and submission; who's a real lesbian (or feminist) and who isn't; and a relatively new entry to the rostrum, the relationship of heterosexuality to the sexuality of committed lesbians – were sparked off again in lesbian discussion of Sheila McLaughlin's film. The other thorny subjects of jealousy, obsession, religion, guilt, repression and voyeurism which *Seeing Things* raises have received scant attention. Huge questions around 'race' (the 'butch' woman, Agatha, is Black while Jo, her 'femme' lover suspected of infidelity with a man, is white) were also initially largely overlooked.

It was abundantly clear therefore that the conflicts at the Summer School, and later during the film's cinema run, only peripherally engaged with the film itself. Instead, the focus of the debate was *whether or not the film should be shown and watched*, thus crystallizing the main strands of lesbian feminist discourse then current: shock, righteousness and prohibitiveness versus the urge, even if very tentative, to explore sexual issues. Polarization is inherent in this scenario. For us, the question arises as to why all these debates around lesbian sexuality are always posed in terms of issues like SM, which are on the whole of marginal concern to most lesbians. It is apparent that this sadomasochistic game, where some women flaunt 'shocking' words and dress and others exhibit shocked reactions, constantly requires the ante to be raised. Extremity is the keynote: the extremity of the subject matter means that both sides, and certainly all in between, get to avoid talking about those problems which really dominate our personal lives, like frustration, loneliness, jealousy and obsessive dependencies; the extremity of the emotional display at these public events and on paper seems to be a displacement of the intensity with which we as women live out our sexual selves.

Yet perhaps the Summer School represented a significant shift in this dynamic, because the women arguing in favour of screening the film were not 'extremists' and did not meet the intensity of the arguments for restriction with any similar emotiveness. The unilateralism of their opponents was thus illuminated in a way which seems to have had considerable impact at grass-roots level.

We're Old Enough to Make Up Our Own Minds

Repercussions and ripples were immediate. The grapevine buzzed with differing tales of what had happened at the Summer School and in our experience most women's reactions were out of synch with the small group of women who had set up a 'safe space for lesbians to come to if they were distressed by the film' after they had failed to stop it being shown. A significant number of women whose political sympathies have been much closer to revolutionary feminism than to socialist feminism, women who have been committed radical feminists for years, women new to the arguments as well as those who may well have been actively opposed to lesbian sadomasochism, were fed up with how the prohibitionists went about their business and the lengths to which they would go to pressure women into following their line. Revolutionary feminists' continual refusal to take real account of race and class has increasingly alienated even those women who have sympathy with other aspects of their politics. At the Summer School this was underscored by the fact that one of the *Seeing Things* organizers was a strong Black lesbian who stood her ground as a *Black feminist* in the face of all the sound and fury. School mistresses may have some purchase on our psyches but rebellion was in the air.

One of the failures of the politics which takes no account of our ongoing struggles with ambiguity, nuance, contradiction and difference is that no one except the élite can sustain it forever. In the end, sustaining a vision of a better future, committing oneself to change, is done while standing in smelly but possibly fertile muck. The summer of '88 signalled a groundswell of openness, an urge to have difficult, knotty discussions. Many women wanted to make up their own minds, draw their own distinctions, find their own place in lesbian-feminist politics. The rarefied purists were experiencing a backlash. To us it seemed as if they were stuck somewhere back in the 1970s, oblivious to new realities.

The Summer School set off a newly articulated move away from past political styles. It had some part in settling the tone of the rest of the summer's lesbian discussions focusing on sexuality and sexual practice.

A Wave or Tolerance

Shortly after the School, attention shifted to American lesbian feminist writer Joan Nestle, here on a speaking tour to mark the British publication of her book *A Restricted Country* (1988). Nestle is that rare creature in America, a committed socialist as well as a sexual radical. She co-founded New York's ground-breaking Lesbian Herstory Archive, and first came to prominence through an article about her own participation in butch/femme bar culture of the 1950s in the notable sex issue of *Heresies* (1981).

Most of Joan Nestle's events were packed out. Nestle is a charming and articulate figure, who speaks openly about her own sexuality, always attempting to link personal experience into wider collective concerns. The events were remarkable for the spirit of exchange apparent between the wide variety of women who attended them. It is ironic that less than a month after the furore about *She Must Be Seeing Things*, exactly the same issues and words (if not more) could be aired so freely. Because Nestle is genuinely concerned with the content of lesbian sexual lives and, importantly, able to talk about it (an upfront American, after all) her frankness deconstructed the discourse of prohibition London had been accustomed to. The motivation for her disclosures is not to polarize or create conflict, but is marked by a willingness to listen to other women without fearfulness, to pull things from the margins to the centre. That such a controversial woman, straight from the 'enemy camp', received such a good hearing and generated so much obviously heartfelt participation indicated how strong the tide for exploration is.

Cross-currents abound, however. It is as though politicized lesbians in London are still reacting against the internal agenda of 'shoulds' and 'shouldn'ts', at the same time as having to respond to external demands and attacks. A lot of energy is being spent in rejecting and defending and not much in paying attention to the substance and direction of the 'new tolerance'.

This seems to have resulted in a stalemate of sorts, nowhere more apparent than at the panel discussion 'Putting the sex back into sexual politics', which Sheba organized at the end of the Joan Nestle tour. An audience of 300 men and women (mainly women) listened to six speakers putting their contrasting views of the 'where to now?' of sexual politics.

There was a definite buzz of anticipation on the evening. No one could remember such large numbers of women and men getting together to talk about sex and politics in years, even taking into account the mixed gay and lesbian actions protesting Section 28 during 1988. Here was a gathering of people across a wide political spectrum: radical feminists, socialist feminists, SM dykes, deconstructionists, gay men of good will, a small but significant number of Black gay men and lesbians, oldies and youngies, the curious, the sceptical, the helpful. Yet hardly any sparks flew on the night. It was almost as if getting ourselves to such an occasion was as far as we could go with any confidence.

Putting the Sex Back into What Politics?

It was interesting to note the way in which the politics of representation – which here focused on the issues of pornography and censorship – had such a firm hold on the panel and the audience. It's true that two women on the panel presented complex radical feminist positions which addressed the state of the world, but it was the discussions around images, meanings of images, symbols, words – *representations* – that dominated the evening. The irony is that this focus on representation is as true for the lesbian feminist anti-pornographers as it is for those gay men and lesbians attempting to open up discussions around ambiguity, who tend to be in the 'sex radicals' camp. The difference in their politics is then played out around how they believe individuals are affected by different representations.

On this occasion, going through all the predictable refrains in the pornography discussion seemed clearly a time-killing exercise. There was an uneasy sense that there were other things to talk about, but no one quite knew what they were. Better stick to the lines we knew by heart in this particular debate. At no time did anyone address the theme question by asking 'which politics can we put sex back into?; there was hardly any reference to the real work campaigns and personal struggles we were involved in. It's as though there was a collective blank-out when it came to articulating anything about the hard times we were (and are) living through. No longer are we sloganizing, no longer are we mindlessly sectarian, no longer are we particularly cynical; perhaps what we are is stupefied.

What struck us most on that evening was the difficulty everyone seemed to have in imaging how a different set of affairs could work. The willingness to open up possibilities was certainly present, but willingness tempered with past experiences was not enough. It seems as if many women and men were holding back, as if the usual patterns of attack and confrontation were not considered suitable behaviour, but what was there to replace them with? The combination of openness, lack of radical new political visions *and* the particular constellation of gender and racial dynamics seemed to confound many.

It was significant that of those present, Black gay men and women were the most provocative and disclosing around sex and sexual politics, speaking from their own experience of the necessity of tussling with contradictions and not relying on simplistic notions of difference. Most white lesbians (in the majority at the event), who previously might have leapt in with both feet, appeared subdued and cautious in response to this. Many white gay men seemed equally at a loss as to how to handle gender differences. So here was a significant event at which nothing particularly significant was said – an indicator of how far things have moved, but how much further there is to go.

And There Was More

Other events took place within this period which added to the sense that talking about sex was the only thing to do as the summer of '88 drew to a close. Initiatives came from all sorts of disparate angles, including a Saturday afternoon video debate on SM for lesbians. Again, anticipation ran high and the mood was one of willingness to explore and understand. Several hundred women packed the hall to listen to a pro and con debate, which didn't eventuate as planned, as a last-minute withdrawal by the anti-SM position left the line unbalanced.

The audience discussion that followed turned into a Chain Reaction Gang question and answer session (Chain Reaction Co-op organizes a disco for lesbian 'sex radicals' and is heavily associated with lesbian SM). This was not so much an exploration of the meaning and practice of SM, as revelations from a very particular group of lesbians with a generally recognized dress style, almost all white and quite young, pleased as punch to be the centre of such curiosity, which was fine but left uncovered vast areas of experience and analysis. Again the urge to talk was evident but the results were disappointing.

What's It All About?

So the summer of 1988 was marked by a turn away from self-policing and attempts to block others but, particularly for lesbian feminists, there was uncertainty as to what to put in its place. There also seems to be some danger that the reaction against restriction will take on an uncritical momentum of its own – so that 'listening to and respecting each other' becomes an end in itself. Already there are signs of a fetishistic tolerance that avoids asking questions as much as the old regime did.

A new blocking mechanism may be set up, where previously forbidden 'words' are more freely used, such as dildo, sex toy, SM, butch/femme, fucking, etc., but we still don't know the relationship of these words to what we actually do sexually, let alone how we negotiate these objects and acts and integrate them into the rest of our lives, physically, emotionally or politically. The thrill or breakdown of fear about saying these words or even being willing to hear other lesbians say them, could set up a new hierarchy more centred on a discourse of prohibition/tolerance than on the content of these words.

Many 'old' problems were evident in the summer's organized events, which no amount of openness could make disappear. The lesbians who flocked to the Summer School, to Joan Nestle's talks, to the panel, the SM debate and the screening of *She Must Be Seeing Things* were over-whelmingly white and relatively young. The questions this raises are certainly not new, but they emphasize yet again the specificity of the current 'we' of any lesbian discussion around sexuality.

Does Anyone Know the Way?

Pornography, censorship, violence against women, and so on, are among the array of pre-existing concerns for feminist sexual politics which are neither outdated nor without resonance for many lesbian feminists. However, we believe that we have reached the state where our experiences, our analysis and the conditions imposed upon us by the state make possible critical formation of a fresh sexual politics. Can we shake off the hold of limiting prohibitions and realize that openness to talking about experiences considered frightening, 'bad' or of no interest is not going to kill us? Can we then go on to ask critical questions without killing the lesbian we question and then go further to revitalize and create a sexual politics which engages many lesbians across acknowledged differences and understood inequalities? We too are caught with the will and the belief but not the formulation.

Afterthought

It's significant that we can talk about *lesbian* sexuality and sexual practice – even if with uncertainty and with awareness of how the intersections of class, race, age and disability structure our lesbian sexualities differently. In some ways our lesbianism does set us apart from 'women', whoever they are. It makes us different and forces us to reflect on our sexuality. This is commonly accepted and understood by both lesbian feminists and most heterosexual feminists. But we're still waiting for individual heterosexual feminists to come out of the closet and discuss and reveal the intricacies of their sexuality and sexual practice, to stop generalizing and get specific, even if it focuses on individuals or small groupings. Is domination and subordination a clear-cut issue in heterosexual sex? Do heterosexual feminists have thoughts on SM? Has anyone sighted a butch het women and femme het man together? Is *Cosmopolitan* correct in telling us that strong, assertive (feminist?) heterosexual women can't bear 'new men' in bed and long to be swept off their feet by machos in the streets? Answers on a postcard please!

An Unpublished Letter to *Lesbian Review of Books*
– MAY 24, 1995

Dear *Lesbian Review*,

I love review publications so I was particularly pleased with the first three issues of *Lesbian Review of Books*. A great idea at the right time. Long may it prosper.

I have been sparked into writing by the four reviews (ranging from highly critical to keenly appreciative) of Sheila Jeffreys' book, *The Lesbian Heresy* in No. 2 (Winter 1994-95) and the four responses to those in No. 3 (Spring 1995). I have been especially stirred up by Jeffreys' own reply to the reviews, in which she makes (yet again) the accusation that one of the two very negative reviews, by Judith Halberstam, made her feel sexually harassed and that she is concerned by the 'practice of sexual harassment of prominent feminists by other women ...'

Sheila Jeffreys' book, *The Lesbian Heresy*, was first published in Australia almost two years ago. It created a bit of a flurry and then, as is the case with the majority of books, settled quietly into its corner in the lesbian and gay bookshops. I must admit, I was rather bemused to find it so prominently reviewed in the *Lesbian Review of Books*. But, hey, who's complaining and the reviews and replies in the next issue made interesting reading to me, a longtime critic of Jeffreys' politics. One of the most intriguing aspects was the palpable anger which emanated from the negative ones. I'm interested in exploring where this anger comes from.

Let me tell you a couple of stories. True stories which may go some way in explaining why for some tempers run so high when Sheila Jeffreys comes into sight. The first story I have told before in *off our backs* in 1990. It concerns the 1990 4th International Feminist Book Fair in Barcelona which I was attending as a publisher and writer. Briefly, after being officially listed in the book fair catalogue as one of the participants on the major lesbian panel and after arriving in Barcelona, out of the blue I was asked to withdraw from it. I was informed that room was needed to include more black lesbians and that the organizers were 'sure I would understand'. Although I was all in favour of breaking through ongoing white feminist dominance, something about the request struck me as weird. Probably some of the weirdness came from the fact that two out of three of the British lesbians left on the panel were white (Sheila Jeffreys and Lilian Mohin), and all three represented lesbian political positions I was in conflict with.

The two white lesbians and Maud Sulter, the black lesbian, were on the other side of an ongoing struggle in Britain around pornography, censorship and the meanings of SM. The more I thought about it, the more angry I became. After the panel was over I was told by two mystified participants from other countries that Sheila Jeffreys had announced she wouldn't take part if I were allowed to speak. They added that she had planned to read some of my writing to 'prove' I was a pornographer but had been persuaded not to. My anger was fuelled by the exclusionary tactics Jeffreys used against me, but I was equally angry about the unforgivable use of race. Using the reality of racism as a ruse to kick me off the panel was an insult to black lesbians and others committed to authentic shifts in power.

I have other stories which reveal reasons for some of the high feelings surrounding Sheila Jeffreys. Here in Melbourne, a young lesbian feminist working in a feminist group with Jeffreys, argued with her about what constituted *consent* in sex between women. The exchange grew heated. The young dyke ended up saying that if while fucking, her girlfriend begged her to slap her on the face, the arm, the legs and she did, was that not *consensual* SM? Jeffreys disagreed.

In a future meeting of the same group which the young woman was not present at, Jeffreys made the accusation that the young woman had sexually harassed her, citing the argument about what constituted consent in sex. In Jeffreys' version, just to *use* these words was an assault on her. Jeffreys also called up at least one organization the woman worked for, suggesting it should not employ her in the future. The shocking thing to me is not that Jeffreys should hold vastly different views on SM to other lesbian feminists and argue her case fiercely; the unnerving thing is to what lengths she is prepared to go in her rush to denounce her opponents.

Another example: in public meeting featuring Jeffreys, a Melbourne lesbian from a non-English speaking background asked her a question about class and race. Jeffreys' answer did not satisfy her and she pursued the question. Jeffreys grew irate, angrily shouting that she knew who had sent the woman to the meeting. The sadomasochists. Of course. Laughable if she weren't so deadly serious.

I don't want to read too much into these incidents. After all, we're big women and political life is not a tea party. However, after my experience at the Barcelona Bookfair I get steamed up when I see or hear Jeffreys going on about personal attacks and playing fair. So my antennae went up when I read her accusation that the review (Winter 1994-95) by Judith Halberstam constituted both unfair play and sexual harassment.

At the end of a long and sustained critical review of Jeffreys' book, Halberstam writes:

> Apparently (and Jeffreys confirms this) a London lesbian erotica firm puts out a dildo named Sheila; the Sheila is dubbed the 'Spinster's Best Friend'. Of course, when Jeffreys in her book tells her reader about the dildo it is to accuse the lesbian sex industry of sexual harassment. In fact, this dildo may be the only worthwhile contribution Sheila Jeffreys has made to lesbian culture. I suggest she strap it on and enjoy the joke. After all, don't lesbian separatists have a sense of humour?

Sheila responds in the next issue, not surprisingly angry at Halberstam's review. She starts out (as is her wont) with the frontal counter-attack. 'When I saw the concluding remarks of Halberstam's review of my book, *The Lesbian Heresy*, I felt sexually harassed and immediately faxed (LRB editor) Loralee (MacPike) about it.' The rest of the letter is a descending series of accusations: 'It is as invasive to be the object of another woman's sexual fantasy as it is to suffer so at the hands of men' and ' ... it should be possible to express anger without personal attack'. It seems almost indecent of Jeffreys to shamelessly cry wolf given her own track record.

When dealing with certain conflicts between feminists it is exacerbating when one 'side' believes without a shred of doubt that they are the righteous, true believers, under attack by turncoats and infiltrators. What I have learned over the years is that it is almost impossible to engage (or rather, try to engage) in face-to-face or direct argument or even simultaneous appearances (i.e. a panel) with feminists like Jeffreys. If you disagree or uphold an oppositional feminist analysis, you are automatically negatively labelled by her.

I'm more and more led to agree with Judith Halberstam in her review that this sort of feminism is a type of fundamentalism. You can't argue with fundamentalists because if you do, you simply prove, over and over, that they are right and you are wrong. They do not recognize that you have any validity. After all, everything is decided, there are no complications, life is a series of right or wrong turns, and god help you if you admit to ambivalence or embrace a contradiction. Because everything is parcelled up neatly, you are clearly one of the enemy, foolish, a dupe, a turncoat, *ad infinitum*, if you disagree of hold differing views.

If, like me, you have been hanging in there, maintaining and questioning feminist, lesbian and anti-racist politics for years, these dismissals are at first hurtful, later infuriating and finally irritating. Feminist principles begin to wear a bit thin when specific lesbians go on attacking and dismissing and even denying that you or other lesbian feminists you admire are feminists. In some situations, what then happens is a kind of frustrated hitting out, sometimes crudely, sometimes with a fair measure of wit and sophistication. Witness Judith Halberstam's play on words with dildos.

(By the way, the difference in wording in Halberstam's dildo throwaway line and Jeffreys' feeling of being sexually harassed by the 'joke' is intriguing. Halberstam suggests that Jeffreys 'strap it on and enjoy the joke', whereas Jeffreys complains that if a man suggested that he would like to see her 'strapped into a dildo', she would have grounds for serious complaint. Look at the way each woman envisages the dildo: Halberstam suggests the lesbian, Jeffreys in this case, strap it on – an active and decisive act. Whereas Jeffreys sees herself in another's eyes, strapped into a dildo. The image is passive and put upon – if not a bit weird. How do you get strapped into a dildo? As well, I imagine that Halberstam is taking the micky with her suggestion – still not very nice, but rather different from Jeffreys' interpretation that she is the object of Halberstam's sexual fantasy. Love and hate may be closer than we like to admit. However, in this instance, the sexualisation of Halberstam's intent and meaning is overstated by Jeffreys.)

The history of frustration which stems from the conflicts I've mentioned also goes some way towards why I felt a little *frisson* of cynicism on reading the admirable Joanna Russ's response to the reviews of Jeffreys' book. Russ wrote that coalitions won't happen 'if people continue to talk past each other'. She continues, 'I think the only way to make our positions intelligible to each other is not by arguing in abstractions, but by recounting experiences and connecting them to our particular ideas, i.e. by consciousness raising.' Later she opines that, 'Once we know about each other's experiences and the ideas which come from them, we can avoid the kind of thing Judith Halberstam does at the end of her review of *The Lesbian Heresy*.' Finally she says, 'We must stop making totalizing statements, employing a double standard of behavior (if one of us does it, it's a human flaw; if it's one of Them, it is a sign of Their evil), and demonizing each other (no matter what They say, I know what They really mean and it's bad).'

Russ presents me with a conundrum. What happens if you agree on some levels with everything she says and have tried your damnedest to do the right thing in light of this and, fuck me, it does not work? What do you do when you talk about your experiences and how they relate to your analysis and they are dismissed as delusions?

Here's an example: Halberstam refers to her as well. Who has shared more of her experiences and connected them to her body, emotions and analysis, than lesbian feminist Joan Nestle? Has this led to Nestle being understood or respected, even if disagreed with, by lesbian feminists like Jeffreys? Absolutely not. Why? Because they respect only the voices of lesbians who prop up their own beliefs. In any case, it's a moot point, as my guess is that Jeffreys would find Russ's plea a manifestation of liberalism and therefore not worthy of serious consideration.

In the end, I also am not happy with a politics based so directly on experience. Resist demonization and denunciation, yes, attempt to listen, fine, but we have to accept that our political positions, our analyses and our priorities for action are more than the sum of our experiences, and that the differences between us must be recognized and addressed. How else do we develop a politics with anything to say outside of our own small backyards? Sadly, I believe the coalitions Russ advocates will have to be forged out of more than proper listening.

My last suggestion is that accusations of foul play from Jeffreys are inevitable. She says in her letter of complaint to the *Review* that, 'It was generally accepted, I thought, that personal attack, aimed at the person of the reviewer rather than the content of the book, was not acceptable.' (I am assuming in the above quote that Jeffreys is referring not to the 'person of the reviewer' but rather to the person of the writer.) Jeffreys goes on to finish off by saying 'there is still a responsibility to ensure fair play.'

Ironically, I believe her accusations are inevitable because the person of the writer and the content of her books are unusually deeply intertwined, so to criticize one is to attack the other. They are also inevitable exactly because of the political analysis Jeffreys espouses. In other words, strong overt disagreement (face-to-face or in print) with

Jeffreys over lesbian sexual matters – be they definitions of porn, adherence to or even critical support of SM, relationships with men, of whatever sort, sex toys, butch/femme etc., etc., can, in the Jeffreys' view of the world, tip ever so easily into what *she* experiences as sexual harassment.

While Russ is correct in pointing out that we do not all experience the same things in the same way, surely that common view cannot be a one way road. For instance, a dildo is not offensive to many dykes, it is to others, and probably the majority don't give a shit. Give lesbians who hate dildos respect and don't deduce it indicates anything about the quality of their sex lives. I find it more difficult to entertain those who insist that a dildo is literally a penis substitute, but I try. In the Russ view, shouldn't lesbians who hate dildos for whatever reason give me some time too?

Mutual respect aside, I claim the right to argue over the meaning and use of dildos when talking about lesbian sex – without having to say over and over that, of course, some dykes are disgusted by dildos or think they are a patriarchal imposition. Sorry, kindness and fairness considered, these are, as the old-fashioned poststructuralists used to say, contested sites, practices and meanings. They are no *more* loaded with painful meaning or feminist importance than other areas we fight and disagree about. I refuse to place a particular lesbian feminist 'take' on certain sexual practices at the top of some peculiar hierarchy of emotional and political importance. Jeffreys has gone for the jugular of too many lesbian feminists she disagrees with for them to pander to her cries of harassment.

Dismiss, disrespect, misrepresent, behave as if other self-proclaimed lesbian feminists are 'the enemy', but don't play the *faux-naive* when some girls lose their tempers and strike back in less than salutary ways. It's called reaping what you sow.

PS: In her response to the reviews of Jeffreys' book, I found Anna Livia's comparison of Judith Butler and Sheila Jeffreys' positions within lesbian feminism amusing. Butler is well known among some American, Australian and British students. Compared to Bulter, Jeffreys is relatively unfamiliar – most feminist academics and hot shot students I know of, rather snobbishly dismiss her – at least in Britain and Australia.

The major point of difference between the place of Butler and Jeffreys within a lesbian-feminist discourse, at least in Britain and Australia, is that Jeffreys' politics are played out more locally and in more direct antagonism to whatever else she believes is going on in lesbian subcultures – whether they are overtly feminist or happening in clubs. For instance, Jeffreys has declared that she couldn't send her Melbourne University innocent young dyke students out to Melbourne lesbian and gay venues because of the horrors they might encounter. She, of course, has actively suggested that any lesbian event which smacks of SM should be closed down. Save us from being saved from sin.

Camille Paglia's *Sex, Art and American Culture*
– FIRST PUBLISHED IN *FEMINIST REVIEW* 49, SPRING 1995

Camille Paglia's writing is often numbingly boring. The problem with reviewing her is that selective quotes make her appear snappy in a fashionably politically incorrect way. Then Camille the public performer and Camille the writer of books get all mixed up. Which is not to say reading *Sex, Art and American Culture* is *only* boring; it is also infuriating. I kept looking ahead to see how much more, oh lord, how much more to go before I was through? Then there were the moments of disgust and anger. And why didn't anyone warn me in one of the numerous hyped-up articles I read about naughty Camille that her writing is repetitious and tediously predictable? I'm bewildered that Paglia has apparently captivated so many with so little, including a swag of gay men and lesbians. In a recent issue of the Australian gay magazine *OutRage*, Peter Blazey practically elevated our Camille to saviour status (Blazey, 1993). It just goes to show, yet again, that being queer is no indicator of political acumen.

At least her first book, *Sexual Personae – Art and Decadence from Nefertiti to Emily Dickinson*, no matter how nauseously undergraduate it tended to be, did focus on famous cultural artefacts and personalities. In it she tells us she is practically single-handedly rescuing us from the aridity of modernism and restoring the unity and continuity of Western culture in an approach which combines the disciplines of literature, art history, psychology and religion. Gee whiz. Her 'method' is a form of sensationalism: 'I try to flesh out intellect with emotion and to induce a wide range of emotion from the reader' (1992: xiii). The aim is continued in this collection of essays, mostly written between 1990 and 1992 after the first book's publication. In it she expounds *ad infinitum* on her main themes, including the news that rape is one of life's little miseries, that paganism and astrology are deep and meaningful, that American academia sucks, French intellectuals suck, feminism sucks, lesbianism sucks, Madonna is fabulous and so is PAGLIA. But the focus is narrow and the weaknesses of her position in relation to popular culture are clearer than in *Sexual Personae*.

Let me make it clear from the start that I am not opposed to Paglia because she: (a) is in favour of pornography; (b) supports sado-masochism but makes sure we know she doesn't practise it; (c) adores gay men; (d) thinks Madonna is the bee's knees; (e) wore Lauren Hutton's Wonderbra for a photo opportunity; (f) is an academic; (g) can't get anyone to fuck her; (h) calls herself a Freudian. All of these might form the basis for an energetic and humorous self-aggrandizement. I loathe her because of the positions she takes about nature, society, men and women, politics, rape, sexuality, feminism, gay men and religion and I am critical of Paglia's world view because of its incredibly reactionary basis.

Paglia claims all sorts of (magnificent) things for herself. She is going where no one else has dared. She reveres Freud. She will reclaim 'Catholicism's ancient, latent paganism' (42). She will persuade us (endlessly) of the inevitable 'Apollonian versus Dionysian dichotomy in the West' (151). She will restore the primacy of never-changing Nature to our understanding of sex. She will ram common sense down our throats. She will make raucous fun of date rape. She will explain that rock and roll heralds democracy. She will extol her 'sixties generation' (47) (over and over) and she will tell you often of Paglia's unique greatness and astuteness when it comes to popular culture. She is also saving feminism from the spoilsport, whiny, middle-class women's studies' academics and their wussy male counterparts on campuses all over America. Each and every one of these places is apparently in the grip of a sorority of po-faced Lacanian, leftist, liberal, anti-pleasure women.

Paglia is pissed off by wishy-washy Rousseauian humanists but she makes sure that we understand that being anti-liberal does not mean she is a neo-conservative. However, just because someone tells you something continuously does not for one second mean that they are telling the truth or achieving what they claim to. Paglia is transparently a libertarian conservative. She doesn't seem to be able to comprehend that it is entirely possible to be pro-sex, pro-porn, pro-abortion, pro-prostitution and be a conservative. Has she never heard of libertarian Tories? Hasn't she got a clue that her much vaunted voices of 'realism' and 'common sense' are exactly those of a variety of conservatisms. The woman is chillingly naive about politics – about political history, currents and analysis.

Paglia is usually out of date, behind the times and definitely not in tune with the streets. She wouldn't know a street if it hit her in the face. It's embarrassing. Her analysis of modern culture is banal and relies heavily on descriptive passages referring to theories, famous traditions, historical buzz words. Because it is posed as central to everything, culture tends to loom. She makes a meal out of how much perversity excites her. Okay, okay. But she comes across as mean-spirited, not as someone interested in taking wing herself. It's as if she has watched American popular culture for the past two or three decades from a college room, from a distance, never from within it. You can imagine her in her student personae as the neurotic swot whose main social intercourse is always with 'mentors' and teachers, covering her needy arse with condescending dismissals of her peers. Yeah, maybe it is a bit sad, but Christ do we have to suffer her as a consequence?

Camille is as vacuously reductive in her boring denunciations of 'the feminists' as any feminist has ever been in her denunciation of patriarchy. Both rely on blanket assertions which ignore the subtle and complex ways in which women have struggled with different feminisms for over ten or fifteen years, acknowledging and analysing the different ways feminists see the world and try to change it. But if she did that she couldn't make the outrageous statements which send the press and anti-feminists into paroxysms of joy. Paglia's style and content depend on selection and wilful ignorance.

As far as Paglia is concerned, feminists make women into victims and attack her for giving women responsibility. 'I am being vilified by feminists for merely having a common-sense attitude about rape' (59). A big lump of this common-sense attitude includes the fact that, 'We cannot regulate male sexuality. The uncontrollable aspect of male sexuality is what makes sex interesting. And yes, it can lead to rape in some situations. What feminists are asking for is for men to be castrated, to make eunuchs out of them. The powerful, uncontrollable force of male sexuality has been censored out of white middle-class homes' (63). She finishes off this astoundingly silly section by throwing out a backhanded racist 'compliment' to two groups who she claims haven't censored male sexual lust by saying, 'But it's still there in black culture, and in Spanish culture'(63).

Camille has long, recurring diatribes about hormones, biology and sex differences. She has the audacity to claim that as well as being a Freudian, she is not a biological determinist. Listen to the lady: 'Dionysus, trivialized by sixties polemicists, is not pleasure but pleasure-pain, the gross continuum of nature, the subordination of all living things to biological necessity' (105). And, 'My theory of nature follows Sade rather than Rousseau: aggression and violence are primarily not learned but instinctual, nature's promptings, bursts of primitive energy from the animal realm that man has never left' (105). She ruminates on why society 'works': 'Despite crime's omnipresence, things work in society, because biology compels it' (107).

Contrary to Paglia's claims, she is about as Freudian as a fried egg. Quite the opposite: she has no deep understanding of those concepts and continuously misrepresents or contradicts her supposedly Freudian understanding of sex. For instance, in her rush to attack anything with a

French whiff to it, from Rousseau to Lacan, she gives us an amazingly unreflective potted history: 'At midlife, I now accept that there are fundamental sex differences based in hormones' (107). As a 'fractious adolescent battling the conformist fifties' she believed sexual differences were 'nothing but convention'. However, 'slowly, step by step, decade by decade, I was forced to acknowledge that even a woman of abnormal will cannot escape her hormonal identity' (107). It is her earlier 'noisy resistance' which has brought her 'full circle back to biology. From my militant history comes a conviction of self-knowledge: I can declare that what *is* female in me comes from nature and not from nurture' (107). Like the hoary ex-communist of the Cold War, Camille trots out her surface 'experiences' to lend credence to her turncoat assertions; there is not a shred of evidence that she has explored the murkier aspects of her psyche. What would a true Freudian analyst make of her?

I won't quote the excessively long paragraphs about 'woman's maternal fate' where I'm afraid that we all (with the exception of one, guess who?) end up in a swamp, engorged, immobilized, gurgling about racial memories while partaking of primal soup. 'From puberty to menopause, women are hormonally mired in the liquid realm to which this book gives the peculiar name the "chthonian swamp", my symbol for unregenerate nature' (109). No such healthy diet for men! Paglia emotes that, 'Male lust, I have written elsewhere, is the energizing factor in culture. Men are the reality principle. They created the world we live in and the luxuries we enjoy. When women cut themselves off from men, they sink backwards into psychological and spiritual stagnancy' (24). After this description it is clear that feminists want too much. 'But feminism was always wrong to pretend that women could "have it all". It is not male society but mother nature who lays the heaviest burden on women. No husband or day-care center can ever adequately substitute for a mother's attention' (89).

Paglia is a woman, but she clearly believes she is not like any other woman. She is more like a man. Except that she is a woman. Poor old Paglia. Now, at the middle point of her rather secluded life she experiences rampaging young men as moving and exciting. Did she ever really know any of the masculine jocks she loves to describe as inhabiting USA college campuses? Pre-feminism, in the same American 1950s and early 1960s she describes, I and my sexy girlfriends did. We avoided them like the plague – brains the size of peas, interests confined to football, and sexual desires about as dark and demonic as fish fingers.

What is it in all this which attracts some gay men? Well, perhaps they are simply conservative. However, I also wonder if it is Paglia's self-proclaimed love of gay men that gives the clue and the libertarian points of her politics. Describing the anti-porn positions of American feminists

Andrea Dworkin and Catherine MacKinnon which Paglia has attacked, Peter Blazey in his *Outrage* article says:

> Paglia denounces both as Stalinists of political correctness, 'fanatics, zealots and fundamentalists of the new feminist religion. Their alliance with the reactionary, anti-porn far right is no coincidence.' This is relevant to Australia, where feminism is becoming reflexively anti-male, humorless and sexphobic; it is particularly suspect on the issue of pornography – which ought to alarm every gay male, since nothing decent ever came out of being in bed with Fred Nile. – (Blazey, 1993:44)

I quote Blazey at length because he appears to buy into Camille *because* she loves gay men *and* makes convenient sweeping nasty statements about women and feminists. The irony of this is that there are large numbers of lesbian feminists in Britain, the United States and Australia who have fought long and hard and often successfully against Dworkinite-style politics.

Does Camille's supposed adoration of homosexuality hold up under scrutiny? What does she really have to say about them? On religion this:

> When feminism and gay activism set themselves against organized religion, they have the obligation to put something better in its place. Hostile intrusions into church services, as undertaken by gay groups in New York and Philadelphia, are infantile, damaging the image of gays and bringing their cause into disrepute. All sacred places, pagan or Christian, should be honored ... Gays must face the fact that, unlike other minority groups, they cannot reproduce themselves. Like artists, their only continuity is through culture, which they have been instrumental in building. Therefore when, by guerrilla tactics, they attack the institutions of culture (including religion), they are sabotaging their own future. – (Paglia, 1992:36)

How revolutionary. 'Our problem is not patriarchy but, in the urban industrialized world, collapsing manhood, which male homosexuality properly remedies by its glamorous cult of the masculine' (36). With a friend like this who needs enemies?

Paglia refers admiringly to the work of John J. Money, an exponent of the 'Born That Way' school of sexual difference, who has been the subject of much detailed criticism. She sets him up in opposition to Foucault, her French *bête noir*: 'For thirty years, the sexual territory between biology and psychology has been far more successfully and sensibly explored on American soil, at the Johns Hopkins University School of Medicine, by John J. Money' (180). And later she asserts quite uncritically that 'The seventies and eighties have seen a worldwide resurgence of research into hormones, comparative anatomy, genetics,

fetal development and brain chemistry, and their relation to sex differences and even personality traits' (185).This is a writer who maintains she
is a Freudian.

Paglia's position on AIDS is quite similar to the one she holds on rape.
The world is full of continuous and universal truths. Nature, dark and
extremely messy, simply is, like it or lump it. Religion, ethical codes,
morality, all are imposed by society. If you rebel against rigid or stultifying
aspects of society, even if for 'good' reasons, well good luck, but don't
come crying and snivelling when you get serious flack, rape, pillage,
lynchings, vigilantes – or AIDS – in response. What is society? Society
simply is, hey nonny no. 'We asked why should I obey the law? and why
shouldn't I act on every sexual impulse? The result was a descent into
barbarism ... And out of the pagan promiscuity of the sixties came AIDS.
Everyone of my generation who preached free love is responsible for
AIDS' (216). Later when our Pag is lighting into Foucault again she says
'If what I have reliably heard about his public behaviour after he knew he
had AIDS is true, then Foucault would deserve the condemnation of
every ethical person' (230).

Paglia has no sense of today's changing sexual scene except through
the worship of Madonna. She claims that 'Homosexuality, more common
as well as more visible, is part of this movement for sexual self-knowledge
and self-definition' (99), in a paragraph which puts the boot into seventies'
androgyny. But she has no understanding or knowledge of the new waves
of sex and gender politics manifest in the groping but often wild and funny
queer politics. Quite hysterically she criticizes the American Absolutely
Queer posters of a few years ago. '"Absolutely Queer." *Absolutely* queer? I
thought we got rid of absolutes! ... Now we've got *gay* people talking about
what is *absolute*? This is fascism! This is fascism!' (276). She doesn't seem to
have a clue that the juxtaposition of 'absolute' and 'queer' contains quite
wittily a critique of any notion of absoluteness.

I cannot bear to go into Camille's ludicrous ideas about lesbianism
which leaves dykes sunk 'backward into psychological and spiritual
stagnancy'. Lesbian sex is 'cozy' and the girls often end up 'in emotion
without sex'. Paglia sometimes claims that she is playing games when she
makes remarks like this. But I think it's another instance of her wilful
ignorance. Who on earth does she hang out with – if anyone? She whinges
about the impossibility of having hot sex with lesbians. My guess is that
Camille is incapable of having hot sex, full stop. Gay men on the other
hand are 'guardians of the masculine impulse. To have anonymous sex in
a dark alleyway is to pay homage to the dream of male freedom' (24). This
is extremely tired, old stuff; there is nothing new in any of this crap.

Paglia is prepared to extrapolate wildly on the nature of human
existence, the meaning of sex, the causes of violence and rape, from an

eccentric but selective look at art, writing and culture through history. It is the extrapolations that infuriate. The way they are juxtaposed is sometimes startling but there is nothing new in the content. And Paglia simply ignores huge chunks of history. She ignores the immensely important movements of women's liberation and Black liberation in the 1970s. She rarely speaks convincingly or with any passion about race or class except to vilify white, middle-class women (she's Italian so none of that counts for her), or to throw out condescending compliments to African-Americans and Hispanics (Paglia talking about rape as white middle-class women's complaint: 'I don't notice so many Hispanic women and African-American women going around and carrying on like this' (268). They know what real sex is. They don't complain about date rape. Anorexia doesn't affect them. They like food. They've got such energy. Their music is so great. Surprise, surprise, these are Camille's attributes too. Camille is loud, therefore she gets on with African-Americans. 'Now I'm loud. Did you notice? I'm very loud. I've had a hell of a time in academe. This is why I usually get along with African-Americans' (271). Wow – a new approach to race relations.

Paglia's own Pagliamania might be forgiven if she delivered the goods. Even her much-touted cheekiness palls after the first chapters, especially as her deep conservatism reveals itself more and more. Surely not all her readers are so ill-read and ignorant of history, feminism, politics and popular culture that they see no flaws, hear no *faux pas* and smell no bullshit coming off her? Surely not all gay men, or pro-pornography, pro-abortion, anti-censorship readers will get cozy with Camille simply because she supports these things. In the end I am left with her monumental pretentiousness and bad style sense. Speaking for the nth time about 'my sixties' Camille proclaims: 'My generation, inspired by the dionysian titanism of rock, attempted something more radical than anything since the French Revolution' (216). Please.

References

Blazey, Peter (1993) *OutRage*. Melbourne No. 116 January, 44-7.
Paglia, Camille (1990) *Sexual Personae – Art and Decadence from Nefertiti to Emily Dickinson*. Yale University Press.
Paglia, Camille (1992) *Sex, Art, and American Culture*. London: Viking.

A Nice Postscript

Has it come to this? Ending my collection with a nasty piece on Camille Paglia? I admit that in the softly lit English autumn of 1995 I am tempted to tantrums. Yet again it's American sexual politics' players who hog the media in Britain and Australia, no matter how skilled, contentious, witty and committed the home grown talent is. Naomi Wolfe has issued a confused call for the foetus's humanity. Conservative mid-Atlantic Andrew Sullivan claims he's written a book (*Virtually Normal*) on gay politics for the 'general reader' and that it doesn't matter that he's white, male and gay, his thoughts are beyond any of these identifying markers. Angela Mason of Britain's Stonewall organization has pointed out that his recommended reading list contains no women. Yet who, if not feminist theorists and activists, have contributed more to our understanding and critiques of sexual politics?

Even further to the right, fundamentalists – Christians, Muslims, take your pick of fundy-flavour – fulminate against lesbians and gay men in the same moment that new style conservatives quietly open the back door a crack for eager gay-cons to breathlessly enter.

But these semi-headline grabbing occurrences are only part of the picture. In 1995 I am moved by women's continuing struggles, by gay resistance, by people's defiance in the face of reaction. Lesbian Avenger actions in the USA and Britain stir me up (and make me feel a wee bit old). Breast cancer activism inspires me and I see a political practice forming which combines experience, activism and an accelerated accruing of knowledge about treatments, research, care and prevention.

Years ago feminists were keen to make connections, needing to forge links between issues and groups. I see this disposition everywhere in my writing in the 1970s and eighties. Grand plans may be declared passé these days, yet right in front of our eyes affairs are occurring which beg to be linked up. Increasingly women living with HIV/AIDS talk about the need to make contact with other women's health groups, concluding their concerns have as much to do with wider issues of women's health as with gay men's considerations. Cancer activists push forward the dirty reality of the toxic world we live in, connecting with environmentalists, demanding that the primary prevention of cancer be addressed, not hidden away under a rhetoric of imminent medical cures.

The women's health movement, so focused on reproduction and sexuality for the past twenty-five years, now nourishes the more specified needs of particular groups of women. For instance, a feminist analysis of health and illness is vital to HIV/AIDS work with women. In turn, the broad experience of gay men organizing around HIV/AIDS informs the new politics of breast cancer activism. And so it continues. Incomplete connections filled with possibilities.

If today the existence of a vital, seemingly unified women's movement is questionable, then seemingly disparate groupings move towards each other. Old-time feminists often bemoan the fact that women's studies are now the major route into feminism for many younger women, worrying that this road is a dead-end for activism. But the arguments and divisions which exist in academia between women's studies, lesbian and gay studies, and new queer developments, continue to throw up contradictions which make the isolation of feminism in ivory towers untenable. Even the most erudite and dense postmodernists seem increasingly compelled to grapple with the day-to-day social reality of women's lives and to ponder the possibilities of struggle and change. Even the odd stubborn radical feminist separatist is appropriating parts of the language of postmodernism.

Unsettling, upsetting, exhilarating: for women, questions of power, exploitation and oppression jostle with those concerning confidence, joy, lust and love. Nothing is solved or resolved for us yet, but nothing is the same as it was at the start of the women's liberation movement in the late 1960s. Hesitantly, then with growing confidence, these concerns and involvements are reflected in my writing in the past, now in the present and, I hope, in the future.

I lied in the book title – I'm still nice but now I'm nasty too. Doing it all simultaneously is awkward but there's no better way. I long for women to comfort and sustain each other but also for inspired risk-taking, tough words, hilarious arguments. I lust after change *and* continuity. Formulaic and institutionalized solutions and coalitions stifle risk-taking; as women we should aim for something far more radical, raunchy and difficult. I hope my writing reveals this now and will continue to in the future because I anticipate remaining a feminist until I pop my clogs.

Index